YEARBOOK IN EARLY CHILDHOOD EDUCATION

Bernard Spodek • Olivia N. Saracho
EDITORS

VOLUME 1
Early Childhood Teacher Preparation
Bernard Spodek and Olivia N. Saracho, Editors

VOLUME 2
Issues in Early Childhood Curriculum
Bernard Spodek and Olivia N. Saracho, Editors

VOLUME 3
Issues in Child Care
Bernard Spodek and Olivia N. Saracho, Editors

VOLUME 4
Language and Literacy in Early Childhood Education
Bernard Spodek and Olivia N. Saracho, Editors

VOLUME 5
Early Childhood Special Education
Philip L. Safford, Editor
with Bernard Spodek and Olivia N. Saracho

VOLUME 6
Meeting the Challenge of Linguistic and Cultural Diversity in Early Childhood Education
Eugene E. García and Barry McLaughlin
with Bernard Spodek and Olivia N. Saracho

VOLUME 7
Issues in Early Childhood Educational Assessment and Evaluation
Bernard Spodek and Olivia N. Saracho, Editors

VOLUME 8
Issues in Early Childhood Educational Research
Bernard Spodek, Olivia N. Saracho, and Anthony D. Pellegrini, Editors

YEARBOOK IN EARLY CHILDHOOD EDUCATION

Editorial Advisory Board

The *Yearbook in Early Childhood Education* is a series of annual publications. Each volume addresses a timely topic of major significance in the field of early childhood education, and contains chapters that present and interpret current knowledge of aspects of that topic, written by experts in the field. Key issues—including concerns about educational equity, multiculturalism, the needs of diverse populations of children and families, and the ethical dimensions of the field—are woven into the organization of each of the volumes.

YEARBOOK
IN
EARLY CHILDHOOD EDUCATION
VOLUME 8

ISSUES IN EARLY CHILDHOOD
EDUCATIONAL RESEARCH

EDITED BY

Bernard Spodek, Olivia N. Saracho,
and Anthony D. Pellegrini

TEACHERS
COLLEGE
PRESS

Teachers College, Columbia University
New York • London

Published by Teachers College Press, 1234 Amsterdam Avenue, New York, NY 10027

Library of Congress Cataloging-in-Publication Data

Issues in early childhood educational research / edited by Bernard
    Spodek, Olivia N. Saracho, and Anthony D. Pellegrini.
        p.   cm. — (Yearbook in early childhood education ; v. 8)
    Includes bibliographical references and index.
    ISBN 0-8077-3765-8 (hardcover : alk. paper)
    1. Early childhood education—Research.   I. Spodek, Bernard.
II. Saracho, Olivia N.   III. Pellegrini, Anthony D.   IV. Series.
LB1139.23.I77   1998
372.21'072—dc21   98-27030

ISBN 0-8077-3765-8 (cloth)

Printed on acid-free paper
Manufactured in the United States of America

05 04 03 02 01 00 99 98   8 7 6 5 4 3 2 1

Contents

Introduction:
Reflections on the Past

Bernard Spodek and Olivia N. Saracho

The interest in research in the field of early childhood education has increased dramatically for more than 15 years. A range of evidence supports this view. Several books as well as journals attest to the current state of affairs. *Handbook of Research in Early Childhood Education* (Spodek, 1982) and *Handbook of Research on the Education of Young Children* (Spodek, 1993) are compendiums of research throughout the field of early childhood education. Similarly, the *Yearbook in Early Childhood Education* series, published by Teachers College Press since 1990, has been reporting the current state of knowledge in the field.

In addition, a number of new journals have been established that are dedicated specifically to reporting on research in early childhood education. *Early Childhood Research Quarterly* and *Early Education and Development* are two journals that have appeared in the United States. The increased interest is not limited to the United States alone, however. The European Early Childhood Education Research Association (EECERA), established only in this decade, publishes the *European Early Childhood Educational Research Journal*. The *International Journal of Early Childhood Education*, devoted to reporting early childhood education research in a number of countries, also began publication in Korea in 1996. Other journals in education and child development also have published reports of research in the field. The appearance of these new research publications and the absence of earlier similar publications suggests that the focus on research on early childhood education is a relatively recent phenomenon.

The field of early childhood education has had a long tradition, stretching back about 200 years to the time when programs specifically designed for young children were developed in Europe. However, the tradition of conducting research in early childhood education is a much shorter one, probably beginning in the 1960s and continuing at an increased pace to the present. Historically, early childhood education has been a field of practice rather than a field of research. Historical models of early childhood education, such as those of Robert

Owen and Friedrich Froebel, were built not on a base of research, but rather on philosophical assumptions. Even the twentieth-century models, such as the progressive kindergarten, the Montessori method, and the nursery school of Margaret Mcmillan, while giving lip service to the importance of research, seldom were built on a foundation of empirical research.

There are a number of possible explanations for the recent upsurge in research production in a field where little or no research was conducted earlier. Relatively little educational research was conducted in general until the 1950s, when the Eisenhower administration supported such research through the U.S. Office of Education. This suggests one explanation: The lack of research on early childhood education in an earlier period was a reflection of the limited amount of research done in all of education.

Another possible explanation for the dearth of research before the 1960s was the belief in the close relationship between child development and early childhood education. As a result of this belief, early educators felt that research done on the development of young children was directly relevant to early childhood education. This belief might have been supported by the fact that most of this child development research was done in the context of preschool programs, or at least with children enrolled in laboratory preschools. These university laboratory nursery schools often were established primarily for the purpose of providing subjects for child development research.

A third possible explanation for the lack of early childhood education research is the limited number of early childhood programs that were supported by public funds and the small number of children enrolled in such programs. In 1966, it was estimated that fewer than 10.5 million 3- to 5-year-old children— fewer than 30% of children of this age—were enrolled in early childhood programs (King, 1975). This compares with an estimated 53% of all 4-year-olds and 86% of all 5-year-olds enrolled in educational programs in 1991 (Snyder & Hoffman, 1992). Thus, there was little call for policy makers to support research in the field until recently.

It was in the 1960s when major changes took place in the field of early childhood education that generated research in the field. Beginning with the "discovery of poverty" in the early 1960s, American society began to search for ways to alleviate poverty and change the structure of society. One way of modifying society, it was felt, was to improve the childhood experiences of children from poor and minority backgrounds. Works by Benjamin Bloom (1964) and J. McVicker Hunt (1961) suggested that we could have the greatest impact on human development by creating intervention programs in the early years. As a result, a number of innovative early childhood programs, aimed primarily at children in poverty, were developed in research centers around the country. Funded primarily by the Ford and Carnegie Foundations, these programs were the forerunners of federal programs such as Head Start and the preschool programs funded under Title I of the Elementary and Secondary Education Acts. The original intervention programs were established within a research framework, often with experimental and control groups, so that program effectiveness could be judged. Research also was done to assess the effectiveness of the later government-funded programs.

Most of the researchers studying early childhood education during this period were from the fields of educational or child psychology. Using research models from these fields, the early researchers based their work primarily on an experimental model, with treatment and control groups. The data collected to determine the effectiveness of the interventions were based either on developmental tests or school readiness tests. In many cases, scores on IQ tests were collected, since these programs were designed to raise intelligence, and intelligence is "what intelligence tests measure."

The range and variety of research being conducted today have been expanded considerably since that time. Some researchers have followed up on these earlier projects, conducting longitudinal studies of the subjects as they have matured. A greater diversity of program outcomes has been studied in these longitudinal studies. In addition, many other aspects of early childhood education have been researched beyond program outcomes, including the physical and social settings of the classroom and the functioning of classroom teachers, including teacher–child and teacher–parent interactions.

The use of standardized tests as a way of collecting data in early childhood research—an early practice—has been widely criticized by researchers such as Samuel Meisels and his colleagues (1993) and Lorrie Shepard and M. Elizabeth Graue (1993; see also Chapter 2 in this volume). Newer research models, growing out of the traditions of fields other than psychology, are now being used to study problems in the field. Since young children are educated primarily in groups, these methods can provide us with information about educational processes that was not available to the field before. The traditions of the field also have been studied using historical methodologies. Seeing where we came from as a field, and the sociocultural elements that influenced practice in earlier times, helps us better understand current practice and the context in which the field functions. Increasingly, research using qualitative methodologies has been done in early childhood education.

An awareness of the increased amount and diversity of research in early childhood education led the editors to develop this volume. A wide range of knowledge has been generated by newer studies, and a great number of issues have been raised. The authors of the chapters that follow describe particular research methodologies and their application to early childhood education. They also raise issues and concerns about research done with particular methodologies.

In the first chapter, which focuses on doing historical research, Barbara Beatty comments on the relative absence of historical research in early child-

hood education, suggesting a number of possible reasons for this lack. She identifies one of the issues in doing such research as the need to identify the historical biases of the author seeking and interpreting primary data sources. Beatty
distinguishes between two types of historical research. She characterizes the
research done by members of the field as inside research, and that done by others as outside research. Inside research often deals with issues of practice, while
outside research tends to place practice, in a historical, social, or economic context. Within her chapter Beatty suggests a wide range of primary and secondary
resources that can be used by those searching for the history of the field. She
also identifies a number of historical issues that are worthy of study.

M. Elizabeth Graue, in Chapter 2, on standardized tests, describes the advantages of using standardized tests in research in early childhood education.
These tests can be used to provide information about attributes, skills, and knowledge that are measurable in children. However, their use also limits what we
can know about children. Graue is concerned that these tests, because of their
inflexibility, ignore children's ways of knowing. Their use is based on a construct
of a universal model of development, which ignores both cultural differences
and individual differences in children. They cause researchers to focus on end
points of experience rather than taking into account the experiences themselves.
These limitations have led educational researchers to look for other ways of
collecting information about children and their experiences.

In Chapter 3, J. Amos Hatch characterizes qualitative research as that being
done in natural settings and seeking to capture the perspectives of the actors in
those settings. This research uses observation, field notes, and the collection of
artifacts as its data sources. It requires long periods of firsthand engagement by
the researcher. The researcher uses the information collected to abstract the
meanings held by those observed. This is done through inductive data analysis.
Qualitative research, of necessity, has an element of subjectivity to it. Hatch presents examples of qualitative research, including participant-observation studies,
interpretive studies, artifact analysis, narrative studies, and poststructuralist
studies. Among the issues Hatch raises about qualitative research is the place of
theory in this research and whether this theory should come from an analysis of
the scholarly literature or should emerge from the study. He also raises the issue
of ethics related to this research, warning against the exploitation of the children and adults being studied. Hatch concludes his chapter with a number of
caveats for those wishing to conduct qualitative research.

Observation techniques can be used in both qualitative and quantitative
research. Anthony D. Pellegrini, in Chapter 4, mentions the importance of observational research in this field because of the need for thorough descriptions.
He also points out the method's roots in the traditions of child study. Pellegrini
discusses the need for a theory to determine what will be observed and how
observations will be categorized. He notes that all researchers enter a field with

at least some form of implicit theory to guide their observations. Three levels of descriptions gained from observations are identified in this chapter: physical description, description of consequences, and relational description. He also discusses the characteristics of good categories used to group description: They are homogeneous, they are mutually exclusive, and they are exhaustive. Pellegrini closes this chapter by identifying the rules for sampling and recording categories of observation behavior.

Peter K. Smith discusses ethological research methods in Chapter 5. He defines ethology as a research method that uses direct observation by nonparticipants to gather data in natural settings. Ethology, which is a method first used in studying animals, is interested in the functional and comparative evolutionary significance of behavior. While there are similarities between ethology and ethnography, both of which use observational techniques, ethology does not use interviews or probe the meanings held by the participants in a setting. Smith reviews a number of ethological studies of early childhood education that have been conducted since the 1970s. He then offers guidelines for doing ethological research in early childhood education. He raises issues about using direct nonparticipant observation in research, about what constitutes natural settings in the study of early childhood education, and about whether experimental manipulations can be used in ethological research. He concludes that ethology can provide a new perspective in studying young children in educational settings.

Richard M. Lerner, Penny Hauser-Cram, and Erez C. Miller look at the assumptions underlying longitudinal research designs in Chapter 6. They suggest that, in addition to issues of convenience, efficiency, and economy, basic theoretical assumptions underlie the determination to study children over time and the selection of a particular longitudinal design in doing research. One possible assumption is the universality of developmental processes. Another is the view that there are connections across life periods. Different views determine different methods and even the number of points at which to collect data in a study. While cross-sectional research can generate information about children, it cannot provide information about developmental pathways. In addition, the more complex the developmental process is considered to be, the more data points are needed and the more kinds of data need to be collected. The spacing of data collection points also is influenced by the ages of the children and the developmental domains being studied. Furthermore, data analysis is influenced by theoretical considerations. The authors suggest that longitudinal researchers consider not only internal influences on development, but contextual influences as well. In this regard they suggest that teachers become researchers as well, since they are most knowledgeable about the school context in which children function.

In Chapter 7, on teachers as researchers, Renee T. Clift and Lillie Albert also consider the issue of insider versus outsider research. From their perspective, however, insider research is that conducted by practitioners on their own practice, while outsider research is conducted by others outside of practice—primarily by researchers as researchers. The authors view teacher research as a way to bridge the gap between research and practice. They assert that teachers know their problems and can investigate them. Teacher research also gives teachers a voice, often not heard in the scholarly discourses about teaching. They suggest that teachers should learn to conduct research as part of their initial preparation. Among the problems these authors identify in teachers doing research are the lack of time to conduct research in one's own classroom, the small number of students that are studied by teachers in their research—typically a single class or even fewer—and the need for reflective analysis in addition to description in this research.

Meta-analysis is a research technique that allows a set of empirical studies to be combined and synthesized. This technique is being used increasingly in research in early childhood education. Marinus H. van IJzendoorn, in Chapter 8, sees meta-analysis as serving the same purpose as narrative reviews of the literature: to make sense of research in an area of the literature. In fact, he notes that there two complementary ways of combining results from many studies. While a good meta-analysis should be embedded in a narrative context, it allows a higher degree of precision and rigor than does a narrative review. Van Ijzendoorn identifies the stages in meta-analytic research as a spiral process, from formulating a specific hypothesis, to systematically collecting the relevant studies, to coding and analyzing the data, to finally interpreting the results. He identifies issues in each of these stages. He then reviews the meta-analyses that have been done in several domains of early childhood education. He concludes that, in general, intervention programs have been effective, suggesting there is enough evidence from the combined studies to recommend early childhood intervention programs as a matter of public policy. He also deals with the criticisms that have been leveled at meta-analyses of early childhood programs, suggesting that the problems that have been identified with these meta-analyses can be easily solved.

In the final chapter, the editors of this volume speculate about the future of early childhood research. In looking to the future, they suggest who might be the subjects of future research and who might be the researchers. They provide suggestions about the issues that might be addressed by future research and where such research should take place. They also discuss the various methodologies and their places in future research.

The chapters, when taken together, help to illuminate many of the significant issues related to research in early childhood education. They should inform the discourse about research in the early childhood education community and should help individuals improve the quality of their research as they study the various aspects of early childhood education.

This volume is the work of many persons. Not only were the chapter authors and the editors involved in the project, but members of the Editorial Advisory Board for the Yearbook on Early Childhood Education series contributed as well. They helped conceptualize this book and reacted to the ideas of the editors. In addition, they individually reviewed drafts of the chapter manuscripts, judging their quality and making suggestions for improvement. The editors would like to acknowledge their work and thank them for the help they have provided.

REFERENCES

Bloom, B. S. (1964). *Stability and change in human characteristics.* New York: Wiley.

Hunt, J. McV. (1961). *Experience and intelligence.* New York: Ronald Press.

King, I. A. (1975). *Preprimary enrollments, 1974.* Washington, DC: Government Printing Office.

Meisels, S. J., Steele, D. M., & Quinn-Leering, K. (1993). Testing, tracking, and retaining young children: An analysis of research and social policy. In B. Spodek (Ed.), *Handbook of research on the education of young children* (pp. 279–292). New York: Macmillan.

Shepard, L. A., & Graue, M. E. (1993). The morass of school readiness screening: Research on test use and test validity. In B. Spodek (Ed.), *Handbook of research on the education of young children* (pp. 293–305). New York: Macmillan.

Snyder, T. D., & Hoffman, C. M. (1992). *Digest of educational statistics (1991).* Washington, DC: National Center for Educational Statistics.

Spodek, B. (1982). *Handbook of research in early childhood education.* New York: Free Press.

Spodek, B. (Ed.). (1993). *Handbook of research on the education of young children.* New York: Macmillan.

CHAPTER 1

From Infant Schools to Project Head Start: Doing Historical Research in Early Childhood Education

Barbara Beatty

Like young children themselves, whose needs often are ignored in public discourse about education, early childhood education, until recently, has been one of the most under-researched fields in the history of education. This is in part because most young children in the past lived their lives within the private sphere of the family or were not accorded public attention. Their education was the responsibility of their parents, who taught them informally in whatever ways they could, or arranged for them to be taught and cared for by relatives, friends, neighbors, servants, or governesses. Older children who received formal education were educated by tutors or attended schools that kept records. Younger children were educated at home, in other people's homes, or in small preschools, which kept few, if any, records.

Lack of records is not the only reason for the lack of history of early childhood education. Low status is also a factor. Preschool education was primarily a women's occupation and was seen as less important than the education of older children. Most historians in the past were men and were either not knowledgeable about, uninterested in, or not rewarded for writing about female teachers and little children. But with the advent of the women's movement and burgeoning empirical research in child development and education, interest in the history of early childhood education has increased. New scholarship links early childhood education to women's history, to labor history, to the history of child and family welfare policies, and to parent education, pediatrics, psychology, and other fields. With the initiation of children's studies as a specialty, more research in the history of early childhood education is likely to be forthcoming. But there is a continuing need for scholarship to fill in the historical record, and to see whether there are lessons from the past that can inform preschool education today. This scholarship also may help increase public awareness of the importance of early childhood education and raise the status of early childhood education as a profession.

Many different historical approaches and methods can be used in this research. Some historians concentrate on intellectual history; others focus on political or economic history, or on the social history of the experiences of different groups and classes within society. Some histories are narratives that tell the story of people and events, while others include quantitative analysis of historical phenomena. Many combine these different foci, forms, and techniques.

The validity of historical research in any field depends on the construction of plausible, logical, significant research questions, and on the marshaling of convincing historical data to answer these questions. Developing research questions that are broad enough to be interesting but focused enough to be researchable, and on which historical data are available, requires much thought and planning. David Hackett Fischer's classic, *Historians' Fallacies* (1970), remains one of the best guides to framing good questions and to avoiding pitfalls in historical research. Reviewing existing literature by other scholars provides an overview of what has been done and of current thinking, and can suggest further questions for research. Thinking about how contemporary historical accounts might or should be revised in the light of new findings or modern issues and concerns is one of the strongest motivations for doing historical research. Modern secondary sources, such as books, journal articles, and chapters in edited volumes— many of which can be located through computerized database searches—also can be useful for getting a sense of a time period or program and for providing additional bibliographical information.

Historians must be very careful when using secondary sources as they may contain inaccurate or unsubstantiated information and may be biased by the personal, political, or historiographical perspective of the author. But this bias is also due to the desire to create accounts of the past that explain significant current topics. This search for significance can lead to presentism—the insertion of modern views and ideas into events and minds in the past—but also can produce historical inquiry that is powerful and relevant.

To answer research questions and confirm hypotheses or interpretations, primary historical sources from the time period must be located and examined. Books, newspaper articles, annual reports, catalogues, letters, diaries, and other primary sources can be found in libraries or archives at colleges, universities, and historical associations. State and federal documents, such as U.S. Office of Education surveys and reports, also provide information and statistics. Historical sources such as census records and school department figures can be used to document enrollments of children of different ages and backgrounds in various types of programs. Sampling techniques and other research designs may be needed to collect and analyze such quantitative data.

The reliability of historical research depends on the quality and quantity of supporting evidence from primary sources. The evidence must be accurate, relevant, and clearly documented. Quotations and other specific factual information must be cited in such a way that other researchers can locate the sources and check their veracity. Historians generally use the citation format of the American Historical Association. Qualifiers such as "may" and "might" are used frequently, to indicate the lack of conclusive evidence and the likelihood of other possible historical interpretations.

Sources should be as representative as possible of the experiences of people from a wide range of backgrounds and regions, or the particular group and locality being discussed must be specified. Providing a balanced account of the past is difficult because most readily available sources document the lives of relatively wealthy, well-educated women and men from urban areas. But there is an increasing amount of data describing the lives of racial, ethnic, and linguistic minorities, and on diverse cultural, regional, and socioeconomic groups. Capturing the experiences of children in the past remains extremely difficult, however, as they are the most silent and silenced of historical actors and usually are spoken for by adults. Sources from material or popular culture, such as toys, clothes, songs, games, photographs, television shows, or films, can provide an effective way of documenting children's culture more directly.

Using primary sources can be difficult, time-consuming, and expensive. Most archives have written or computerized finding aids that describe in detail what their collections contain. Researchers can call or write to have copies of specific finding aids sent to them and should contact an archive in advance of visiting. Some primary source documents are on microfilm and for a fee, will be copied or mailed to researchers. Grants are sometimes available to support these research costs.

Analysis of the influence of external historical events on early childhood education is very important. For instance, public funding and support for early childhood education frequently have been driven by external societal issues such as immigration, war, economic trends, prevention of poverty and crime, and so on, rather than by concern about the intrinsic needs of children and families. Works by scholars outside of early childhood education often contain more of this contextual information and tend to be more critical and analytical. The tendencies of historians to see progress or decline, to portray persons in the past as active agents or powerless victims, and to empathize with or criticize historical actors and actions are key historiographical choices. Some "outsider" histories portray educational programs as intrusive social engineering, or as racially segregated, class-biased means of reproducing the existing stratified power structure. Similarly, particular historical personages sometimes are depicted in an unsympathetic fashion. Biographies of Maria Montessori, for instance, show how differently historians may interpret the life of an historical figure (Kramer, 1976; Standing, 1957). Not all external histories are negative, however, but critical perspective is healthy as it forces re-examination of the effects and larger role of early childhood education in society.

Internal histories also can be helpful. "Insider" research by scholars from within the field often focuses on the history of pedagogical methods and classroom techniques and can provide a more detailed analysis of the specific issues and tensions that occupied the attention of early childhood educators in a particular time period. Internal histories sometimes do a better job describing the texture and timing of events in early childhood education, which did not always coincide with the generalizations and periodicity used by other historians. But "insider" histories often lack historical context. They tend to present early childhood education uncritically, as a noble, humanitarian crusade, with uniformly positive effects, and to portray early childhood educators as selfless heroines or heroes. Although not all "insider" histories lack this critical perspective, some are unanalytical and reinforce the marginality that has prevented early childhood education from receiving the serious, mainstream attention it deserves.

"Real" history is complex. To the extent that there can be objectivity in a subjective narrative—a topic of much current scholarly discussion—a balanced assessment of both positive and negative aspects of a subject should be attempted. It is thus very important for researchers to read widely and to think about different historiographical approaches (Cronon, 1992; Novick, 1988; Seixas, 1996).

This chapter provides guidelines for doing historical research in early childhood education, as well as a brief review of existing research and information on locating sources. The history of early childhood education can be divided into five overlapping time periods: (1) early history prior to the beginning of organized, extrafamilial preschools; (2) the infant school movement of the early 1800s; (3) the kindergarten movement, from the 1830s to the present; (4) the day nursery, nursery school, and Montessori movements, from the mid-nineteenth century to the present; and (5) the public preschool movement, from the 1920s to the present. Summaries of these historical movements follow, along with some possible research questions. Researchers should look especially for continuities and discontinuities among these movements and time periods, and for the effects of gender, social class, race, ethnicity, and economic and cultural variables in the history of educational programs for young children.

EARLY HISTORY OF EARLY CHILDHOOD EDUCATION

Relatively little is known about the history of early childhood education from ancient times until the 1600s, when writing about educating young children began to appear. Robert Ulich (1947) and others document that the Greeks, Romans, and other ancient civilizations had concepts of "ages of man," or periods of life from birth to old age, and Giovanni Levi and Jean-Claude Schmitt (1997) have edited a volume on the history of youth in Western European culture from the Greeks to Fascism in modern Italy and Germany. But the question of when childhood began to be seen as a unique period of life requiring special care and education is a topic of debate. Philippe Aries (1962) argues that the "discovery" of childhood began in the seventeenth century; he uses paintings of the infant Jesus, clothing, and other material artifacts as primary sources to document this change. Other secondary sources contain information about family life and child-rearing practices, such as swaddling, breast feeding, and the use of wet nurses. Research also is being done on the history of early childhood education in non-Western countries. International journals such as *Paedagogica Historica* include some of this work, and more information is available through organizations such as the International Standing Conference on the History of Education and by contacting historians and educators in other countries.

It is known that in the past many young children were treated very badly and suffered horribly. Infanticide and abandonment were common, and many children died from disease or were enslaved, malnourished, maimed, or otherwise abused. Others spent their youth in orphanages, poor houses, factories, or fields, or on the streets. Much research remains to be done on the early history of early childhood education, particularly in non-Western cultures, where child labor remains a common phenomenon. Researchers should pay close attention to questions of the effect on young children of variations in family structure, kinship, religious beliefs, economic production, and advances in medicine and public health. Questions about how concepts of childhood evolved at different times in different cultures and of culturally specific expectations for child behavior are particularly interesting topics for study.

The discovery of childhood appears to have been well under way in colonial America. Children from birth to age 6, called "infants," were dressed and treated differently from older children. Unlike today, colonists thought even very young children were capable of early intellectual development. Because of religious pressure for children to learn the Scriptures as soon as possible as a requirement for salvation, didactic instruction began at a very young age and took place in a home environment. Early education consisted primarily of teaching children, especially boys, to recite the catechism and to read the Bible. Fathers were initially responsible for these important tasks, although mothers increasingly took charge of the education of young children.

Young children in colonial America were educated in a variety of private settings before they began attending public grammar school around the age of 7. Some were taught at home by their parents or by governesses or servants. Others were taught in the homes of relatives or friends if they were boarded out, or in their masters' homes if they were apprenticed. Increasingly, however, both little boys and little girls were taught in schools. They attended petty or dame schools run by neighborhood women or private schools run by schoolmasters, who charged relatively low fees and accepted children from a range of backgrounds. There appears to have been considerable variability and flexibility in the age at which children began going to school. Many young children went to the rural district schools attended by their older brothers and sisters, and were allowed to be present in and around classrooms with older children (Vinovskis, 1972).

Primary sources on early childhood education in colonial America include material culture such as paintings, clothing, and toys. There are collections of family papers in archives and at state and local historical associations. Secondary sources focus on family life, child-rearing practices, and religion (Beales, 1979; Hiner, 1979; Mintz & Kellogg, 1988). Gerald Moran and Maris Vinovskis (1986) have written about early education in Puritan New England, but little work has been done on the mid-Atlantic or southern colonies. More study of dame schools would be especially helpful, and information might be available in primary sources such as town records or in diaries or letters in local archives. Older secondary sources contain descriptions of some of these early, home-based preschools (Earle, 1899; Seybolt, 1935). We need answers to questions such as how much time there was for play, how coming to the New World changed child-rearing and educational practices, how adult expectations about early cognitive ability affected children's development and learning, and how religious and sectarian differences influenced concepts of early education.

THE INFANT SCHOOL MOVEMENT

The notion that young children could benefit from education outside of the home, and should be educated differently from older children, grew out of the changing conditions and ideas that transformed Europe in the seventeenth and eighteenth centuries. Protestant ministers and Enlightenment and Romantic philosophers, such as Johann Amos Comenius (1592–1670), John Locke (1632–1704), and Jean Jacques Rousseau (1712–1778), wrote treatises advocating more child-centered, naturalistic approaches to education. Educators and social reformers such as Johann Heinrich Pestalozzi (1746–1827) and Robert Owen (1771–1858) organized special programs called infant schools to educate and care for the young children of the working classes and the poor. The concept of extrafamilial education for young children became popular among the upper classes as well, and private infant schools were started in major cities in Europe. Educational methods in these programs varied greatly, but most utilized structured games and periods of outdoor play and physical exercise. Infant school pedagogy emphasized the importance of showing affection and using gentler disciplinary techniques with younger children. Some of these programs, such as Owen's communitarian experiments, were explicitly utopian and sought to revolutionize society by changing the way young children were socialized and educated (Forest, 1927; Harrison, 1968; Rusk, 1933).

Followers of Pestalozzi and Owen introduced the idea of infant schools to America, and infant schools were opened in most cities along the eastern seaboard in the 1820s and 1830s. Infant school societies, often female auxiliaries of the men's evangelical Sunday School groups that started the first public or "common" primary schools during the same period, sponsored charity programs to educate poor children and proselytize their families. Private infant schools were begun for wealthier children and enjoyed a brief heyday in the 1830s. Many young children in the early nineteenth century attended primary schools, some of which initially accepted children as young as 3 or 4 (Kaestle & Vinovskis, 1980). But a new American child-rearing literature that encouraged mothers to educate their children at home, concerns about the dangers of precocity, and the expense of running programs cut the infant school movement short. Very few were left in the United States after 1840, and primary school attendance by younger children declined as well (Beatty, 1995; Kuhn, 1947; May & Vinovskis, 1977; Ryan, 1982; Vinovskis, 1972; Wishy, 1968).

A growing body of historical research describes these first formal early childhood education programs. Primary sources include annual reports and magazine articles on infant school societies in Boston, Philadelphia, New York, and elsewhere, and writings about infant education by Bronson Alcott (1830) and others (e.g., "Infant Education," 1829). Research in archives may turn up records of infant school societies in other cities. There are numerous examples of American child-rearing guides from the 1830s and 1840s, and local school records document the attendance of younger children during this period (Child, 1830; Humphrey, 1840; Vinovskis, 1972).

Secondary sources on the infant school movement include studies by Dean May and Maris Vinovskis (1977), Alan Pence (1986), and Charles Strickland (1982). Carl Kaestle and Maris Vinovskis (1980) have analyzed school enrollment patterns for young children in nineteenth-century Massachusetts. It would be interesting to know more about why the idea of educating young children outside of the home caught on and then faded so quickly, how the infant school movement affected the lower grades in public primary schools, and how changing conceptions of young children's intellectual abilities and needs were communicated to, understood, and put into practice or not by different groups of American parents and educators.

THE KINDERGARTEN MOVEMENT

Kindergartens are well known because they gradually succeeded in becoming institutionalized within the public schools. The kindergarten movement began at about the same time the infant school movement was ending, in the 1830s, in what is now Germany. Friedrich Froebel (1782–1852), who had studied with Pestalozzi, started what he felicitously called a kindergarten (child's garden or garden of children) in 1837 in Blankenburg, in Thuringia, near Keilhau. He developed special, sequenced kindergarten materials, activities, finger plays, and games, called "gifts," "occupations," and "mother plays," and wrote books explaining his methods in copious detail (Froebel, 1895). The kindergarten was linked with German liberalism and social reform and was taken up as a cause by educated middle- and upper-class women and men, such as the Baroness Bertha von Marenholtz-Bulow and others, who became ardent supporters and followers of Froebel. Although kindergartens were banned for a period by Prussian authorities, they spread to England and other parts of Europe and became an international movement.

Kindergartens were brought to the United States in the 1850s by German immigrants, and German-speaking kindergartens were begun in cities and towns with large German populations. The first kindergarten in the United States was probably started by Margarethe Meyer Schurz (1833–1876), in her home in Watertown, Wisconsin, in 1856, although there were other early German kindergartens. Elizabeth Peabody (1804–1894) opened the first English-speaking kindergarten in America in Boston in 1860 and immediately wrote a kindergarten guide (Peabody, 1863). Peabody invited German "kindergartners" (as the teachers, not the children, were called) to come to America, many of whom started training schools and wrote kindergarten guides (e.g., Kraus-Boelte & Kraus, 1877). Peabody (1893) founded a kindergarten association, the American Froebel Union, started a journal, *The Kindergarten Messenger*, gave numerous lectures, and actively promoted kindergarten teaching as a vocation for American women. These efforts; the work of William Hailmann, Henry Barnard, and others; and the exhibits and model kindergarten at the 1876 Centennial Exposition in St. Louis did much to popularize the movement. Private kindergartens serving children from middle- and upper-class backgrounds were begun in most major American cities in the 1880s and 1890s.

Charity or "free kindergarten" associations also were started, to provide kindergarten education for the children of the poor and immigrants who crowded American cities in the 1880s and 1890s. Beginning in New York and Boston, free kindergartens, often supported by the wives of wealthy industrialists, spread to Chicago and other parts of the Midwest and West. Charity kindergartens in Boston were the site of child study experiments in the 1880s by the pioneering psychologist G. Stanley Hall (1893). John Dewey (1900) included a kindergarten-like class at his laboratory school at the University of Chicago in the 1890s. The first program at Hull House, Jane Addams's famous settlement house in Chicago, was a kindergarten. Anna Bryan (1838–1901) and Patty Smith Hill (1868–1946) of the Louisville Free Kindergarten Association, Alice Putnam (1841–1919) of the Chicago Free Kindergarten Association, and others began modernizing Froebel's German kindergarten methods to fit the needs of American children and to align Froebelianism with the principles of the emerging science of developmental psychology.

Training mothers to use kindergarten methods was also a key part of Froebel's original concept, and mothers' classes on a broad range of topics were a central aspect of the kindergarten movement. Elizabeth Harrison (1849–1927) of the Chicago Kindergarten College (now National Louis University) and other kindergartners wrote enormously popular books for mothers. Harrison's efforts culminated in the 1894 Chicago Conference of Mothers, the forerunner of the National Congress of Mothers and Parent–Teacher Associations (Harrison, 1895).

Early public kindergarten experiments were started in St. Louis and Boston in the 1870s. Susan Blow (1843–1916) convinced Superintendent of Schools William Torrey Harris, a Hegelian and also a kindergarten supporter, to begin kindergartens in the St. Louis schools in 1873. Blow became a well-known kindergarten trainer and leader of the Froebelian faction that insisted on strict adherence to the original German kindergarten methods. Some kindergartners, such as Kate Douglas Wiggin (1856–1923), who taught at the Silver Street Kindergarten in San Francisco and later wrote *Rebecca of Sunnybrook Farm*, promoted the idea of children's rights and worked to universalize kindergarten education for all children. Beginning in the late 1880s, free kindergarten associations petitioned school boards for support and gradually were incorporated into the public schools in major American cities. The National Kindergarten Association, a political action group founded in New York City in 1909 by Bessie Locke, coordinated a campaign to establish public kindergartens throughout the country. The South and rural areas in the West were late in adopting kindergartens, and very few public kindergartens served African American children. By 1912 about 350,000 children, approximately 9% of those of kindergarten age, were enrolled in public kindergartens; by 1922 some 12% of eligible 5-year-olds were enrolled, and the number of public kindergartens continued to grow slowly (Spodek, 1980; U.S. Department of the Interior, Bureau of Education, 1914).

Primary Historical Sources on Kindergartens

Primary historical sources on German and international kindergartens include Froebel's writings, most of which have been translated into English, and those of other German kindergartners. Prominent nineteenth-century American educator and editor Henry Barnard (1851) collected and published a number of documents and papers on the kindergarten, including Froebel's autobiographical letter to the Duke of Meiningen. Ann Taylor Allen's (1991) excellent book on the German kindergarten movement contains extensive information about other German sources. Archives at the Froebel Institute College in London and the English Froebel Society hold useful information, as do archives and other sources in countries such as China, Japan, and Australia. There may be additional information on kindergartens internationally in the records of the missionary societies that sponsored many foreign kindergartens. Some sources on the international kindergarten movement exist in the archives of the Association for Childhood Education International (ACEI), located in McKeldin Library at the University of Maryland in College Park.

Numerous primary sources are available on the American kindergarten movement. The ACEI archives contain the largest single collection of historical materials on early childhood education, including originals or copies of most key documents, articles, and books. They also contain an extensive collection of old photographs, a set of most of Froebel's gifts and occupations, and other artifacts.

Libraries, historical societies, and archives contain the papers of many American kindergartners. Elizabeth Peabody's letters are held in the Peabody Collection at the Concord Free Public Library in Concord, Massachusetts, and in the Henry W. Berg and Albert A. Berg Collection at the New York Public Library in New York City. The most useful source, Peabody's correspondence with William Torrey Harris, is held at the Missouri Historical Society in St. Louis. Bruce Ronda (1984) has edited a collection of Peabody's letters. Some of Susan Blow's letters are in the William Torrey Harris Papers, the ACEI archives, and in the Blow family papers at the Missouri Historical Society. Patty Smith Hill's papers are at the Filson Club in Louisville, Kentucky, and in the Patty Smith Hill Collection in the archives at Teachers College Library at Columbia University in New York City. Elizabeth Harrison's papers are at National Louis University in Evanston, Illinois. Kate Douglas Wiggin's papers are held in the Bowdoin College Library in Brunswick, Maine. The William Hailmann Collection is in the Department of Special Collections in the University Research Library at the University of California at Los Angeles. Papers of other "kindergartners" are available in archives around the country, notably those of Sarah B. Cooper, among the Sarah Ingersoll Cooper papers in the Cornell University Archives in Ithaca, New York, and of Lucy Wheelock in the archives at Wheelock College in Boston. Numerous articles by these and other kindergartners can be found in journals such as *The Kindergarten*, *Kindergarten Magazine*, and *Kindergarten Review*, held in many university libraries. Articles on the kindergarten also appear in other nineteenth- and twentieth-century education journals and newspapers.

The records of free kindergarten associations located in archives and historical associations around the country provide additional primary historical information about the kindergarten movement. Records of the charity kindergartens sponsored by Pauline Agassiz Shaw (1841–1917) in Boston are at the Schlesinger Library on the History of Women in America at Radcliffe College in Cambridge, Massachusetts. Documents on free kindergartens in Chicago can be found in the Chicago Women's Club Records at the Chicago Historical Society. The Cincinnati Historical Society holds records of the Cincinnati Free Kindergarten Association. Annual Reports of the Louisville Free Kindergarten Association are available at the Gutman Library at the Harvard Graduate School of Education in Cambridge, Massachusetts, as well as at the Filson Club in Louisville. The records of the Silver Street Kindergarten Society and the Golden Gate Kindergarten Society in San Francisco are at the Bancroft Library at the University of California at Berkeley and are available on microfilm. The Bancroft also holds the papers of Phoebe Apperson Hearst, who sponsored kindergartens in San Francisco and elsewhere. The best source of information on what few kindergartens there were in the South is the Southern History Collection in the library of the University of North Carolina at Chapel Hill. There are undoubtedly more free kindergarten association records to be found in local archives around the country.

The records of professional associations and of training programs are another useful primary historical source. The Proceedings of the Kindergarten Department of the National Education Association, available in most university libraries, contain much information, as do the records of the International Kindergarten Union, held in the ACEI archives. Records of the Grand Rapids Kindergarten Training School are in the Michigan Historical Collections at the University of Michigan in Ann Arbor; California Kindergarten Training School records are at the Bancroft Library at Berkeley. The archives of Hampton University in Virginia contain information on and striking photographs of the kindergarten for African American children at Hampton Institute. By the turn of the twentieth century, most colleges of education and departments of education in colleges and universities offered kindergarten courses, which were listed in their catalogues and bulletins. There were also various kindergarten teacher preparation institutes, such as the Clark University Summer School in Worcester, Massachusetts, and others, about which information is available. The records of the National Kindergarten Association are held in the Teachers College Archives at Columbia University.

Records on public kindergartens are available in various forms in school systems and state and public libraries throughout the country. Minutes of local school board meetings and reports of local school superintendents contain debates over the establishment of public kindergartens and information on costs, facilities, enrollments, and other topics. State boards of education and state superintendents or commissioners of education also kept records about kindergartens. The U.S. Bureau of Education published periodic kindergarten circulars and reports and collected statistics on kindergartens nationwide.

Secondary Historical Sources on Kindergartens

There are a number of good secondary sources on the kindergarten movement, including biographies, comprehensive histories, and monographs. Robert Downs's (1978) biography of Froebel is the most useful. Ruth Baylor (1965) and Hersha S. Fisher (1980) have written biographies of Elizabeth Peabody. Biographical information on Susan Blow, Patty Smith Hill, and other kindergartners can be found in *Pioneers of the Kindergarten in America* (International Kindergarten Union, 1924), *Notable American Women* (James & James, 1971), and other biographical dictionaries and encyclopedias. Both Susan Blow and Patty Smith Hill led interesting, long lives and would be excellent subjects for full-length biographies.

The best comprehensive history of the early kindergarten movement in America remains Nina Vandewalker's *The Kindergarten in American Education*, published in 1908. Other more recent books on the kindergarten movement include *The Kindergarten: Its Encounter with Educational Thought in America* by Evelyn Weber (1969); *The Kindergarten Crusade* by Elizabeth Dale Ross (1976); and *Child's Garden: The Kindergarten Movement from Froebel to Dewey* by Michael Steven Shapiro (1983), which provides a sophisticated account of the kindergarten in the context of American culture and intellectual history. The kindergarten also is covered in some detail in *Preschool Education in America: The Culture of Young Children from the Colonial Era to the Present* (Beatty, 1995). Shorter treatments include articles in *History of Education Quarterly* by Marvin Lazerson (1971), Dominic Cavallo (1976), Ann Taylor Allen (1988), and Caroline Winterer (1992). Dorothy Hewes's (1990) overview of the history of kindergarten teacher preparation in the first volume of Spodek and Saracho's *Yearbook in Early Childhood Education* is very useful, as are chapters on early childhood education as a profession by Barbara Finkelstein (1988) in Spodek, Saracho, and Peters's *Professionalism in Early Childhood Education* and by Beatty in Antler and Biklen's *Changing Education* (1990). Marianne N. Bloch's (1987) chapter on the history of early childhood education in Popkewitz's *The Formation of School Subjects* also provides a good summary of the kindergarten.

Much research remains to be done on the history of the kindergarten movement. We need to know more about regional and cultural differences in kindergarten pedagogy and in the spread of kindergartens. How were different groups of Americans convinced to add an additional year of nonacademic education to their local public schools? How were objections to the cost of kindergartens overcome? How did kindergarten directors and teachers interact with mothers, children, and families from different class, ethnic, and racial backgrounds? Are there lessons about the role of parent involvement in educational reform to be learned from the kindergarten's mobilization of mothers as supporters and advocates? How did kindergartning evolve as a profession and how was it affected by the dominance of women and by its perception as women's work? What was the relationship between the kindergarten and other movements and organizations? How did kindergarten directors and teachers relate to public school personnel and how did kindergartens change or how were they changed by the public schools? How have kindergarten programs and curricula changed in the past 50 years? The wealth of primary source material briefly noted in this chapter has not been fully utilized and should be useful in providing more detailed answers to some of these questions.

THE DAY NURSERY, NURSERY SCHOOL, AND MONTESSORI MOVEMENTS

In the mid-nineteenth century, at around the same time as the infant school and kindergarten movements, day nurseries also were started in America. Like the crèches begun in France in the late eighteenth century for the children of working mothers, day nurseries provided physical care for young children. It is questionable, however, whether early day nurseries had an educational curriculum, as infant schools and kindergartens did. Some in the field, such as Rose Alschuler, tried to make day nurseries more educational, and daycare shares some of preschool education's long history (Michel, 1986). Daycare socialized young children, but, as the term suggests, it was designed as a custodial service for the children of poor and working mothers, rather than as preschool education for young children (see Rothman, 1973). Although this distinction is somewhat artificial, the difference in function and clientele signified real historical differences in quality, methods, and perceptions. Day nurseries were often woefully crowded, ill-equipped, unstimulating environments, despite the efforts of their committed, hard-working staffs. Preschool teachers historically distanced themselves from daycare personnel, who called themselves nurses and then workers, and who initially identified with nursing organizations and then with trade unions, rather than with professional education associations. Public perceptions of day nurseries stigmatized them as charities or poverty programs.

The first day nursery in the United States was started in Boston in 1838 by Mrs. Joseph Hale for the children of seamen's wives and widows. In 1854 New York Hospital opened a Nursery for the Children of Poor Women, for the children of wet nurses and women who had been patients (Kerr, 1973). Day nurseries were begun in major American cities in the 1880s and 1890s, sometimes in conjunction with charity kindergartens, and the National Federation of Day Nurseries was founded in 1898 (O'Connor, 1995). Local daycare groups, such as the Association of Day Nurseries in New York, also were started. The day nursery movement enjoyed a heyday in the years before World War I. By 1910 as many as 5,000 children were enrolled in day nurseries in New York City (Kerr,

1973), and female philanthropists such as Mabel Dodge and others supported both day nurseries and charity kindergartens (Cahan, 1989).

Following World War I, day nurseries were criticized by the National Conference of Social Work and other child welfare groups. Daycare became pathologized as a service for poor and abnormal children whose mothers could not care adequately for them. Social workers argued it was better for mothers to stay home, and working mothers were seen as harming their children (Michel, 1986). Supported as a response to crises during World War I and II, daycare re-emerged in the 1960s with federal money from Aid for Dependent Children and what became Title XX-funded child-care programs for the children of women on welfare (Roby, 1973). Feminism and the entry of large numbers of middle- and upper-class women into the labor market in the 1970s and 1980s helped bring daycare into the mainstream. Early childhood education professionals increasingly see preschool and child-care programs as jointly providing services that should be of high quality to children and families (Caldwell & Freyer, 1982; Prochner, 1996).

Like the infant school and kindergarten movements, the nursery school movement had European origins. In 1913 British socialist reformer and Independent Labor Party member Margaret McMillan (1860–1931) started an "open air" nursery school for children from 1 to 6 years of age in the London slum of Deptford. McMillan developed a nursery school pedagogy based on the importance of physical health, cleanliness, outdoor play, and sensorial experiences (McMillan, 1921; Stevinson, 1923). In 1918 the British Parliament passed the Fisher Act, which enabled local education authorities to fund nursery schools, and the nursery school movement then spread throughout England. Americans Abigail Eliot and Edna Noble White attended McMillan's training program in the early 1920s and returned to start nursery schools in the United States (Braun & Edwards, 1972).

In America nursery schools were part of a broad new configuration of fields and professions dealing with young children and families. Psychologists, physicians, social workers, home economists, and parent and nursery school educators collaborated as "experts" concerned with child welfare issues. Much of the intense interest in young children and families in the years following World War I came from newly organized, foundation-based private philanthropy, especially the Laura Spelman Rockefeller Memorial. Lawrence K. Frank, who administered the Memorial's programs for children and families, wanted to make children a legitimate topic of academic research. In the 1920s Frank disbursed more than a million dollars of Rockefeller Foundation money to child study, child development, child guidance, child welfare, parent education, and nursery education projects, and many psychologists became involved in preschool-related research (Schlossman, 1981).

Nursery schools with different emphases received Rockefeller funding in the 1920s. The Bureau of Educational Experiments nursery school, started in

1919 in New York City by Caroline Pratt, Harriet Johnson, and Lucy Sprague Mitchell, focused on socioemotional development and on liberating children from adult oppression. The Yale Psycho-Guidance Clinic Nursery School begun by Arnold Gesell in New Haven in 1920 focused on treating young children with emotional and behavioral problems. The Preschool Laboratories at the Iowa Child Welfare Research Station at the University of Iowa in Iowa City, which opened in the early 1920s, served as a site for research studies on the development of normal children. The Ruggles Street Nursery School and Training Center, started in Boston in 1922 by Abigail Eliot, emphasized parent involvement. The nursery school at the Merrill–Palmer Institute in Detroit, started in 1922 by Edna Noble White, became a national center for parent education. The Smith College Cooperative Nursery School, begun in 1926 by Ethel Puffer Howes as part of the Institute for the Coordination of Women's Interests at Smith College in Northampton, Massachusetts, was designed to meet the needs of educated mothers who wanted to have careers. Many other nursery schools were started on college and university campuses, and private nursery schools and parent cooperatives were begun throughout the country in the 1920s, 1930s, and 1940s (Beatty, 1995; National Society for the Study of Education, 1929; Tank, 1980).

Other pedagogical methods and programs for young children were begun in the early twentieth century as well. Maria Montessori (1870–1952), an Italian physician, started the Casa dei Bambini for poor children in Rome and developed a highly structured, sensorially based sequence of educational techniques and materials. Montessori's ideas spread and were introduced to the United States in 1906 by the American author Dorothy Canfield Fisher and popularized through articles in *McClure's Magazine* (Fisher, 1912; Kramer, 1976; Montessori, 1917; Rambusch, 1993). Montessori toured the United States in 1911, but was concerned that influential Americans such as Alexander Graham Bell, his wife, and others were changing her methods. Desirous of controlling her innovation, Montessori rejected American support and in turn was rejected by American psychologists such as William Heard Kilpatrick, whose 1914 critique condemned her techniques as unscientific. This curtailed the first round of American interest in her work. Montessori's ideas were adopted in other countries around the world, especially in India, and enjoyed a renaissance in the United States in the 1960s after her death. A disparate group of American educators, including progressives and Catholics, began espousing and Americanizing Montessori's pedagogy. Aided by the efforts of Nancy Rambusch, who taught at the Whitby School in Greenwich, Connecticut, and became the leader of the American Montessori Society, Montessori Schools and methods spread throughout the United States and became firmly established as a preschool education model (Chattin-McNichols, 1992; Hainstock, 1997; Rambusch, 1993).

Primary and Secondary Sources on Day Nurseries, Nursery Schools, and Montessori

Primary sources on the history of daycare have been underutilized. Chicago Day Nursery Association records are held in the Chicago Women's Club Collection at the Chicago Historical Institute. Additional day nursery association records are available in local historical association archives around the country. Sonya Michel's (1986) doctoral dissertation contains an extensive listing of primary sources. Other secondary sources include Mary Keyserling's *Windows on Daycare* (1972), Margaret Steinfels's *Who's Minding the Children?* (1973), Virginia Kerr's chapter "Child Care's Long American History," in Pamela Roby's *Child Care—Who Cares?* (1973); Sheila Rothman's, "Other People's Children" (1973); Victoria Getis and Maris Vinovskis's chapter "History of Child Care in the United States Before 1850" (1992); Roger Neugebauer's "Child Care's Long and Colorful Past" (1990); and Geraldine Youcha's *Minding the Children* (1995).

Primary and secondary sources on the history of the British nursery school movement include Margaret McMillan's *The Nursery School* (1921), Emily Stevinson's *The Open-Air Nursery School* (1923), and other books by British nursery educators. Elizabeth Bradburn's *Margaret McMillan: Portrait of a Pioneer* (1989) and Carolyn Steedman's very interesting *Childhood, Culture, and Class in Britain: Margaret McMillan, 1860–1931* (1990) provide information on McMillan's life and list primary source references. On the British nursery school movement generally, see Ilse Forest, *Preschool Education: A Historical and Critical Study* (1927); Education Enquiry Committee, *The Case for Nursery Schools* (1929); and Nanette Whitbread, *The Evolution of the Nursery-Infant School: A History of Infant and Nursery Education in Britain, 1800–1970* (1972).

The best general primary sources on the American nursery school movement are the National Society for the Study of Education's Twenty-Eighth Yearbook, Preschool and Parental Education (1929); the White House Conference report, *Nursery Education* (1931); and the U.S. Office of Education Bulletins published in the 1930s (e.g., Davis & Hansen, 1933). The Rockefeller Archive Center (1988) in North Tarrytown, New York, holds the records of the Laura Spelman Rockefeller Memorial and has published *A Survey of Sources in the History of Child Study*, outlining the foundation's holdings on its projects for children, including the nursery school–related programs funded by Lawrence Frank. Frank's papers are at the Rockefeller Archive Center as well as at the History of Medicine Division of the National Library of Medicine in Bethesda, Maryland. Also at the National Library of Medicine are the papers of Helen Woolley Thompson and the oral histories collected by Milton Senn on other psychologists involved in child development and nursery school–related research.

Other primary sources on nursery schools include Harriet Johnson's (1928, 1933, 1936) books about the Bureau of Educational Experiments nursery school and Caroline Pratt's (1948) fascinating autobiography about her work with young children. Arnold Gesell (1923) wrote a book on preschools, *The Pre-School Child*, and did numerous studies on the development of nursery school–age children. Researchers at the Iowa Child Welfare Station produced an enormous amount of data on preschool-age children, including a popular textbook on nursery school methods by Ruth Updegraff (1938). Abigail Eliot's extensive papers are at the Schlesinger Library at Radcliffe College; the records of the Ruggles Street Nursery School and Training Center are in the Eliot–Pearson files in the archives at Tufts University in Medford, Massachusetts. Edna Noble White (1940) wrote a published report on the history of the Merrill–Palmer School, and her papers and the nursery school's records are in various collections in the Merrill–Palmer archives at the Walter P. Reuther Library at Wayne State University in Detroit, Michigan. The Reuther Library also holds an oral history collection of transcribed interviews with early childhood educators from the Detroit area in the 1920s, 1930s, and 1940s. The records of the Smith College Cooperative Nursery School are held in the Institute for the Coordination of Women's Interests Collection in the Smith College Archives in Northampton, Massachusetts. The archives of Pacific Oaks College in Pasadena, California, have materials on nursery schools, and there is information on college and university nursery schools in campus archives around the country.

Additional sources on the history of nursery schools are available in the ACEI Archives at the University of Maryland. The records of the National Association for Nursery Education, now the National Association for the Education of Young Children (NAEYC) are held in NAEYC's national office in Washington, DC, and in the NAEYC Archives in the Cunningham Memorial Library at Indiana State University in Terre Haute, Indiana. Dorothy Hewes's *NAEYC's First Half Century, 1926–1976* (1976/1996) provides a helpful overview of the organization's history. James Hymes (1978–1979) has published a three-volume book of oral history interviews with leaders of the nursery school movement. There are also articles on nursery schools published in the 1920s and 1930s in journals such as *Childhood Education*. Primary sources on the Montessori movement include Maria Montessori's own books, and early appreciations and critiques of her work. Secondary sources include biographies of Montessori by E. M. Standing (1957), Rita Kramer (1976), and others, and books and chapters on Montessori methods and the American Montessori movement by Nancy Rambusch (1993), Elizabeth Hainstock (1997), and others. The records of the American Montessori Society are in the Teachers College Archives at Columbia University in New York City.

Despite this wealth of primary and secondary material, there is no comprehensive secondary source on the history of the American nursery school movement. The history of nursery schools is treated in Samuel Braun and Esther Edwards's *History and Theory of Early Childhood Education* (1972); in Beatty, *Preschool Education in America* (1995); and in articles by Stephen Schlossman

(1976, 1981) and others. Questions that historians might pursue include the impact on parents of nursery school-related child-rearing advice; the ways in which nursery school teachers' and parents' questions and needs helped shape the agenda for child development research; and how pluralistic and competing psychological constructions of child development affected nursery schools. It also would be useful to investigate attempts to gain public support for nursery schools and to analyze why nursery schools failed to become universalized, as the kindergarten did. There are books on the history of child care, but the inter-relationship of and tensions between day nurseries and nursery schools should be examined in more detail. The relationships, or lack thereof, between nursery educators and child-care personnel, and among different types of public pro-grams and funding sources, should be explored as a way of understanding the class-biased, two-tiered system of child care and early childhood education that evolved in the United States, which affects children, families, and teachers today. Reasons for the recent resurgence of interest in Maria Montessori's meth-ods also would be worth investigating, along with analysis of the social class, cul-tural, and religious associations of the Montessori movement.

PUBLIC PRESCHOOLS, PROJECT HEAD START, AND RECENT GROWTH IN EARLY CHILDHOOD EDUCATION

Like daycare, support for public preschools for children under kinder-garten entrance age in the United States has been associated with national emergencies. The rationales for public preschool funding have focused more on providing employment for adults, war-related child care, combatting pov-erty, or ending welfare than on educating young children. There have been some exceptions for young children in need, but even poor or disabled chil-dren have received only limited public support. And during national emer-gencies, support for all eligible children has not been guaranteed (Beatty, 1995; Lazerson, 1972). Many of the educators and psychologists involved in the nursery school movement of the 1920s also were involved in the public pre-school programs funded by the federal government during the Depression and World War II. A few public preschool experiments existed in the 1920s prior to these government programs. Funded in part by the Chicago Women's Club, a public nursery school for young children with mental health and behavior problems was begun by Rose Alschuler in 1925, at the Franklin School in Chicago. Alschuler (1937) also coordinated a public nursery school experiment in the Winnetka Public Schools. In the 1920s the public schools of Grand Rapids, Michigan, sponsored a few nursery schools. Some public high school home economics departments started preschools as preparental education programs, a trend that increased (Beatty, 1995).

Beginning in 1933 the federal government sponsored Depression-era emergency nursery schools as part of President Franklin D. Roosevelt's New Deal. Targeted at children between the ages of 2 and 5 whose families were on relief, these Works Progress Administration (WPA) nursery schools, many of which were housed in public school buildings, were meant to employ out-of-work teachers, janitors, cooks, and other service workers. Supervised by a National Advisory Committee made up of prominent nursery school educators and directed by Mary Dabney Davis of the U.S. Office of Education, the WPA nursery schools grew quickly. By 1934–35 about 75,000 children were enrolled nationwide, although this was only a fraction of the more than 2 million eligible preschoolers with unemployed parents (Langdon, 1935; Tank, 1980). Nursery educators such as Abigail Eliot, George Stoddard, and Grace Langdon made supervisory visits to emergency nursery schools and hoped federal support would continue after the Depression was over. By 1942, however, when the program was nearing its end, there were only 944 WPA nursery schools enrolling 38,375 children, down from a high of almost 3,000 schools with about 500,000 children at the program's peak (Goodykoontz, Davis, & Gabbard, 1947).

The onset of World War II revivified federal support for preschool education and kept the emergency nursery schools from extinction. As mothers of young children joined the work force for the first time in large numbers, the need for child care for the children of women working in war-related industries became a pressing national concern. In 1943 the Lanham Act, which had been passed by Congress in 1941 to provide funding for facilities in war-impacted communities, was extended to include child-care programs. A National Commission for Young Children was appointed, headed by Rose Alschuler (1942), and prominent nursery educators again were involved in the operation and supervision of wartime children's centers. The best known and documented of the wartime children's centers were the quasi-private, industry-based child service centers directed by Lois Meek Stolz and James L. Hymes at the Kaiser Shipbuilding Company in Portland, Oregon (Stolz, 1978). Although there is disagreement over how many children attended the wartime children's centers, with figures ranging from somewhat over 100,000 to a million, again only a percentage of the children needing care were served (Tank, 1980; Vinovskis, 1993). Again nursery educators hoped children's centers would receive federal support after the war, but President Truman soon terminated Lanham Act child-care funding, although California and Washington, DC, continued to provide public support for children's centers for some children from lower-income families (Grubb & Lazerson, 1977).

Federal support for preschool education started up again in 1965 with Project Head Start, part of President Lyndon B. Johnson's War on Poverty. Experimental preschool programs in the early 1960s, such as Susan Gray's Early Training Project in Murfreesboro, Tennessee, and Martin and Cynthia Deutsch's program in New York City, provided models for Head Start. The Ford Foundation funded an influential experimental preschool in New Haven under the direction of Jeannette Galambos Stone (Zigler & Muenchow, 1992; Zigler & Valentine, 1979). Administered by the Office of Economic Opportunity, not the Office of Education, Head Start was founded as a comprehensive, community-based program for disadvantaged 3- to 5-year-olds and included health care, parent education, and other services in addition to preschool education.

Some early Head Start programs, such as that sponsored by the Child Development Group of Mississippi, were part of radical community organizing and civil rights work (Greenberg, 1969). Head Start expanded quickly from a summer to a year-round program and by 1975 enrolled approximately 350,000 children at an annual cost of $392 billion (Cravens, 1993). Head Start sponsored other initiatives such as the Follow Through program, Parent and Child Centers, and Home Start. Early research on the effects of Head Start and on the different Head Start Planned-Variation curriculum models showed many positive results. But the goal of increasing IQ scores overshadowed other objectives. In 1969 the Westinghouse Learning Corporation Study (Cicirelli, 1967) indicated that IQ gains from Head Start attendance faded in the elementary grades (Westinghouse Learning Corporation, 1969). Despite recent concerns about quality, Head Start remains very popular and has demonstrated beneficial effects for children as well as for parents and families of children in the program (National Head Start Association, 1995).

Since the mid-1980s there has been a great increase in support for early childhood education. The publication in 1980 of the findings of David Weikart's cost-effective Perry preschool program in Ypsilanti, Michigan, provided an enormous boost for the movement to institute publicly funded preschools (Berrueta-Clement et al., 1984; Schweinhart, Barnes, & Weikart, 1980). Weikart's high-quality program showed evidence of increasing high school graduation rates, college attendance, employment, and other positive outcomes, and of decreasing teenage pregnancy and arrests. Although subject to debate, these and other studies indicated the potential efficacy and long-term benefits of early childhood education. New programs integrating preschool education into the public schools were begun in many states and localities, and community-based preschool programs have grown as well (Mitchell, Seligson, & Marx, 1989). But preschool education in America remains a patchwork, with quality determined largely by family income and location, and by the variability of state guidelines, accreditation, training, and funds for program development.

Sources on Public Preschools, Head Start, and Recent Growth in Early Childhood Education

Extensive primary sources exist on public preschools, particularly on the WPA nursery schools and on Project Head Start. The Chicago Women's Club Collection at the Chicago Historical Society contains the records of the Franklin Public Nursery School. Rose Alschuler wrote a description of this early experimental public preschool for the National Society for the Study of Education's Twenty-Eighth Yearbook (1929). Alschuler's book, *Two to Six* (1937), describes the Winnetka public nursery schools.

The wonderfully detailed typescripts of Grace Langdon's supervisory visits to WPA nursery schools around the country are one of the highlights of the enormous amount of primary source information about the Depression-era emergency nursery schools contained in the WPA Collection held at the National Archives in Washington, DC. The published reports of the National Advisory Committee on Emergency Nursery Schools (1934, 1935) include useful statistical data, as does Langdon's (1935) short article, "The Facts About Emergency Nursery Schools," and other pieces in *Childhood Education*. Discussion of the emergency nursery schools appears in the *Proceedings of the Sixth Conference of the National Association for Nursery Education* (1933), in James L. Hymes's (1978–1979) interview with Christine Heinig, and in Ruby Takanishi's (1977a) interview with Lois Meek Stolz, copies of which are at the National Library of Medicine in Bethesda and in the Schlesinger Library at Radcliffe College in Cambridge.

Some primary source material on the wartime children's centers can be found in the WPA files in the National Archives, as emergency nursery schools received continuation funding during the war under the Lanham Act. Hymes's (1978–1979) interview with Lois Meek Stolz focuses on her and his work at the Kaiser child service centers in Portland, Oregon. The issue of wartime child care was the topic of Congressional hearings in the Senate over the War Area Child Care Act, called the "Thomas Bill," in 1943, and discussion of wartime child care appears in issues of the *Bulletin of the Child Welfare League of America* for 1943 and 1944.

Older collections and overviews of early childhood education provide information on some of the early and ongoing experimental preschool programs that began before Head Start. Of these volumes, *Early Childhood Education* edited by Bernard Spodek (1973) and *As the Twig Is Bent* edited by Robert Anderson and Harold Shane (1971) are particularly useful. Reports of the High/Scope Foundation in Ypsilanti, Michigan, contain data on the origins of the Perry preschool program (Schweinhart, Barnes, & Weikart, 1980, 1993). Sue Bredekamp's (1996) review of the history of the Perry preschool program provides a useful analysis of why this predecessor to Head Start has had such a powerful and continuing effect on recent American preschool policy. Since the norms of psychological research, unlike historical research, require confidentiality of subjects, individual case records of children in these experimental programs are not available. There are longitudinal studies comparing some of these projects (Lazar & Darlington, 1982; Ryan, 1974). Spodek's *Handbook of Research in Early Childhood Education* (1982) provides a useful overview of the field.

The overwhelming amount of data on Project Head Start can be divided into two types: primary and secondary sources on the history of Head Start, and research studies and statistics on Head Start programs and their effects. Memoranda and other administrative data on the history of Head Start are held in the Administration for Children, Youth, and Families in the Office of Health and Human Services in Washington, DC. The National Head Start Association is conducting an oral history project on Head Start personnel and programs, and has published a collection of "success stories" with excerpts from interviews with graduates, parents, and teachers from different periods in the program's history (National Head Start Association, 1995). Transcripts of some of the interviews and other files are held at the Association's offices in Alexandria, Virginia. James Hymes's (1978–1979) interview with Keith Osborn is also a source of information on the early history of the program.

The most interesting secondary source on the early days of Head Start is Polly Greenberg's detailed, admittedly biased account of the Child Development Group of Mississippi, *The Devil Has Slippery Shoes* (1969). The most detailed secondary source on the origins of Head Start remains Edward Zigler and Jeanette Valentine's edited volume, *Project Head Start* (1979). Edward Zigler and Susan Muenchow's book, *Head Start* (1992), contains Ziegler's personal perspective as one of the founders and first directors of the program. Maris Vinovskis's article, "Early Childhood Education: Then and Now" (1993), provides a useful short overview of the history of Head Start, and there are brief treatments of Head Start in many other sources. Various data synthesis projects currently under way will provide guidelines to the mountain of psychological research data on Head Start.

Some general secondary sources contain information on different kinds of public programs for young children, including preschools. Gilbert Steiner's *The Children's Cause* (1976) and W. Norton Grubb and Marvin Lazerson's *Broken Promises* (1982) provide overviews of the long history of attempts to secure public support for children, as does Robert Tank's dissertation, "Young Children, Families, and Society in America since the 1820s" (1980); Ruby Takanishi's chapter, "Federal Involvement in Early Childhood Education, 1933–1973: The Need for Historical Perspectives" (1977b); and Marianne N. Bloch's, "Becoming Scientific and Professional: An Historical Perspective on the Aims and Effects of Early Education" (1987). Anne Mitchell, Michelle Seligson, and Fern Marx's *Early Childhood Programs and the Public Schools* (1989) documents the recent growth of public preschools. Other sources, including surveys and reports on the need for increased public support for early childhood education, also contain information on current trends (Boyer, 1992; Carnegie Corporation of New York, 1996; Committee for Economic Development, 1991).

FURTHER SUGGESTIONS FOR RESEARCH
IN EARLY CHILDHOOD EDUCATION

This chapter includes a number of suggested research questions for different historical periods and movements in the history of early childhood education. For public preschools, much more research is needed on the history of Head Start. Cultural, linguistic, racial, gender, and economic issues in the history of preschool programs also require much more analysis. A general history of the early childhood education movement since the 1960s, with studies of the many experimental preschool projects, would be very helpful. Researchers should focus on the reciprocal relationships between psychology and preschool education, on the positive and negative effects of this reciprocity, and on how research agendas and practical needs have been interdependent. A recent example of the relationship of science and policy is the new push for expanding access to preschool programs based on brain research showing the importance of early learning in cognitive development. The intertwining of early childhood education with home economics, social work, pediatrics, and other professions should be explored. The role of political advocacy for early childhood education programs and funding also should be examined, along with the complicated relationship of early childhood education and feminism, labor market segmentation, welfare reform, and child welfare.

The larger story of the long-term effects of not providing universal access to preschool education in America and the impact of this policy on K–12 education is a fascinating topic for speculation. Many aspects of the history of early childhood education remain to be researched; it is a fertile field in need of focused studies and monographs as well as large syntheses. The history of the education of young children in America is just beginning to be told.

Acknowledgments. The author would like to thank Michael Eanes, Dorothy Hewes, Greg Powell, Adele Rosenthal, Lawrence Schweinhart, and Sheldon H. White for their help with this chapter.

REFERENCES

Alcott, B. (1830). *Observations on the principles and methods of infant education.* Boston: Carter & Hendee.

Allen, A. (1988). Let us live with our children: Kindergarten movements in Germany and the United States, 1840–1914. *History of Education Quarterly, 28,* 23–48.

Allen, A. (1991). *Feminism and motherhood in Germany, 1800–1914.* New Brunswick, NJ: Rutgers University Press.

Alschuler, R. (1937). *Two to six: Suggestions for parents and teachers of young children.* New York: Morrow.

Alschuler, R. (1942). *Children's centers.* New York: Morrow.

Anderson, R., & Shane, H. G. (Eds.). (1971). *As the twig is bent.* Boston: Houghton Mifflin.

Aries, P. (1962). *Centuries of childhood: A social history of family life.* New York: Vintage.

Barnard, H. (Ed.). (1851). *Papers on Froebel's kindergarten.* Hartford: Office of Barnard's American Journal of Education.

Baylor, R. M. (1965). *Elizabeth Palmer Peabody: Kindergarten pioneer.* Philadelphia: University of Pennsylvania Press.

Beales, R. W. (1979). Anne Bradstreet and her children. In B. Finkelstein (Ed.), *Regulated children, liberated children: Education in psychohistorical perspective* (pp. 10–23). New York: Psychohistory Press.

Beatty, B. (1990). A vocation from on high: Kindergartning as an occupation for American women. In J. Antler & S. K. Biklen (Eds.), *Changing education: Women as radicals and conservators* (pp. 35–59). Albany: State University of New York Press.

Beatty, B. (1995). *Preschool education in America: The culture of young children from the colonial era to the present.* New Haven: Yale University Press.

Berrueta-Clement, J. R., et al. (1984). *Changed lives.* Ypsilanti, MI: High/Scope Press.

Bloch, M. N. (1987). Becoming scientific and professional: An historical perspective on the aims and effects of early childhood education. In T. S. Popkewitz (Ed.), *The formation of school subjects* (pp. 25–61). New York: Falmer Press.

Boyer, E. L. (1992). *Ready to learn.* Princeton: Carnegie Council on the Advancement of Teaching.

Bradburn, E. (1989). *Margaret McMillan: Portrait of a pioneer.* London: Routledge.

Braun, S., & Edwards, E. (1972). *History and theory of early childhood education.* Worthington, OH: Charles A. Jones.

Bredekamp, S. (1996). 25 years of educating young children: The High/Scope approach to preschool education. *Young Children, 51,* 57–61.

Cahan, E. D. (1989). *Past caring: A history of U.S. preschool care and education for the poor, 1820–1965.* New York: National Center for Children in Poverty, Columbia University.

Caldwell, B., & Freyer, M. (1982). Day care and early education. In B. Spodek (Ed.), *Handbook of research in early childhood education* (pp. 341–374). New York: Free Press.

Carnegie Corporation of New York. (1996). *Years of promise.* New York: Author.

Cavallo, D. (1976). From perfection to habit: Moral training in the American kindergarten. *History of Education Quarterly, 16,* 147–161.

Chattin-McNichols, J. (1992). *The Montessori controversy.* Albany: Delmar.

Child, L. M. (1830). *The mother's book.* Boston: Carter & Hendee.

Cicirelli, V. G. (1969). *The impact of Head Start: An evaluation of the effects of Head Start on children's cognitive and affective development.* Athens, OH: Ohio University.

Committee for Economic Development. (1991). *The unfinished agenda.* New York: Author.

Cravens, H. (1993). *Before Head Start: The Iowa station and America's children.* Chapel Hill: University of North Carolina Press.

Cronon, W. (1992). A place for stories: Nature, history, and narrative. *Journal of American History, 78,* 1347–1376.

Davis, M., & Hansen, R. (1933). *Nursery schools, their development and current practices in the United States*. U.S. Department of the Interior, Office of Education Bulletin No. 9. Washington, DC: Government Printing Office.

Dewey, J. (1900). Froebel's educational principles. *Elementary School Record, 1,* 147–160.

Downs, R. B. (1978). *Friedrich Froebel*. Boston: Twayne.

Earle, A. M. (1899). *Child life in colonial days*. New York: Macmillan.

Education Enquiry Committee. (1929). *The case for nursery schools*. London: George Philip & Son.

Finkelstein, B. (1988). The revolt against selfishness: Women and the dilemmas of professionalism in early childhood education. In B. Spodek, O. N. Saracho, & D. Peters (Eds.), *Professionalism in early childhood education* (pp. 10–28). New York: Teachers College Press.

Fischer, D. H. (1970). *Historians' fallacies: Toward a logic of historical thought*. New York: Harper Torchbooks.

Fisher, D. C. (1912). *A Montessori mother*. Chicago: Richardson.

Fisher, H. S. (1980). *The education of Elizabeth Peabody*. Unpublished doctoral dissertation, Harvard Graduate School of Education, Cambridge, MA.

Forest, I. (1927). *Preschool education: A historical and critical study*. New York: Macmillan.

Froebel, F. (1895). *Pedagogics of the kindergarten* (J. Jarvis, Trans.). New York: Appleton.

Gesell, A. (1923). *The pre-school child*. New York: Houghton Mifflin.

Getis, V., & Vinovskis, M. (1992). History of child care in the United States before 1850. In M. E. Lamb, K. J. Sternberg, C. Hwang, & A. G. Broberg (Eds.), *Child care in context: Cross-cultural perspectives* (pp. 185–206). Hillsdale, NJ: Erlbaum.

Goodykoontz, B., Davis, M. D., & Gabbard, H. F. (1947). Recent history and present status of education for young children. In *Forty-sixth yearbook of the National Society for the Study of Education: Vol. 2. Early childhood education* (pp. 59–120). Chicago: University of Chicago Press.

Greenberg, P. (1969). *The devil has slippery shoes: A biased biography of the child development group of Mississippi*. New York: Macmillan.

Grubb, W. N., & Lazerson, M. (1977). Child care, government financing, and the public schools: Lessons from the California children's centers. *School Review, 86,* 5–37.

Grubb, W. N., & Lazerson, M. (1982). *Broken promises: How Americans fail their children*. New York: Basic Books.

Hainstock, E. C. (1997) *The essential Montessori: An introduction to the woman, the writings, the method, and the movement*. New York: Plume.

Hall, G. S. (1893). *The contents of children's minds on entering school*. New York: Kellogg.

Harrison, E. (1895). *A study of child nature from the kindergarten standpoint*. Chicago: Chicago Kindergarten College.

Harrison, J. F. C. (1968). *Utopianism and education: Robert Owen and the Owenites*. New York: Teachers College Press.

Hewes, D. W. (1990). Historical foundations of early childhood teacher training: The evolution of kindergarten teacher preparation. In B. Spodek, & O. N. Saracho (Eds.), *Yearbook in early childhood education: Vol. 1. Early childhood teacher preparation* (pp. 1–22). New York: Teachers College Press.

Hewes, D. W. (1996). *NAEYC's first half century, 1926–1976*. Washington, DC: NAEYC. (Original work published 1976)

Hiner, N. R. (1979). Cotton Mather and his children. In B. Finkelstein (Ed.), *Regulated children, liberated children: Education in psychohistorical perspective* (pp. 24–43). New York: Psychohistory Press.

Humphrey, H. (1840). *Domestic education.* Amherst, MA: Adams.

Hymes, J. L., Jr. (Ed.). (1978–1979). *Living history interviews* (Vols. 1–3). Carmel, CA: Hacienda Press.

Infant education. (1829). *Ladies' Magazine, 2,* 89.

International Kindergarten Union. Committee of Nineteen. (1924). *Pioneers of the kindergarten in America.* New York: Century.

James, E. T., & James, J. W. (Eds.). (1971). *Notable American women, 1607–1950.* Cambridge, MA: Harvard University Press.

Johnson, H. (1928). *Children in the nursery school.* New York: John Day.

Johnson, H. (1933). *The art of blockbuilding.* New York: John Day.

Johnson, H. (1936). *School begins at two.* New York: New Republic.

Kaestle, C., & Vinovskis, M. (1980). From apron strings to ABCs: School entry in nineteenth-century Massachusetts. In C. Kaestle & M. Vinovskis (Eds.), *Education and social change in nineteenth-century Massachusetts* (pp. 46–71). Cambridge: Cambridge University Press.

Kerr, V. (1973). One step forward—two steps back: Child care's long American history. In P. Roby (Ed.), *Child care—who cares? Foreign and domestic infant and early childhood development policies* (pp. 85–99). New York: Basic Books.

Keyserling, M. D. (1972). *Windows on daycare.* Washington, DC: National Council of Jewish Women.

Kilpatrick, W. H. (1914). *The Montessori system examined.* Boston: Houghton Mifflin.

Kramer, R. (1976). *Maria Montessori: A biography.* New York: Putnam.

Kraus-Boelte, M., & Kraus, J. (1877). *The kindergarten.* New York: E. Steiger.

Kuhn, A. L. (1947). *The mother's role in childhood education: New England concepts, 1830–1860.* New Haven: Yale University Press.

Langdon, G. (1935). The facts about emergency nursery schools. *Childhood Education, 11,* 253–258.

Lazar, I., & Darlington, R.B. (1982). Lasting effects of early education. *Monographs of the Society for Research in Child Development, 47* (2–3).

Lazerson, M. (1971). Urban reform and the schools: Kindergartens in Massachusetts, 1870–1915. *History of Education Quarterly, 11,* 115–142.

Lazerson, M. (1972). The historical antecedents of early childhood education. In I. J. Gordon (Ed.), *Early childhood education* (pp. 33–54). Chicago: University of Chicago Press.

Levi, G., & Schmitt, J.-C. (Eds.). (1997). *A history of young people* (Vols. I–II). Cambridge, MA: Harvard University Press.

May, D., & Vinovskis, M. (1977). A ray of millennial light: Early education and social reform in the infant school movement in Massachusetts, 1826–1840. In T. Hareven (Ed.), *Family and kin in urban communities, 1700–1930* (pp. 62–99). New York: New Viewpoints.

McMillan, M. (1921). *The nursery school.* New York: Dutton.

Michel, S. (1986). *Children's interests/mothers' rights: Women, professionals, and the*

American family, 1920–1945. Unpublished doctoral dissertation, Brown University, Providence, RI.

Mintz, S., & Kellogg, S. (1988). *Domestic revolutions: A social history of American family life.* New York: Free Press.

Mitchell, A., Seligson, M., & Marx, F. (1989). *Early childhood programs and the public schools.* Dover, MA: Auburn House.

Montessori, M. (1917). *The advanced Montessori method.* New York: Frederick A. Stokes.

Moran, G. F., & Vinovskis, M. A. (1986). The great care of Godly parents: Early childhood education in Puritan New England. In A. B. Smuts & J. W. Hagen (Eds.), History and research in child development. *Monographs of the Society for Research in Child Development, 50* (4–5, pp. 24–37).

National Advisory Committee on Emergency Nursery Schools. (1934). *Emergency nursery schools during the first year.* Washington, DC: Author.

National Association for Nursery Education. (1933). *Proceedings of the Sixth Conference of the National Association for Nursery Education.* New York: Author.

National Head Start Association. (1995). *Head Start success stories.* Washington, DC: Author.

National Society for the Study of Education. (1929). *Twenty-eighth yearbook: Preschool and parental education.* Bloomington, IL: Public School Publishing.

Neugebauer, R. (1990). Child care's long and colorful past. *Child Care Information Exchange, 76,* 5–9.

Novick, P. (1988). *That noble dream: "Objectivity" and the American historical profession.* New York: Cambridge University Press.

O'Connor, S. M. (1995). Mothering in public: The division of organized child care in the kindergarten and day nursery, St. Louis, 1886–1920. *Early Childhood Research Quarterly, 10,* 63–80.

Peabody, E. (1863). Kindergarten guide. In E. Peabody & M. Mann (Eds.), *Moral culture of infancy, and kindergarten guide.* Boston: T. O. P. Burnham.

Peabody, E. (1893). *Lectures in the training schools for kindergartners.* Boston: Heath.

Pence, A. (1986). Infant schools in North America, 1825–1840. In S. Kilmer (Ed.), *Advances in early childhood education and day care* (Vol. 4, pp. 1–25). Greenwich: JAI Press.

Pratt, C. (1948). *I learn from children: An adventure in progressive education.* New York: Simon & Schuster.

Prochner, L. (1996). Quality of care in historical perspective. *Early Childhood Research Quarterly, 11,* 5–17.

Rambusch, N. M. (1993). Montessori in America today. In M. H. Loeffler (Ed.), *Montessori in contemporary American culture* (pp. 7–16). Portsmouth, NH: Heinemann.

Roby, P. (Ed.). (1973). *Child care—who cares? Foreign and domestic infant and early childhood development policies.* New York: Basic Books.

Rockefeller Archive Center. (1988). *A survey of sources in the history of child study.* North Tarrytown, NY: Author.

Ronda, B. A. (Ed.). (1984). *Letters of Elizabeth Palmer Peabody: American renaissance woman.* Middletown, CT: Wesleyan University Press.

Ross, E. D. (1976). *The kindergarten crusade*. Athens: Ohio University Press.

Rothman, S. (1973). Other people's children: The day care experience in America. *Public Interest, 30*, 11–27.

Rusk, R. R. (1933). *A history of infant education*. London: University of London Press.

Ryan, M. P. (1982). *The empire of the mother: American writing about domesticity, 1830–1860*. New York: Institute for Research in History and Haworth Press.

Ryan, S. (1974). *A report on longitudinal evaluations of preschool programs* (DHEW Publication No. 76, pp. 306–324). Washington, DC: Government Printing Office.

Schlossman, S. L. (1976). Before Home Start: Notes toward a history of parent education in America, 1897–1929. *Harvard Educational Review, 46*, 436–467.

Schlossman, S. L. (1981). Philanthropy and the gospel of child development. *History of Education Quarterly, 21*, 275–300.

Schweinhart, L. J., Barnes, H. V., & Weikart, D. P. (1980). *Young children grow up: The effects of the Perry Preschool program on youth through age 15*. Ypsilanti, MI: High/Scope Press.

Schweinhart, L. J., Barnes, H. V., & Weikart, D. P. (1993). *Significant benefits: The High/Scope Perry Preschool study through age 27*. Ypsilanti, MI: High/Scope Press.

Seixas, P. (1996). Conceptualizing the growth of historical understanding. In D. R. Olson & N. Torrance (Eds.), *The handbook of education and human development* (pp. 765–783). Cambridge: Blackwell.

Seybolt, R. F. (1935). *The private schools of colonial Boston*. Cambridge, MA: Harvard University Press.

Shapiro, M. S. (1983). *Child's garden: The kindergarten movement from Froebel to Dewey*. University Park: Pennsylvania State University Press.

Spodek, B. (Ed.). (1973). *Early childhood education*. Englewood Cliffs, NJ: Prentice-Hall.

Spodek, B. (1980). The kindergarten: A retrospective and contemporary view. In L. Katz (Ed.), *Current topics in early childhood education* (pp. 173–192). Norwood, NJ: Ablex.

Spodek, B. (1982). *Handbook of research in early childhood education*. New York: Free Press.

Standing, E. M. (1957). *Maria Montessori: Her life and work*. Fresno, CA: Academy Library Guild.

Steedman, C. (1990). *Childhood, culture, and class in Britain: Margaret McMillan, 1860–1931*. New Brunswick, NJ: Rutgers University Press.

Steiner, G. (1976). *The children's cause*. Washington, DC: Brookings.

Steinfels, M. (1973). *Who's minding the children? The history and politics of day care in America*. New York: Simon & Schuster.

Stevinson, E. (1923). *The open-air nursery school*. London: Dent.

Stolz, L. M. (1978). The Kaiser Child Service Centers. In. J. L. Hymes, Jr. (Ed.), *Living history interviews: Vol. 2. Care of the children of working mothers* (pp. 26–56). Carmel, CA: Hacienda Press.

Strickland, C. E. (1982). Paths not taken: Seminal models of early childhood education in Jacksonian America. In B. Spodek (Ed.), *Handbook of research in early childhood education* (pp. 321–340). New York: Free Press.

Takanishi, R. (1977a). *An American child development pioneer, Lois Meek Stolz* [Interview typescript]. Schlesinger Library, Radcliffe College, Cambridge, MA.

Takanishi, R. (1977b). Federal involvement in early childhood education, 1933–1973: The need for historical perspectives. In L. Katz (Ed.), *Current issues in early childhood education* (pp. 139–161). Norwood, NJ: Ablex.

Tank, R. M. (1980). *Young children, families, and society in America since the 1820s: The evolution of health, education, and programs for preschool children.* Unpublished doctoral dissertation, University of Michigan–Ann Arbor.

Ulich, R. (Ed.). (1947). *Three thousand years of educational wisdom.* Cambridge, MA: Harvard University Press.

Updegraff, R. (1938). *Practice in preschool education.* New York: McGraw-Hill.

U. S. Department of the Interior, Bureau of Education. (1914). *Kindergarten Circular No. 6.* Washington, DC: Government Printing Office.

Vandewalker, N. C. (1908). *The kindergarten in American education.* New York: Macmillan.

Vinovskis, M. A. (1972). Trends in Massachusetts education. *History of Education Quarterly, 12,* 501–529.

Vinovskis, M. A. (1993). Early childhood education: Then and now. *Daedalus, 122* (1), 151–176.

Weber, E. (1969). *The kindergarten: Its encounter with educational thought in America.* New York: Teachers College Press.

White, E. N. (1940). *The Merrill–Palmer school: A report of twenty years, 1920–1940.* Detroit: Merrill–Palmer School.

Whitbread, N. (1972). *The evolution of the nursery-infant school: A history of infant and nursery education in Britain, 1800–1970.* London: Routledge & Kegan Paul.

White House Conference on Child Health and Protection, Committee on the Education and Training of the Infant and Preschool Child. (1931). *Nursery education.* New York: Century.

Winterer, C. (1992). Avoiding a "hothouse system of education": Nineteenth-century early childhood education from the infant school to the kindergarten. *History of Education Quarterly, 32,* 289–314.

Wishy, B. (1968). *The child and the republic: The dawn of modern American child nurture.* Philadelphia: University of Pennsylvania Press.

Youcha, G. (1995). *Minding the children: Child care in America from colonial times to the present.* New York: Scribner.

Zigler, E., & Muenchow, S. (1992). *Head Start: The inside story of America's most successful educational experiment.* New York: Basic Books.

Zigler, E., & Valentine, J. (Eds.). (1979). *Project Head Start: A legacy of the war on poverty.* New York: Free Press.

CHAPTER 2

Through a Small Window: Knowing Children and Research Through Standardized Tests

M. Elizabeth Graue

Standardized tests have been a prominent part of the educational landscape for years, ranging from individual markers of academic identity to high-stakes measures of efficacy for both individuals and institutions. Within the realm of early childhood curriculum, the use of standardized tests has received much attention, for both its potential to improve practice and its related deleterious effects. As practitioners, policy makers, and politicians increasingly have relied on tests, we have seen tests used as gateways for student entrance and promotion in elementary schooling, a narrowing of curriculum that mirrors the content and format of tests, instructional time used for test preparation, and intense pressure placed on school people to produce good test scores (Gnezda & Bolig, 1988; Shepard, 1991).

Awareness of these trends and the outcomes they promoted prompted the early childhood community to call for the development of standards for evaluating the validity of tests used with young children (Bredekamp & Shepard, 1989; Kamii, 1990; National Association for the Education of Young Children, 1988; Shepard, 1991). In addition, there has been increased attention to alternatives to traditional standardized measures for young children, with multisource, contextualized data generation at its core (e.g., Bredekamp & Rosegrant, 1992, 1995; Genishi, 1992; Hills, 1992; Meisels, 1994; Wolf, Bixby, Glenn, & Gardner, 1991). It is clear that the public voice of early childhood education speaks without wavering on the issue of use of standardized measures with young children—

they typically are seen as having limited value for developing curriculum or for generating information about individual or groups of children, and carry with them significant potential for misuse.

But curricular and evaluation uses are not the only contexts in which standardized tests are employed in early childhood education. In this chapter, I will explore another, and perhaps more pervasive, use of these tools—the use of standardized tests in early childhood research. I will explore the assumptions and values that ground the employment of standardized tests, how their use shapes knowledge production and standards for scholarship in the field, and how they frame research–practice connections.

I examine these issues theoretically by looking at standardized tests as tools that shape research, scholars, practitioners, practice, and policy. From this perspective, these tools represent the ideas in the field and at the same time, through this representation, come to fashion the field as well. In particular, I am interested in how our use of standardized tests has provided opportunities to understand the practice of early childhood education and the experiences of children, as well as how it has crowded out other understandings that might enrich our work. To do this we must utilize and reach beyond the prevailing psychometric criteria for evaluating the use of testing instruments so that our consideration of the benefits and limitations are not constrained by the discourse and ideology that have framed the field of testing. I try to provide a balanced view across modes of thinking about testing and research, but realize that to include the various perspectives, I must confine my discussion to broad issues. I refer readers to a well-established literature on early childhood testing if they are interested in pursuing the psychometric dimension more fully (Bredekamp & Shepard, 1989; Gullo, 1994; Kamii, 1990; Meisels, 1985, 1994; National Association for the Education of Young Children [NAEYC], 1988; Powell & Sigel, 1991; Scarr, 1981; Shepard, 1991; Wortham, 1990).

WHAT IS A STANDARDIZED INSTRUMENT?

There are many ways of knowing in research, from measures of human attributes amenable to quantitative summarization, to participant-observations and narratives of human experience. The field of early childhood research has broadened its evidentiary base in recent years (Bowman, 1993; Walsh, Tobin, & Graue, 1993), but the scholarly community is still defined predominantly by quantitative measures of predefined attributes (Swadener & Kessler, 1991). I later explore the academic and ideological frames that underlie these tools; here it is important to define how I am using the idea of standardized tests.

A *standardized test* is an instrument with specified content that has fixed procedures for administration and scoring designed to measure an individual's knowledge, skills, or development. This measure is accomplished by taking a sample and inferring the state of being from that sample. For this reason, a test is a representation of what someone can do, be, or become (Hanson, 1993). The fixed content and direction for administration are thought to provide all children with equal access to the test items, as well as to make interpretation of results unambiguous and therefore objective. The test provides a means of comparison among individuals and groups on the attribute measured by the scale that is summarized quantitatively (Green, 1981; Gullo, 1994; Wortham, 1990). Standardized instruments vary immensely in focus and format, but should meet standards of validity and reliability established for psychometric precision and for appropriateness with young children (American Educational Research Association, American Psychological Association, & National Council on Measurement in Education, 1985; NAEYC, 1988).

The early childhood research community has utilized a number of types of standardized instruments in practice and research, with a muddied history of misuse of instruments (Meisels, 1985). *Achievement tests*, such as the Comprehensive Test of Basic Skills (CTB/McGraw-Hill, 1990) or the Iowa Test of Basic Skills (Hieronymus et al., 1990), measure mastery of particular content or skill as the result of instruction. Research uses include measures of outcomes related to a myriad of instructional methods and contexts, organizational strategies, and demographic influences. *Readiness tests*, such as the Metropolitan Readiness Test (Nurss & McGauvran, 1986) or the Boehm Test of Basic Concepts (Boehm, 1986), assess skills seen as needed for a particular instructional program. They might be used as pretests or as outcome measures for instructional programs or demographic characteristics such as school entrance age. *Developmental screening tests*, such as the Denver Developmental Screening Test (Frankenburg, Dodds, Fandal, Kazuk, & Cohrs, 1975) or the Early Screening Inventory (Meisels & Wiske, 1983), are the first step in the process of identifying children with special needs, who would benefit from more in-depth, multidisciplinary assessment. Developmental screening tests have been used by researchers to map developmental markers and connect them to environmental, physical, or instructional contexts. This next step is accomplished by *diagnostic assessments*, such as the McCarthy Scales of Children's Abilities (McCarthy, 1972) or the Battelle Developmental Inventory (Newborg, Stock, Wnek, Guidubaldi, & Sninicki, 1984), which serve to identify children with special needs and point to programming that can address developmental problems attendant to those needs. Finally, *intelligence tests*, such as the Stanford–Binet Intelligence Scale (Thorndike, Hagen, & Sattler, 1986) or the Wechsler Preschool and Primary Scale of Intelligence (Wechsler, 1989), are measures of cognitive functioning derived from problem-solving activities. In research they often are used either as outcome measures related to some treatment or as covariates to establish the initial equivalence of groups examined comparatively. All of these instruments share a focus on individual development in relation to some task or context. They come out of ways of knowing about the world that have a quite coherent philosophy and history.

The science of mental testing rests on certain assumptions about the nature of reality, the movement of children within it, and the development of our understandings of it. These assumptions dictate the development of particular kinds of evidence. One of the key assumptions that ground standardized instruments is that important characteristics of young children can and should be measured. The construction of testing instruments and their use and interpretation are centered on the basic idea of *measurability*, with a premium placed on those skills, abilities, and activities that can be described by test items. From these items, the measures are used to *differentiate among individuals* (Hopkins & Stanley, 1981). Inherent in this conception of differentiation is the idea that comparative information is useful; that we can know more about individuals if we look at them relative to some other group—whether it is a representative norming group or developmental (e.g., age cohort) set. In addition, it is assumed that *the characteristic of interest is differentiated in a patterned way* in the comparison group. Typically, this pattern is a normal distribution, symmetrical with predictable relations of spread among scores that provide information about where an individual's score lies relative to the scores of others. The fixed format of standardized tests is designed to buffer the testing process from bias by eliminating variation in administration, scoring, and interpretation. All subjects receive the same directions to answer the questions or perform the tasks, and all meaning making from the results of the test is prescribed. The task, rather than the interaction between test taker and test giver, mediates the child's understanding.

PREVALENCE OF TESTS IN EARLY CHILDHOOD RESEARCH

The use of standardized tests in early childhood curriculum has been explored and critiqued by several scholars. What do we know about the use of standardized tests in early childhood research? One way we could examine the issue is to look at how historians have described the foundations of early childhood research and practice, with an eye to the sources of evidence used to build the knowledge base that has become our history. Historians have examined how the field of early childhood education came out of a psychological tradition that relied on "scientific" data collection, analysis, and dissemination (Bloch, 1991; Kliebard, 1986). Marianne Bloch (1991) has described the initial development of the child study movement and G. Stanley Hall's promotion of

(a) faith in scientific (objective, rational, empirical) methods; (b) that psychological studies of individuals and individual development and behavior were important; (c) that observed natural development of children, their needs, interests, and impulses could be used to inform pedagogy; and (d) that philosophy should be, to some extent, separated from the science of psychology, child development research and knowledge; and educational pedagogy. (pp. 100–101)

Although the enthusiasm for child study waned, the field of early childhood education became connected with areas that relied on psychological theory, method, and philosophy. A pivotal aspect of this perspective is its use of standardized tools for generating a knowledge base. The field focused on causal relations, with attention to understanding both patterning in development and its production through educational and care settings. This in turn generated a need for instruments that could measure skills, cognition, and behaviors across large numbers of children. Researchers applied experimental treatments, then measured outcomes or followed prespecified observation guidelines of "naturalistic" behavior in laboratory settings. Confined to these methods, tightly controlled instruments for understanding children have been the norm in the early childhood field until recently. The need for objective, comparative data on the development of children dictated the use of tools that would provide such information. Standardized tests are one such tool.

WHAT DO STANDARDIZED TESTS TELL US ABOUT EARLY CHILDHOOD RESEARCH?

Standardized tests are used within spheres of practice that are complex. To evaluate their use and influence, one could focus on the tests themselves, exploring their technical properties and what they allow us to see. This perspective examines the utility of tools-in-action and is the typical focus of psychometric examinations of instruments. In contrast, we could examine how standardized tests mark the field of early childhood education. How do these tools define the activity of early childhood researchers and subsequently the practice of working with young children? This view illuminates meanings-in-action. Although these two dimensions can be used to understand a single entity, they are perspectives situated within very different value structures and goals. What is seen as a strength or a weakness, a cost or a benefit of the use of standardized tests, is dictated by the perspective of the viewer. In the next section of the chapter, I look at the use of standardized tests from the vantage points of both tools-in-action and meanings-in-action, exploring how each perspective sets us up to value testing in different ways and to look for divergent outcomes.

Tools-in-Action

The long-held interest in mapping development and the causal network be-tween actions with children and developmental outcomes produced a reliance on instruments that could measure constructs in that domain of knowledge. Those who value the use of standardized instruments situate most of their argu-ments within the realm of psychometric and empirical-analytic considerations. They focus on the attributes of tests that allow for comparison, generalization, and consistency across settings.

At a general level, early childhood researchers needed to measure the con-struct of interest (validity) in a consistent manner (reliability) without concern about variations in administration or access to tasks (bias). The positive attributes of tests that allow researchers to have confidence in measures have been out-lined by Sue Wortham (1990). The attributes do not stand alone, however. The meanings created by the attributes—the goals, outcomes, and motives that are connected with these characteristics—also are considered.

Because of the way they are constructed, standardized tests have *uniform administration* procedures that make the scripted language and action related to the test comparable in all settings. This uniformity should rule out concerns about bias in administration. A second advantage seen by Wortham is that the standardized tests produce *quantifiable scores*, which makes scoring more ob-jective and allows particular kinds of comparisons among individual and group performance. In addition, the numerical score can be transformed in a variety of ways to facilitate these comparisons. A third advantage is the typical use of *norm referencing* to situate test performance in a larger universe of meaning. A child's test results can be compared with the test results of the norming group to provide a relative picture of being. This is very helpful when researchers are interested in understanding the production of individual differences through various early care and educational settings or instructional strategies. Finally, standardized tests are characterized by a focus on *reliability and validity*, at-tributes that assess the ability of a measure to depict the construct of interest consistently and precisely. When tests are seen as reliable and valid, users can have greater confidence in the results as measured and the inferences made from those results.

All of these characteristics of standardized tests make them good tools for doing particular kinds of work to help us understand children and their develop-ment. Standardized tests can give us information about children's measurable attributes—their language (often focused on vocabulary), concepts, thinking and problem-solving skills, and sometimes physical skills. From these measured at-tributes, we can derive understandings about patterns of development—who can do what in which early education contexts. These patterns are end-point snapshots that presumably are related to the construct to which we hope to make the causal inference. We can evaluate the efficacy of an instructional treatment by who scores better on a test. We can compare the costs and benefits of a treatment relative to the score increment derived from the test. This allows us to determine who should receive limited resources for various services and programs. With sufficient information about patterns, prediction becomes possible—given this constellation of developmental skills and abilities, what kind of setting will provide optimal growth?

These characteristics of standardized tests provide a context for research that has clear rules for procedures and evidence. As a field, we know how to construct measures and how to apply them in research contexts to generate information about the development and experiences of children. The use of these measures provides a cultural context in which we socialize new researchers, establish standards for judging the adequacy of emerging research, and promote confidence in the development of a knowledge base for the field. Standardized tests provide material for building the evidentiary base for our scholarship and practice—research can be evaluated for its faithfulness to technical principles and its coherence to existing knowledge. They illustrate the authoritative discourse of scientific portrayals of children, their care, and their education—univocal, strong, unequivocal.

These advantages are characterized by their technical nature—they are defined by their effects on the ability to measure within a psychometric model. Attributes and meanings are one and the same; they justify themselves in a system in which salient outcomes are procedurally oriented. Bias in testing is related to loose administrative control; rendering quantitative scores is an unquestioned benefit. The system of rationalization is efficient, self-confirming, and complete, with rules that buffer alternative explanations from consideration.

These characteristics and meanings have dimensions other than the technical aspects, if considered from what Gordon and Terrell (1981) call the sociopolitical context. From this perspective the very attributes that are positive within the psychometric view are open to debate. In the next section, I explore the gaps that can be seen in these attributes and how these gaps shape what we can know in early childhood education. My discussion is organized by levels of knowing or meanings produced by tests. It needs to be acknowledged, however, that from the sociopolitical perspective, these levels cannot be considered independently. Technical issues are never purely technical but rest instead on the interplay of social and political issues that frame their use. Although organizationally I present them as separate, I want to remind the reader that they constitute each other.

Meanings-in-Action

At the basic level is the knowledge about and of the *instrument*—how does the test produce data and what can we know from it? The next level is that of *construct*—what constructs do the tests promote and what outcomes do they entail? Finally, I explore the level of *ideology*—what ideology is represented by the instrument and constructs, and how does this ideology shape the field of early childhood research?

Instruments. The use of uniform procedures works from the assumption that variations in procedures introduce additional influences, beyond item difficulty and child performance levels, into the scoring. This perspective represents a belief that the meaning of an activity exists within the script of the task—that the language and action comprise the construction of meaning for test takers. Further, variation produces bias and therefore advantage for certain individuals and groups. This viewpoint ignores a growing concern for individual and cultural construction of meaning that occurs within a task, shaped by past experience and the interaction among test taker, administrator, and task (Garcia & Pearson, 1994). It is also curiously counterintuitive to what might be seen as standard early childhood practice—attending to individual needs of children in activity (Bredekamp, 1987). When we rely solely on scripts of standardized tests, we make assumptions, which may or may not be warranted, about how children are making meaning of a task. That may, in fact, produce more bias in results than do strictly scripted and evenly applied directions. This is more than a developmental matter that affects younger children more than older ones because of their sophistication of language and cognition. It is a matter of shared meanings or intersubjectivity.

The reliance on quantitative scores has made quantification not only a means of understanding children and their experiences but also an end. In test construction, the mode of displaying information through comparative, numerical representation (which is essentially what quantification allows) dictates the form of depiction used for performance on a task. It must be amenable to a categorical representation (yes, it exists; no, it doesn't), or it represents degrees of an entity (above, at, or below age level, or 58th percentile). Tasks must be designed to elicit data in these forms, and reporting must be framed with numbers in mind. Other ways of knowing children—through case descriptions, compilations of anecdotal descriptions, portfolios, interviews—do not fit. A narrow window on an even narrower band of child life is provided.

The comparative aspect of norm referencing, so attractive for its relative portraits of performance, has its downside as well. Built on assumptions of normal distributions of characteristics in populations, standardized tests are designed to spread out the performances of individuals. This process often produces tautological results because the test construction relies on producing arrays of performance, which then are interpreted as telling us that performance is distributed in a pseudo-normal way.

The strengths of standardized tests are also their weaknesses. They are developed by clear methods with standards for what counts as data, contributing to a solid foundation of knowledge. But the clarity and prescriptive nature of tests for research are also indicative of a lack of flexibility, of only structural attention to meaning construction for tasks, of narrow conceptions of representing child experience, and of reliance on distributional assumptions that may or may not be defensible. While these technical issues are important, they lead us to discussion of a broader issue—the constructs that are portrayed by standardized tests.

Constructs. Standardized tests are used to measure the existence, within an individual, of certain constructs. The construct, while abstract and unobservable, is inferred from test performance. In the area of early childhood education, we traditionally have been interested in using tests to help us describe patterns related to social characteristics such as sex or age for constructs such as readiness, language development, or IQ. These social characteristics and test measures are used as markers on the developmental map. The links between standardized tests and conceptions of development have been mutually reinforcing, with development used as a metaphor (Kessler, 1991) and framework for thinking about children, and tests used to sharpen our understanding of developmental trends and outcomes.

This focus on development as a basis for early childhood education has been a foundational aspect of research and practice, and has been described as a tool for the professionalization of the field (Bloch, 1987). It has provided a context for focusing on the patterned aspects of child growth over time and has propelled activity in all aspects of the early childhood field. This reliance on the notion of development recently has been the focus of critique by scholars representing a variety of perspectives. It has been articulated beautifully in the literature (Bloch, 1991; Burman, 1994; Danziger, 1990; Lubeck, 1996; Walsh, 1991), but I will briefly summarize the aspects of the argument related to the use of standardized tests.

The construct of development is pivotal to the work of educational research on young children—tests are used to delineate it and to describe the effects of interventions posed by early educators. But its use as a construct to guide research and practice is suspect for a variety of reasons. The use of the notion of development and its portrayal through the interpretation of standardized tests is based on the assumption that development is one thing for all children in all settings in all activities. Development, as portrayed in standardized tests, is singular, with paths and predictors that are universal and unidimensional. The image it invokes might be a flowchart with if–then statements. But development is much messier than this image suggests. There are multiple ideas about what constitutes development— the field has diverse conceptions about how children grow and learn (Walsh, 1991). Further, development does not "develop" in a cookie cutter fashion in every context (Lubeck, 1996; Walsh, 1991). It is situated in social and cultural practices.

Because development is seen as universal, children are seen as universal as well. For this reason, the samples on which developmental knowledge has been based (and many times the instruments as well) are not seen as bound by cultural, contextual, historical, or political considerations. The foundational work of development, on which the construction of many standardized measures are based, was completed with groups of very privileged European American, middle-class children—a group that is not representative of all children by any means. The baseline for what constitutes normal development historically has been skewed in a direction of middle-class values and experiences (Bloch, 1991; Lubeck, 1996). This argument continues today in critiques and revisions of policy documents on developmentally appropriate practice (DAP) (Bredekamp, 1987; Bredekamp & Copple, 1997; Lubeck, 1994; Mallory & New, 1994; Walsh, 1991).

A personal experience portrays this in its connection to standardized tests. As part of a research project on readiness, I helped school personnel administer their kindergarten entrance readiness screening test, one aspect of the Early Prevention of School Failure program (Werner, 1989). In a section that assessed language, children were shown pictures of objects and asked their function. When I pointed to a picture of a four-pane window, the child was to tell me that the window let the sunshine in (or an approximation of this idea). Javier got that item wrong. The son of migrant workers who had lived what many of us would call a challenging life, Javier told me that the window kept the bad guys out. The manual did not find that to be a suitable answer. The expectations for the experiences and knowledge base that framed the test's idea of school readiness came out of particular views of normal development. These ideas clashed with Javier's life. Because the construct was represented in the instrument in this narrow way, Javier was put outside the realm of readiness.

Historical views of development have had a pervasive individual focus, with the unit of analysis being an individual child in interaction with the environment. In its most pronounced form this individual focus is described by Bruner (1986) as "some inherently individualistic Self that develops, determined by the universal nature of man, and that is beyond culture. In some deep sense, this Self is assumed to be ineffable, private" (p. 85). This view runs counter to current social views of learning, which portray development as mediated through social interaction with others in a complex, culturally situated environment (Bruner, 1986; Bruner & Haste, 1987; Cole & Cole, 1989; Vygotsky, 1978; Walsh, 1991).

While this shift in conceptualizing development has had important implications for curriculum and teaching, its ramifications for measuring individual progress or for portraying the educational experiences of groups have been especially profound. The institution of mental testing, which produced the tool of standardized tests, is built on the individualist view of children, their learning, and their evaluation. The roots for today's measurement practices can be traced to the work of Francis Galton, described by Danziger (1990) as follows:

> What Galton's testing situation produced was essentially a set of individual *performances* that could be compared with each other. They had to be *individual* performances—collaborative performances were not countenanced in this situation. . . . The performances therefore defined characteristics of independent, socially isolated individuals and these characteristics were designated as "abilities." An ability was what a person could do on his own, and the object of interest was either the individual defined as an assembly of such abilities or the distribution of performance abilities in a population. (p. 56)

The construct of development, conceived as an individual act, was linked inextricably to the technology of measuring it (Burman, 1994). The use of traditionally structured standardized tests will continue to provide information for a model of development that is no longer held as appropriate by many. We will get answers to old questions, questions that lead us in directions we do not necessarily want to go.

A particular problem related to standardized tests is that they produce and reify the constructs they purport to measure and describe (Hanson, 1993). At the level of instrumentation, constructs often become confused with what is measurable and, in turn, come to define the construct itself. Standards for validity require that items measure entities that are clearly defined and that discriminate among individuals in unbiased ways that can be understood through psychometric principles. Tasks then are chosen that have those characteristics. But the interpretation of those tasks, individually and in combination to depict a construct, often conflates measurability with meaning. We therefore test what is easier to measure, then define what we are looking for in terms of what is on the test. Forgetting that tests are representations of an idea, we allow them to become the idea in ways that drive research and practice.

This is a classic characteristic of traditional work on readiness (Graue, 1993), which explored relations between performance on readiness tests and school achievement, either at the end of a school year (typically kindergarten) or at a more distant point. The purpose of most readiness tests, as used in the literature and in practice, was to determine who was capable of succeeding in a formal school context—a threshold view of who might profit from the efforts of school people. The tests were composed of tasks that were easy to administer and score—for example, vocabulary, fine motor skills such as cutting, body awareness through drawing a man, and gross motor skills such as standing on one foot. The construct of readiness then *became* those tasks as they were operationalized in research and practice. Researchers proposed work that tightened the link between test items and outcome measures, with practice shaped through the results of this work. Some intervention efforts even developed curriculum directly from narrowly construed test items, heightening the opportunity for improving performance as the result of participation in the program (Shepard, 1991).

The culture of measurability, fostered by the use of standardized tests, produced attention to certain kinds of child characteristics. Simultaneously, the attention of the research community was directed to particular kinds of problems, knowable through the tools of tests. The technology and tools made certain programs of inquiry possible and, in fact, more probable. Given limited resources in the academic world and restricted understandings of diverse ways of knowing, tools constrained the research act so that the field advanced in certain ways but was seriously constrained in others. These possibilities and constraints represent ways of thinking about the world that have ideological and cultural implications for the field.

Ideology. Discussions that take into account the sociopolitical context situate the technical within the political, language forms (such as psychometric jargon) within cultural contexts, and practices within social dynamics that provide privilege to some and disadvantage to others. In this section, I will explore how the use of standardized testing in research in early childhood education represents particular ideas about children and their caregivers and how these ideas shape the field.

A focus on the individual, which is inscribed in measurement practices and traditional views of development, provides the field with individually oriented explanations and excuses for outcomes of research and practice. We "fix" individual children and families through research-based interventions; therefore, the problems we have defined for these children exist in or, even more problematically, are produced by individuals. This approach has limited the explanatory power we have for many of the inequities plaguing children in today's society. Further, it has constrained remedies to one-person-at-a-time programs. Danziger (1990) explained the problem in this way:

> The characterization of individuals in terms of their degree of conformity to criteria of performance within specific social contexts made it easy to redefine the problems of institutions, or even the problems of society, as individual problems. If all social problems were nothing more than the aggregate of individual problems, they could be handled by appropriate treatment of individuals and required no questioning of the social order. (pp. 109–110)

Bloch (1991) illustrates the ramifications of such a view:

> With little attention to the complexity of the influences on the opportunities for development and success, we as a field continue to blame individuals. The constrained and/or narrow way in which early education research and policy has developed over time limits its ability to direct action at appropriate levels, and helps to reinforce inequities that the field claims it works against. (p. 106)

Our use of tests continues to direct our attention to the individual—whether it is to individual children and their growth in particular early childhood contexts or to their parents and teachers, who should produce this growth through professionally endorsed educational practices. Our efforts to change the life chances of individuals or groups of children are targeted to programs that shift the predictors of development (cognitive support, health and nutrition services if they are lucky) and produce changes measured in terms of improvement in test performance. We have no way to explore what Bloch (1991) calls the "complexity of influences" that set up certain interactions and opportunities, no way to change the dynamic of history that is recalled through individualistic perspectives on living.

The use of standardized tests instantiates a hierarchical view of development, producing normality and, as a result, abnormality. Views of children are created that are relational only in distributions of performance on test tasks. Meaning is created by comparison. Whether or not differences in performance have "natural" implications for children, importance is produced through its description by a test:

> The psychological individual was a highly specified and studied entity whose mental qualities and development were understood by virtue of comparison with the general population. So knowledge of the individual and the general went hand in hand; each required the other, and each was defined in terms of the other. (Burman, 1994, p. 14)

A child becomes a person through distinctions in social characteristics like age or grade level relative to peers. Understandings that are adequate in one context become deficient in the interpretation of test results.

Individual children and their experiences in real time and real situations disappear, stripped of meaning without the anchor point of a statistical norm. This norm is a fictitious entity—an aggregation of the reactions of many, many children to scripted situations created for psychometric not pedagogical reasons. Testing allows us to create images of children that place them in a framework of more or less developed so that we can move them along to the next stage, the next skill, the next level of development. And this creation is not purely technical, without implication:

> What is perhaps different about standardised testing is that the moral evaluation that underlies the description is rendered invisible and incontrovertible through the apparent impartiality of statistical norms and administration through the power of the institutions that can enforce statistical description as moral-political prescription. There is a central ambivalence here about the relation between the natural and the nurtured that mirrors the tension between scientific objectivity and social applications structuring psychological

research; it seems that the natural course of development has been carefully monitored, supported and even corrected in order to emerge appropriately. That which is designated as natural or spontaneous arising is in fact constructed or even forced. (Burman, 1994, p. 19)

Those who are defined as deficient are often the least powerful in the educational establishment: those without financial resources, those from cultural groups other than White, middle class (Burman, 1994; Lubeck, 1996). The cultural practices that produce tests are forgotten as we pursue goals whose attainment is framed in terms of increases in test performance.

Our use of standardized tests as evidence in research focuses attention on end points or snapshots of performance. Combined with the notion of development as moving toward some end, early childhood education gets made into a production mechanism, something that produces benefit *later*. All things are examined in terms of benefits somewhere down the line rather than respecting their value in the here and now. We look at curriculum options through the prism of child outcomes, evaluating teaching practices by what will most greatly enhance development at the end of some time increment. This evaluation, particularly for curricula related to primary education, most frequently is made on the basis of standardized tests.

In addition, their use crowds out attention to questions of process or descriptions of experience. This is a classic difference between empirical-analytic and interpretive work, and one that has been played out over and over again in the early childhood research community. We trade attention to experiences for a focus on outcomes because they are seen as more precise and also more cost-effective. But in the process, we miss knowledge of the mechanisms that set the stage for the tested outcomes. One reason for this may be that we assume that we know which processes produce what results, given the universalization of thought about the production of development. Discussions that have focused new attention to the cultural context of child growth and development (see, for example, Corsaro & Miller, 1992) should open up opportunities for pursuing questions of context and process, but the early childhood community will remain anchored to outcome-oriented perspectives if it continues to rely on measures that are standardized.

According to Danziger (1990), "Particular scientific communities are characterized by their commitment to certain scientific goals and this commitment determines the nature of their members' investigative practice" (p. 12). Researchers use the tools and ways of knowing familiar to them, and the reliance on standardized tests has perpetuated the maintenance of a research culture dominated by psychological models and quantitative measures:

Definitions of good science and research affected and continue to affect the legitimacy, value, and expression of knowledge and the perceived importance of different aims and effects. Many early childhood programs are still evaluated on the basis of quantitative IQ and achievement test results, whether or not these are the most appropriate indicators of program effectiveness. Early educators continue to look to psychological theory and research to form appropriate theoretical models and to serve as standards for valuable, good, and important research. The fact that there are varying definitions of knowledge, and good scientific research should be recognized by those in early education and used to formulate broader more flexible, and, at times, more appropriate standards for the field. (Bloch, 1987, p. 57)

To utilize these kinds of tools, new researchers must be educated to understand their characteristics, potential, and contributions. But in this case it is more than "training." Early childhood researchers *socialize* new scholars to value and use tools like standardized tests, imparting value to them by making them the core of research projects that are judged for inclusion in the discourse of the academy, through publication in journals, presentations at conferences, and inclusion in textbooks. Having the "right" kind of evidence is key to getting funded or publishing work, and traditionally standardized tests have been seen as appropriate. They then become part of the lexicon of "good research," closing the circle so that other kinds of research are less likely to find their way into our discussions.

Further, their value to policy makers and the general public is reinforced by the field's use. In policy statements such as *Developmentally Appropriate Practice in Early Childhood Programs* (Bredekamp, 1987; Bredekamp & Copple, 1997), much value is placed on research-based knowledge to guide practice. The field's reliance on this way of knowing about children and teaching heightens the desire for authoritative tools, tools that speak clearly and provide definitive answers. The forms and functions of standardized tests provide that kind of voice.

CONCLUSION

Standardized tests are naturally constrained images of ability/behavior/development. By their structure, they limit the possibilities for children to share their knowledge and experience. This is necessary to get a precise image of what they are measuring. Standardized tests have served the field of early childhood education for many years, helping us map out the terrain of the land we are trying to conquer—the development of children. They have guided research programs, educational programs for children, education for teachers, and the training of prospective scholars.

But that land is much more complicated, and the politics of past mapping now has been questioned by many. At the level of research, the ability of standardized tests to provide information about entities such as programs and curricula is bounded by their structure. They are built from a universe of content that is general enough to be probable in a variety of contexts. Their use also constrains the kinds of questions we can explore—we are confined to what fits the tool and we conceptualize problems only within the realm of possibility for measurement:

> We have as a field too often restricted ourselves to questions that can be best answered using a narrow range of quantitative methods—questions concerning educational outcomes, as measured by tests, and measures of individual and group differences. Those aspects of life that cannot be readily measured have been dismissed as unimportant, or worse, they have been operationalized in most questionable fashion. (Walsh, Tobin, & Graue, 1993, p. 465)

Early childhood researchers need to move to a new era of reflexivity in their work, examining their tools for technical suitability but looking deeper to the newer concerns for consequential validity, which embodies outcomes related to instrument use. Typically this is defined as immediate consequences for individuals, but as researchers we must realize that our work has ramifications that operate beyond the confines of the interactions of those involved in our projects. The use of tests in early childhood research sets in motion particular sets of possibilities for children, as we seek to understand their experiences through the frameworks provided by these tools. Respecting the potential benefits we can attain from using tests, while critically analyzing the ways their use constrains our knowing, should provide a more balanced approach to early childhood research and its focus on children.

REFERENCES

American Educational Research Association, American Psychological Association, & National Council on Measurement in Education. (1985). *Standards for educational and psychological tests*. Washington, DC: Author.

Bloch, M. N. (1987). Becoming scientific and professional: An historical perspective on the aims and effects of early education. In T. Popkewitz (Ed.), *The formation of school subjects: The struggle for an American institution* (pp. 25–62). London: Falmer Press.

Bloch, M. N. (1991). Critical science and the history of child development's influence on early education research. *Early Education and Development, 2*, 95–108.

Boehm, A. E. (1986). *Boehm test of basic concepts*. Cleveland: Psychological Corporation.

Bowman, B. (1993). Early childhood education. In *Review of research in education* (pp. 101–134). Washington, DC: American Educational Research Association.

Bredekamp, S. (Ed.). (1987). *Developmentally appropriate practice in early childhood programs serving children from birth through age 8.* Washington, DC: National Association for the Education of Young Children.

Bredekamp, S., & Copple, C. (Eds.). (1997). *Developmentally appropriate practice in early childhood programs* (rev. ed.). Washington, DC: National Association for the Education of Young Children.

Bredekamp, S., & Rosegrant, T. (Eds.). (1992). *Reaching potentials: Appropriate curriculum and assessment for young children* (Vol. 1). Washington, DC: National Association for the Education of Young Children.

Bredekamp, S., & Rosegrant, T. (Eds.). (1995). *Reaching potentials: Appropriate curriculum and assessment for young children* (Vol. 2). Washington, DC: National Association for the Education of Young Children.

Bredekamp, S., & Shepard, L. A. (1989). How best to protect children from inappropriate school expectations, practices, and policies. *Young Children, 44*(3), 14–25.

Bruner, J. (1986). *Actual minds, possible worlds.* Cambridge, MA: Harvard University Press.

Bruner, J., & Haste, H. (Eds.). (1987). *Making sense: The child's construction of the world.* New York: Methuen.

Burman, E. (1994). *Deconstructing developmental psychology.* London: Routledge.

Cole, M., & Cole, S. R. (1989). *The development of children.* New York: Scientific American Press.

Corsaro, W. A., & Miller, P. J. (Eds.). (1992). *Interpretive approaches to children's socialization* (New directions in child development, No. 58). San Francisco: Jossey-Bass.

CTB/McGraw-Hill. (1990). *Comprehensive tests of basic skills.* Monterey, CA: Author.

Danziger, K. (1990). *Constructing the subject: Historical origins of psychological research.* Cambridge: Cambridge University Press.

Frankenburg, W. F., Dodds, J., Fandal, A., Kazuk, E., & Cohrs, M. (1975). *Denver developmental screening test.* Denver: Denver Developmental Materials.

Garcia, G. E., & Pearson, P. D. (1994). Assessment and diversity. In L. Darling-Hammond (Ed.), *Review of research in education* (Vol. 20, pp. 337–391). Washington, DC: American Educational Research Association.

Genishi, C. C. (Ed.). (1992). *Ways of assessing children and curriculum: Stories of early childhood practice.* New York: Teachers College Press.

Gnezda, M. T., & Bolig, R. (1988). *A national survey of public school testing of prekindergarten and kindergarten children.* Washington, DC: National Forum on the Future of Children and Families, National Research Council.

Gordon, E. W., & Terrell, M. D. (1981). The changed social context of testing. *American Psychologist, 36*(10), 1167–1171.

Graue, M. E. (1993). *Ready for what? Constructing meanings of readiness for kindergarten?* Albany: State University of New York Press.

Green, B. F. (1981). A primer of testing. *American Psychologist, 36*(10), 1001–1011.

Gullo, D. F. (1994). *Understanding assessment and evaluation in early childhood education.* New York: Teachers College Press.

Hanson, F. A. (1993). *Testing testing: Social consequences of the examined life.* Berkeley: University of California Press.

Hieronymus, A. M., Hoover, H. D., Oberley, K. R., Cantor, N. K., Frisbie, D. A., Dunbar, S. B., Lewis, J. C., & Linquist, E. F. (1990). *Iowa tests of basic skills.* Chicago: Riverside Publishing.

Hills, T. W. (1992). Reaching potentials through appropriate assessment. In S. Bredekamp & T. Rosegrant (Eds.), *Reaching potentials: Appropriate curriculum and assessment for young children* (Vol. 1, pp. 43–65). Washington, DC: National Association for the Education of Young Children.

Hopkins, K. D., & Stanley, J. C. (1981). *Educational and psychological measurement and evaluation* (6th ed.). Englewood Cliffs, NJ: Prentice-Hall.

Kamii, C. (Ed.). (1990). *Achievement testing in the early grades: The games grown-ups play.* Washington, DC: National Association for the Education of Young Children.

Kessler, S. (1991). Early childhood education as development: Critique of the metaphor. *Early Education and Development, 2*(2), 137–152.

Kliebard, H. (1986). *The struggle for the American curriculum.* London: Routledge & Kegan Paul.

Lubeck, S. (1994). The politics of developmentally appropriate practice: Exploring issues of culture, class, and curriculum. In B. L. Mallory & R. S. New (Eds.), *Diversity and developmentally appropriate practices* (pp. 17–43). New York: Teachers College Press.

Lubeck, S. (1996). Deconstructing "child development knowledge" and "teacher preparation." *Early Childhood Research Quarterly, 11,* 147–168.

Mallory, B. L., & New, R. S. (Eds.). (1994). *Diversity and developmentally appropriate practices.* New York: Teachers College Press.

McCarthy, D. (1972). *McCarthy scales of children's abilities.* Cleveland: Psychological Corporation.

Meisels, S. J. (1985). *Developmental screening in early childhood: A guide.* Washington, DC: National Association for the Education of Young Children.

Meisels, S. J. (1994). Designing meaningful measurements for early childhood. In B. L. Mallory & R. S. New (Eds.), *Diversity and developmentally appropriate practices* (pp. 202–222). New York: Teachers College Press.

Meisels, S. J., & Wiske, M. S. (1983). *Early screening inventory.* New York: Teachers College Press.

National Association for the Education of Young Children. (1988). NAEYC position statement on standardized testing of young children 3 through 8 years of age. *Young Children, 43*(3), 42–47.

Newborg, J., Stock, J., Wnek, L., Guidubaldi, J., & Sninicki, J. (1984). *The Battelle developmental inventory.* Allen, TX: DLM Teaching Resources.

Nurss, J., & McGauvran, M. (1986). *The metropolitan readiness test.* New York: Psychological Corporation.

Powell, D. R., & Sigel, I. (1991). Searches for validity in evaluating young children and early childhood programs. In B. Spodek & O. N. Saracho (Eds.), *Yearbook in early childhood education: Vol. 2. Issues in early childhood curriculum* (pp. 190–212). New York: Teachers College Press.

Scarr, S. (1981). Testing for children: Assessment and the many determinants of intellectual competence. *American Psychologist, 36*(10), 1159–1166.

Shepard, L. A. (1991). The influence of standardized tests on the early childhood curriculum, teachers, and children. In B. Spodek & O. N. Saracho (Eds.), *Yearbook in early childhood education: Vol. 2. Issues in early childhood curriculum* (pp. 166–189). New York: Teachers College Press.

Swadener, B. B., & Kessler, S. (Eds). (1991). Reconceptualizing early childhood education [Special issue]. *Early Education and Development, 2*(2).

Thorndike, R. L., Hagen, E. P., & Sattler, J. M. (1986). *Stanford–Binet intelligence scale—Fourth edition*. Chicago: Riverside Publishing.

Vygotsky, L. S. (1978). *Mind in society: The development of higher psychological processes*. Cambridge, MA: Harvard University Press.

Walsh, D. J. (1991). Reconstructing the discourse on development appropriateness: A developmental perspective. *Early Education and Development, 2*, 109–119.

Walsh, D. J., Tobin, J. J., & Graue, M. E. (1993). The interpretive voice: Qualitative research in early childhood education. In B. Spodek (Ed.), *Handbook of research on the education of young children* (pp. 464–476). New York: Macmillan.

Wechsler, D. (1989). *Wechsler preschool and primary scale of intelligence—Revised*. New York: Psychological Corporation.

Werner, L. (1989). *Early prevention of school failure*. Washington, DC: U.S. Department of Education.

Wolf, D., Bixby, J., Glenn, J., & Gardner, H. (1991). To use their minds well: Investigating new forms of student assessment. In L. Darling-Hammond (Ed.), *Review of research in education* (Vol. 17, pp. 31–74). Washington, DC: American Educational Research Association.

Wortham, S. C. (1990). *Tests and measurement in early childhood education*. Columbus: Merrill.

CHAPTER 3

Qualitative Research in Early Childhood Education

J. Amos Hatch

Qualitative research has many faces. A distinguishing feature of qualitative inquiry is its inductive nature, so the starting place for qualitative researchers is not a null hypothesis to retain or reject. Because its goal is to reveal the lived experience of real people in real contexts and because those experiences and contexts are dynamic in nature, research questions sometimes change, research designs frequently are adjusted, and data collection strategies often are altered *as studies evolve*. The quality of qualitative work is not judged by how well it approximates prescribed research models, applies standardized control procedures, or utilizes sophisticated statistical packages, so the design of every qualitative study is in some ways created during the research process. This inductive/creative dimension makes qualitative research powerful for exploring the dynamic and complex nature of human activity, but makes it difficult to describe, even in a chapter limited to a discussion of early childhood research.

My objective in this chapter is to *introduce* the reader to the field of qualitative research in early childhood. After a brief overview of qualitative research and the emerging field of early childhood qualitative research, I present characteristics that distinguish qualitative research methods, then use examples to illustrate several types of qualitative studies. The idea is not to identify every kind of study or list every important researcher, but to show examples of work using a variety of qualitative approaches. I next present discussions of theory, issues, and ethics related to the field and conclude with some caveats for new qualitative researchers and a brief treatment of the usefulness and purposes of qualitative research in early childhood.

OVERVIEW

Qualitative research approaches have well-established histories in the social sciences, especially in anthropology and sociology. The theoretical roots of these approaches can be traced to the German intellectual tradition following Kant, Dilthey, and Weber. As the social sciences were struggling to find identities separate from the natural sciences, these roots competed with the mostly French, positivist social science positionings of Decartes, Comte, and Durkheim (see Erickson, 1986; Hamilton, 1994; Vidich & Lyman, 1994). The positivist stance assumes an objective world that has order independent of human perceptions; and the purpose of science from this perspective is to use carefully controlled observation, experimentation, comparison, and prediction to construct generalizations, theories, and laws that explain that inherent order. In contrast, scientists in the qualitative tradition argue that knowledge is symbolically constructed and necessarily subjective; and their goal is to discover how reality is experienced by participants in particular, contextualized settings. The tension between these two competing paradigmatic camps, what I playfully have called the "quantoids" and the "smooshes" (Hatch, 1985, 1995c), continues today.

The anthropological work of Franz Boas and the emergence of the Sociology Department of the University of Chicago, both in the 1890s, represent benchmarks in the application of qualitative research methods (Hamilton, 1994). Anthropologists developed a pattern of spending extended periods of time as participant observers living among "primitive" peoples in remote places. Then, in the tradition of Malinowski and Margaret Mead, these social scientists translated their field notes into ethnographies, monograph-length descriptions of the lifeways of the people they studied. Sociologists of the Chicago school and those who followed their lead utilized participant observation and informant interviewing, producing ethnographies that captured the everyday lives and values of mostly working-class migrant groups in large U.S. cities (see Erickson, 1986). After World War II, as the contributions of anthropologists and qualitative sociologists were recognized and accepted, their methods were adapted by social scientists from other disciplines, including education.

The application of qualitative methods to studies of education settings began in the mid-1950s. Erickson (1986) traces the roots of this recent phenomenon to the work of Spindler at Stanford University, Kimball at Teachers College, Columbia University, and Stenhouse at the Universities of Durham and East Anglia in England. Qualitative work in early childhood education has an even shorter history and, to date, has not been associated with particular individuals or universities. Based on a review of qualitative studies done in early childhood settings, Pamela Browning and I concluded that the number of such studies was relatively small and that "much of the work in this new area of inquiry has been done by researchers from disciplines other than education" (Browning & Hatch,

1995, p. 99). An examination of early childhood sessions at American Educational Research Association annual meetings or of the pages of journals publishing early childhood research indicates that qualitative research is making some headway. The inclusion of a chapter on interpretive research (Walsh, Tobin, & Graue, 1993) in Spodek's *Handbook of Research on the Education of Young Children* and this chapter's publication in this volume are examples of the movement of qualitative research toward the mainstream.

CHARACTERISTICS

Qualitative research in the social sciences has changed markedly since the days of the early anthropologists doing ethnographic studies in faraway lands. When I was designing my dissertation study at the University of Florida in the early 1980s, I was told, "You're not an anthropologist, so this can't be ethnography." I quickly learned that not all qualitative work is ethnography. I called my dissertation research "naturalistic inquiry" and discovered that, even if it wasn't ethnography proper, it still could be rigorous and generate valuable information. Later in the chapter, I will use examples of early childhood studies to illustrate the variety of approaches that have evolved from traditional ethnographic methods.

In this section, I pull together a variety of descriptors that characterize and distinguish qualitative research approaches. The following list of characteristics was drawn from a review of several widely cited texts on qualitative research. My intent is not to provide a definitive list of characteristics that must be present for a study to be considered good qualitative work. Different research approaches within the qualitative paradigm emphasize different characteristics, adding dimensions, altering emphases, and offering alternative characteristics. The goal is to give readers new to qualitative research a sense of what makes such approaches different from more traditional research methodologies. My descriptions are brief, and readers are invited to search out original sources for more comprehensive discussion.

Natural Settings. Qualitative researchers seek to study social phenomena as they naturally occur in everyday life. They believe that human behavior cannot be understood outside the contexts of its natural occurrence and that studying social phenomena in controlled, artificial circumstances distorts the findings of most quantitative studies—they become, in effect, studies of human behavior in controlled, artificial circumstances (Bogdan & Biklen, 1982; Erickson, 1986; Hammersley & Atkinson, 1983; Jacob, 1988; Lincoln & Guba, 1985).

Participants' Perspectives. Capturing the perspectives of the actors in specific social settings is a primary concern of qualitative work. Erickson (1986) identifies the key questions of qualitative research in classroom settings as: "What is happening here, specifically? What do these happenings mean to the people engaged in them?" (p. 124). In much qualitative work, researchers find ways to give participants opportunities to review and respond to the research findings in an effort to improve the accuracy of published descriptions (Bogdan & Biklen, 1982; Hammersley & Atkinson, 1983; Jacob, 1988; Lincoln & Guba, 1985).

Researcher as Data-Gathering Instrument. The principal data of qualitative research are gathered directly by the researchers themselves. These data usually include field notes from participant observations, notes or transcriptions of interviews with informants, and artifacts collected from the context under investigation. When mechanical devices such as video cameras or tape recorders are used to supplement observation, these records have no inherent meaning until they have been analyzed and interpreted by the researcher. Qualitative researchers argue that the human capabilities necessary to participate in social life are the same capacities that make it possible for qualitative researchers to observe and make sense of the actions and intentions of those under investigation (Bogdan & Biklen, 1982; Hammersley & Atkinson, 1983; Lincoln & Guba, 1985; Spradley, 1980). In the words of Hymes (1982), "Our ability to learn ethnographically is an extension of what every human must do, that is, learn the meanings, norms, patterns of a way of life" (p. 29).

Extended Firsthand Engagement. Since understanding social phenomena within particular contexts is the essence of qualitative studies, long periods of direct engagement within those contexts are vital. The fieldwork tradition in qualitative research remains strong, and critics of the rising popularity of qualitative methods are concerned that some researchers are applying data-gathering methods from ethnography but spending far too little time in the contexts they are studying. In 1980, Rist used the term "Blitzkrieg Ethnography" to label this phenomenon. Having just completed 4 years of editing the *International Journal of Qualitative Studies in Education*, I can testify that it is still a problem in the late 1990s. Long-term, sustained engagement with participants in their natural settings is a distinguishing characteristic of good qualitative work (Erickson, 1986; Spindler, 1982; Walsh et al., 1993; Wolcott, 1992). It is difficult to say exactly how long is long enough. The "rule" when I was in graduate school was at least 1 year in the field and an additional year for analysis and writing up the findings. As I advise my own graduate students, I recommend that time in the field be sufficient to answer the questions they are asking. If their goal is to produce an ethnography of a classroom, school, or community, one full school year seems like the bare minimum. If their objectives are more modest, less time may be acceptable. A helpful rule of thumb from Wolcott (1995) is that "anyone contemplating fieldwork should be present at least through a full cycle of activity" (p. 77). The effort to examine social phenomena from participant perspectives requires that researchers be in the scene long enough to observe how the phenomena are experienced in their full expression.

Centrality of Meaning. From the German tradition, *verstehen* (understanding) is the goal of social science. Understanding the meanings that individuals use to make sense of their social surroundings is the goal of qualitative research. Blumer (1969) contributed the theory and method of symbolic interactionism as tools for systematically exploring participant understandings. Three basic premises from symbolic interactionism signal the central importance of meaning: (a) Human beings act toward things on the basis of the meaning that the things have for them; (b) the meaning of such things is derived from, or arises out of, the social interaction that one has with one's fellows; and (c) these meanings are handled in, and sometimes modified through, an interpretive process used by the person in dealing with the things (s)he encounters. Not all qualitative research is undertaken from a symbolic interactionist perspective, but all qualitative research is about understanding the meanings humans construct to make sense of their social lives (Bogdan & Biklen, 1982; Erickson, 1986; Lincoln & Guba, 1985; Schwartz & Jacobs, 1979).

Description and Complexity. This type of work assumes that social settings are unique, dynamic, and complex. The methods allow researchers to explore these settings in ways that focus on the whole rather than reducing them to a set of incomplete and disconnected components. Qualitative data are words, pictures, or objects that cannot be reduced to numbers without losing the essence of the social meanings they represent. Qualitative reports are typically complex descriptive narratives that include examples of actual data and take the reader into the context and build a case for the researcher's interpretations (Bogdan & Biklen, 1982; Erickson, 1986; Hammersley & Atkinson, 1983; Peshkin, 1988).

Subjectivity. Qualitative work gives as much attention to inner as it does to outer states of human activity. Since these inner states are not directly observable, bringing them to light requires subjective judgment on the part of the researcher. Wolcott (1994) distinguishes among qualitative studies that emphasize description, analysis, or interpretation. All three require the application of subjective judgment but in different measures. More subjectivity is applied as researchers move from description toward interpretation. Most qualitative researchers, but not all (see the discussion of poststructural research below), argue that all their findings, including interpretations, are based on carefully gathered empirical evidence captured in the data. Most qualitative researchers would deny the possibility of pure objectivity in any scientific endeavor; instead of pretending to be objective, they concentrate on reflexively applying their own subjectivities in ways that make understanding the tacit motives and assumptions of others possible (Hamilton, 1994; Jacob, 1987; Lincoln & Guba, 1985).

Emergent Design. Lincoln and Guba (1985) describe the rationale for qualitative researchers' reliance on flexible research designs as follows:

> [The naturalist] elects to allow the research design to emerge (flow, cascade, unfold) rather than construct it preordinately (a priori) because it is inconceivable that enough could be known ahead of time about the many multiple realities to devise the design adequately; because what emerges as a function of the interaction between the inquirer and phenomenon is largely unpredictable in advance; because the inquirer cannot know sufficiently well the patterns of mutual shaping that are likely to exist; and because the various value systems involved (including the inquirer's own) interact in unpredictable ways to influence the outcome. (p. 41)

Although qualitative researchers argue about the extent to which research designs should be left to emerge (cf. Wolcott, 1992), most would agree that it is characteristic that research questions and methods are altered as qualitative studies unfold (Jacob, 1988).

Inductive Data Analysis. Qualitative data are usually detailed accounts of specific events or interactions. In data analysis, the job of the researcher is to find relationships or patterns among the specifics. A qualitative researcher does not begin with a theory or hypothesis to prove. In Bogdan and Biklen's (1982) words, "You are not putting together a puzzle, whose picture you already know. You are constructing a picture which takes shape as you collect and examine the parts" (p. 29). Theories generated from this inductive process are said to be grounded in the data; that is, theories develop from the ground up, "from the many disparate pieces of collected evidence that are interconnected" (Bogdan & Biklen, 1982, p. 29). The processes of qualitative data analysis and theory building involve an interplay between inductive and deductive reasoning. As potential patterns or relationships are identified inductively in the data, tentative, hypothetical categories are formed; the data then are read deductively to see if those categories are supported by the data (see Erickson, 1986). Still, the overall pattern of qualitative data analysis is decidedly inductive in nature (Lincoln & Guba, 1985).

Reflexivity. In qualitative research, the knower and the known are inseparable, and it is understood that the act of observing influences what will be observed. Researchers are part of the world they study. For Hammersley and Atkinson (1983), "this is not a matter of methodological commitment, it is an existential fact. There is no way we can escape the social world in order to study it; nor, fortunately, is that necessary" (p. 15). It is the human capacity to be reflexive, to monitor one's influence on a setting, to bracket one's biases, and to recognize one's emotional responses that allows researchers to get close enough to the social action to learn what is actually going on. This closeness means that researchers will form special relationships with participants in their studies, and part of their reflexive responsibility includes monitoring these relationships so that participants are treated with fairness and respect (Lincoln & Guba, 1985; Walsh et al., 1993).

Again, this discussion of characteristics is meant to be general and not exhaustive. I have tried to give readers a sense of what makes qualitative research distinct and valuable. Not all qualitative approaches will include all of the attributes listed, and some approaches will emphasize characteristics not included. In the sample of methodological approaches described below, some approaches will match up very well with these characteristics, some will emphasize some of the characteristics listed and de-emphasize others, and some will include some of the attributes listed but get their distinctive character from features that are not on the listing.

EXAMPLES OF EARLY CHILDHOOD
QUALITATIVE RESEARCH

As Donmoyer (1996) has written, "Qualitative researchers do not now hold—and, in fact, never held—a monolithic view of research and its place in the world" (p. 22). Some would argue that there are as many qualitative research approaches are there are qualitative researchers. Still, there are several identifiable methodological camps within the qualitative tradition, and a number of scholars have developed taxonomies that attempt to categorize qualitative methodologies along various dimensions (e.g., Denzin & Lincoln, 1994; Jacob, 1987, 1988; Patton, 1990; Tesch, 1990; Wolcott, 1992).

As I contemplated putting this section together, I considered using one of the taxonomies as a basis for identifying early childhood studies—in effect, looking for examples of studies that identified themselves with certain labels and fit certain methodological criteria. I opted for a more inductive approach. I began by searching the early childhood and qualitative research literatures for articles and books published since 1989. Having collected these publications, I sorted them into categories based on methodological approach. This process yielded 15 different "methods" (see Other Qualitative Approaches below). Because of space limitations in this chapter and because of occasional ambiguity and frequent overlap within the methodological descriptions in the articles and books examined, I decided to organize the examples presented into the following six categories: (a) studies emphasizing participant-observation; (b) studies emphasizing interviewing; (c) studies emphasizing artifact analysis; (d) narrative studies; (e) feminist studies; and (f) poststructuralist studies. The first three are not "methods" per se, but represent groupings of studies in which one of the three basic data-gathering strategies of qualitative research—what Wolcott (1992) calls "experiencing, enquiring, and examining" (p. 23)—is emphasized. The last three are from more distinct methodological camps and offer examples of approaches that are "pushing the envelope" of traditional qualitative work. What follows, then, are not all the possibilities for qualitative research in early childhood education, but explanations of selected research approaches and examples of what has been published over the past few years.

Participant-Observation Studies

Few of the studies examined billed themselves as participant-observation studies; they were more likely to call themselves ethnographies, ethnographic studies, or case studies. None of the studies in this category relied on observation as the only data collection strategy, but they all emphasized participant observation as the principal feature in their design.

The goal of participant observation is to understand the culture, or setting, being studied from the perspective of the participants. In their efforts to "reconstruct the reality" of social interactants, participant observers attempt to enter the perceptions of those they study, to acquire "members' knowledge and consequently understand from the participants' point of view what motivated the participants to do what the researcher has observed them doing and what these acts meant to them at the time" (Schwartz & Jacobs, 1979, p. 8). Researchers participate as members of the culture to some degree and keep careful written records or field notes. Degrees of involvement vary from study to study. Spradley (1980) classifies five types of participation: complete, active, moderate, passive, and nonparticipation. In the example below, the researcher utilized an active level of involvement.

Robyn Holmes (1995) reported findings from a 6-year study of kindergartners' perceptions of race and ethnic identity in a book entitled *How Young Children Perceive Race*. Holmes conducted informal interviews with children and collected their artwork, but participant observation was her primary data collection tool. She asked teachers to introduce her and treat her as a new student when she first entered the five kindergarten settings of her study. Her goal was to come to understand race from children's perspectives, and she made a concerted effort to participate as a student and relate to her informants as a peer in order to "gain a clear understanding of their world" (p. 8). Holmes used a tape recorder and took field notes, and data from these sources were transcribed and filled in at the end of each observation. Her analyses revealed that children's view of their universe is dualistic in nature—that is, they see the world in terms of antithetical pairs: boy/girl, black/white, are friends/aren't friends, big/little, grown-ups/kids, good/bad. The children's classification schemes for groups of people relied on color words and ethnic terms (e.g., Black, White, Japanese, Spanish), and "because the children exist in a world that is absolute, membership in a category was unconditional, and members were believed to be homogeneous" (p. 41). African American children included references to skin color in self-descriptions, while European Americans rarely did so; and children who held negative perceptions of other groups (e.g., "White people are mean") did not apply those generalizations when they selected friends in the classroom. Holmes concludes that giving young children opportunities to interact with peers from cultural groups different from their own is essential for acquiring knowledge about matters of racial identity and social cognition.

Interview Studies

Interviewing cultural insiders is a research technique that often supplements or complements intensive participant observation, but many qualitative studies are designed with interviewing as the prime data collection technique. Of the studies identified as emphasizing interviews, all of those examined relied on other data sources as well (e.g., school records, photographs, observations, and collection of artifacts).

Not all research interviews are qualitative in nature. Most interviews in quantitative studies are really closed-ended questionnaires (with forced choices, yes/no questions, and Likert-scale categories) administered in person or over the phone. Qualitative researchers use interviews as a means to uncover the meaning structures participants use to make sense of their worlds. These meanings frequently are hidden from direct observation and taken for granted by the participants, and open-ended interviewing provides a tool for bringing these meanings to the surface. Spradley (1979) summarizes the stance of qualitative researchers in relation to their interview informants:

> By word and by action, in subtle ways and in direct statements, [researchers] say, "I want to understand the world from your point of view. I want to know what you know in the way you know it. I want to understand the meaning of your experience, to walk in your shoes, to feel things as you feel them, to explain things as you explain them. Will you become my teacher and help me understand?" (p. 34)

Interviewers enter interview situations with questions in mind but remain sensitive to questions that emerge from the interview interaction, the social context being considered, and the degree of rapport established.

As part of a larger study of kindergarten retention in one school district, Mary Lee Smith (1989) conducted an interview study of teachers' beliefs about retention. Smith's goal was to capture kindergarten teachers' practical knowledge "in the form of stories of particular events and particular children in specific circumstances" (p. 133) and through analysis of the stories to infer their beliefs about retention. Interviews were tape recorded and transcribed, lists of categories were generated through inductive data analysis, data were coded according to the categories, and findings were triangulated with data from classroom observations and district documents on retention rates. Smith identified a typology of teacher beliefs, including: *nativists*, who believe that "within some normal range of environments, children become prepared for school according to an evolutionary, physiological unfolding of abilities" (p. 136); *remediationists*, who believe that "children of legal age . . . are ready for school and can be taught" (p. 137); *diagnostic-prescriptive teachers*, who believe that inadequacies in school readiness can be explained because one or more "distinct traits necessary for learning and attention . . . is not intact" (p. 137); and *interactionists*, who believe "in a complex pattern of interactions between the psychological nature of the child and the environments provided by teachers" (p. 138). Further analysis revealed that nativist teachers were far more likely to retain their kindergarten students than the other three "nonnativist" groups, but that teachers of all belief types, those who retained many and those who retained very few, endorsed retention as an effective solution to a perceived problem. Smith explains this apparent inconsistency in terms of the conflict between teachers' practical knowledge and what the research literature says regarding the disadvantages of retention.

Artifact Analysis

The collection of unobtrusive, artifact data is a part of many qualitative studies, but it is unusual for artifacts to be utilized as the primary source of information in other than text-based analyses such as archival studies, literary critiques, content analyses, policy studies, or historical studies. Among those found in the literature search for this chapter, several policy and historical studies were identified; however, only one study emphasized the collection and analysis of artifacts in an effort to explore a contemporary phenomenon in early childhood education.

Hodder (1994) argues that the analysis of artifacts is not a trivial pursuit but that artifacts, "the intended and unintended residues of human activity, give alternative insights into the ways in which people perceive and fashion their lives" (p. 394). Artifact collection is the gathering of "indicators" such as official documents, children's school work, or any nonreactive measures of group or individual life (Schwartz & Jacobs, 1979). The main advantage of this type of data collection is that it does not influence the social setting under investigation. The major disadvantage, according to Hodder (1994), is that the objects cannot "speak back; . . . there are no 'member checks' because the artifacts themselves are mute" (pp. 398–399). It is the responsibility of the researcher to interpret the significance and meaning of artifacts by (a) identifying the contexts within which artifacts had meaning; (b) recognizing meaningful similarities and differences within contexts; and (c) judging the relevance of theories to the data at hand (Hodder, 1994, p. 399).

As part of a larger qualitative study of philosophies and practices of kindergarten educators, Evelyn Freeman and I (Freeman & Hatch, 1989) completed an artifact analysis study of kindergarten report cards. As part of the larger study, we interviewed teachers, principals, and supervisors, and collected curriculum materials and report cards from representative schools across the state of Ohio. Reflecting on the power of report cards to influence practice and express educational and social values, we decided to do a formal analysis of the 61 district report cards collected. Our analysis was guided by the following questions:

(1) How were report cards organized? (What categories were used and what elements were included in the categories?) (2) How was information reported? (What marking procedures were used?) (3) What were children expected to know and to be able to do? (Based on the evaluation categories of the report cards, what were the expectations for students?) (4) What philosophies of early childhood education or theoretical orientations were evident? (Did the report cards reflect maturationist, behaviorist, or interactionist perspectives?) (pp. 597–598)

The analysis revealed that report cards were organized in three basic ways: chronological lists (4.9%); skills lists (6.6%); and strands of skills, attributes, and/or attitudes (88.5%). A wide variety of marking schemes were used, but virtually all reported children's relative progress against an assumed standard. Students were expected to master specific skills in the areas of work habits and reading and math readiness. A behaviorist theoretical orientation dominated the content and structure of the report cards examined. While 41% of the cards were classified as completely behaviorist, all of the remaining cards included elements indicating a behaviorist orientation. Findings were discussed in relation to theories of socialization, cognitive development, and self-esteem.

Narrative Studies

There is a surge of interest in inquiry in which "stories are used to describe human action" (Polkinghorne, 1995, p. 5). This genre, centered on stories, goes by several names, including life history, life story research, biography, personal experience methods, and narrative inquiry. While I know that early childhood researchers are interested in narrative methods, few published reports were identified in my literature search. This may reflect a wider pattern in the broad area of qualitative research: More people are writing *about* narrative research than are actually doing it (see Hatch & Wisniewski, 1995).

Basic to narrative inquiry is the notion that humans make sense of their lives through story. Bruner (1986) distinguished between *paradigmatic* ways of knowing (the traditional logical-scientific mode) and *narrative* (storied) ways of knowing. Bruner argued that one is not inherently better than the other. Narrative inquiry focuses on storied knowledge and seeks to capture stories as ways to understand how individuals make sense of their life worlds:

> Narrative cognition, even though it has been ignored or devalued by proponents of more "scientific" approaches, is the way each of us comes to understand and communicate human action. Narrative knowledge is organized as stories, and this knowledge is best expressed in storied forms. The processes of doing narrative inquiry involve sharing narrative knowledge through the telling of stories; the products are the stories . . . we choose to tell. (Hatch & Wisniewski, 1995, p. 126)

Clandinin and Connelly (1994) identify the following methods for generating what they call "field texts" (i.e., the data of narrative studies): oral history; annals and chronicles; family stories; photographs, memory boxes, other personal/family artifacts; research interviews; journals; autobiographical writing; letters; conversations; and field notes and other stories from the field.

William Ayers (1989) used several of these data-gathering strategies and some others as he collected the "life-narratives" (p. 8) of six preschool teachers in a book entitled *The Good Preschool Teacher: Six Teachers Reflect on Their Lives*. Ayers collected data in two phases. In the first, he conducted active participant observation in each of the six preschool settings, constructing ethnographic descriptions of each. In the second phase, he used a variety of techniques to encourage the teachers to "reflect on their lives as they affect their teaching practices" (p. 6). Informal interviews, written correspondence (in which the teacher was encouraged to respond to researcher inquiries in the form of vignettes), and nonlinear, interpretive activities were utilized during this phase. Interpretive activities were designed to disengage the teachers from conscious thought by providing familiar materials (e.g., paper, clay, paint) and asking them to use the materials to represent ideas, feelings, and images about themselves and teaching. From the data collected, Ayers put together six distinct portraits, telling the stories of six teachers' lives. Looking across the six life-narratives, Ayers summarized:

> "Teaching as identity" is the clearest theme to emerge in this inquiry, and "teaching as identity" is the frame through which each portrait makes sense. In these portraits, there is no clear line delineating the person and the teacher.

Rather there is a seamless web between teaching and being, between teacher and person. Teaching is not simply what one does, it is who one is. Teaching is a life, a way of being in the world, an intentional circle for these six outstanding teachers. (p. 130)

Feminist Studies

While the data-gathering strategies employed in studies that are labeled feminist or poststructuralist (taken up in the next section) are usually participant-observation, interviewing, and artifact collection, the analytical and interpretive dimensions of each of these types of studies give them a distinctive character that merits separate exposition. Feminist perspectives can make particular contributions to early childhood qualitative research because the overwhelming majority of early childhood workers are women, and caring for and teaching young children historically has been considered "women's work."

As with the other genres sampled in this chapter, it is dangerous business to attempt brief descriptions of complex, multifaceted research areas like feminist studies. Feminism is not a unitary concept; there are many feminisms with multiple political, disciplinary, and philosophical roots (Olesen, 1994). Not all research done by women is feminist research, and not all feminist researchers are women; but the defining characteristic of feminist research is its focus on the distinctive experience of women and on gender-related values that have tended to privilege males (Neilsen, 1990; Tomm, 1989). Other features associated with, but not unique to, feminist research include: a fundamental political and moral orientation toward social change; suspicion of subject–object dualism; recognition that all knowledge is partial and local; and acknowledgment of the importance of self-scrutiny, especially in relation to interactions with those being studied (Henwood, 1996; King, 1996; Tomm, 1989).

From the 1970s, qualitative research undertaken within feminist frameworks has revealed the absence or invisibility of women in certain contexts and exposed the inequalities in these settings because of social and economic patterns of male dominance. Later, feminist standpoint research, which takes women's perspectives as particular and privileged, emerged in Britain and the United States. Olesen (1994) identifies the goals of such research as: "to understand [the] everyday world of women as it is known by women who continually create and shape it within the materialist context" (p. 163). Feminist qualitative work of this type has been useful in bringing to light "women's ways of knowing" (Belenky, Clichy, Goldberger, & Tarule, 1987) and other traits often associated with women. Feminist qualitative research also has provided a powerful tool for explaining the processes of socialization for women and girls, revealing how women are subjugated within social, economic, and political systems, and generating an action framework for moving toward social justice for women.

Deborah Ceglowski (1994) investigated Head Start salary policies in a feminist analysis of interviews with Head Start teachers and administrators. Ceglowski conducted individual interviews with three administrators and focus group interviews (see Reinharz, 1992) with 10 teachers over a year's time. Focus group sessions were held with groups of two or three teachers; all interviews were taped, transcribed, and returned to participants so they could be checked for accuracy. Ceglowski's analysis revealed two distinct groups among the teachers, and composites of "low-income" and "middle-income" teachers were constructed to represent these groups. Both low- and middle-income teachers agreed that their salaries were low, that their work was important, and that they cared for their students and the students' families. However, the low-income teachers, who depended on their salaries for economic survival, held different views of the value of their work to themselves and society than did middle-income teachers whose salaries served to supplement those of their husbands. Low-income teachers argued that society devalues Head Start teaching and that their administrators were not committed to improving salaries. Middle-income teachers valued the positive identity associated with working with others and were more likely to see increases in their salaries as detrimental to the overall structure of the social agencies in which their Head Start program was situated. Ceglowski discusses her findings in terms of "women's work." As in other gender-segregated fields, caring for children is "natural" for women, requiring no special knowledge or expertise and, therefore, is devalued by society. Women's commitment to children and the program turns out to work to their disadvantage when it comes to salary considerations. In this study, one of the administrators pointed out: "In some ways, our employees are helping to fund the program we have because we offer them low salaries, we pay them low salaries, so we put the money into the programming aspects" (p. 380). The study points out the human side of salary discussions in early childhood; and the feminist perspective taken in the analysis reveals some of the complexity in the discourses of women's work, socioeconomic status, caring, and early childhood teaching.

Poststructuralist Studies

Poststructuralist perspectives are the subject of widespread and heated debate in fields as diverse as physics and literary criticism. The long-term impact on qualitative research is hard to measure because the debate rages on. Tobin (1995) has pointed out rightly that early childhood education and poststructuralist thought are unlikely partners, and few early childhood studies that claimed or evidenced a poststructuralist framework were found in my literature search. Still, it seems important to include this perspective because the larger scholarly community presently is expending so much energy, thought, and angst dealing with the poststructuralist critique.

Poststructuralists have pointed out that traditional "postpositivist" qualitative research perspectives have much in common with the positivist research they frequently railed against (see Hatch, 1995b). Virtually all quantitative, positivist research and most qualitative, naturalistic studies are based on structuralist assumptions. For example, I have argued for years that my research is empirical (that it generates knowledge based on careful direct observation), although not statistical. Further, I have presented the findings of most of my studies as "analytic generalizations" that purport to reveal the categories of meaning that participants use to make sense of their social worlds. The poststructural critique has helped me see that, for better or worse, my assumptions about legitimate sources of knowledge and the ways knowledge can be structured were parallel to those of my quantitatively oriented counterparts.

Tobin (1995) highlights the differences between structural and poststructural positions within early childhood qualitative work:

> Most qualitative research in early childhood education reflects the belief that people mean pretty much what they say, that texts have stable meaning, and that the reality of a classroom can be captured by a careful ethnographer. Poststructural research, in contrast, is characterized by a suspicion of the meaning of words and actions, a lack of belief in the stability of textual meaning, and a cynicism about the claims of ethnography and other naturalistic methods. (p. 226)

Poststructuralists regard "Truth" as an illusion. Poststructuralist thinkers argue that "we can never lift ourselves out of the framework within which we speak, live, and work, and that all our forms of knowledge, including scientific knowledge, are subjective" (Elkind, 1994, p. 20). They remind us to be "skeptical about beliefs concerning truth, knowledge, power, the self, and language that are often taken for granted and serve as legitimation for Western culture" (Flax, 1987, p. 624). This skepticism does not translate directly into a set of qualitative methods, but it does provide a frame through which the nonunitary nature of human experience can be interpreted. If meaning is always in flux, poststructuralism becomes a tool for analyzing the processes through which meanings and individual identities are constructed and modified through human discourse.

Bronwyn Davies is a poststructuralist early childhood researcher from Australia. Her book, *Frogs and Snails and Feminist Tales* (Davies, 1989), describes a study of preschool children's gender identity socialization. She used a poststructuralist (and feminist) framework for analyzing and interpreting children's understandings of feminist tales (i.e., stories in which girls or women successfully take on nontraditional role behaviors). In the first phase of the study, Davies spent hundreds of hours reading and discussing selected feminist tales with eight young children. These experiences were recorded, transcribed, and analyzed. In a second phase, she spent 2 years doing participant observation, while continuing the reading/discussing processes, with 40 children in three distinct Australian preschool settings. As a poststructuralist, Davies studied the ongoing processes whereby individuals take themselves up as persons. She argues:

> Individuals, through learning the discursive practices of a society, are able to position themselves within those practices in multiple ways, and to develop subjectivities both in concert with and in opposition to the ways in which others choose to position them. By focusing on the multiple subject positions that a person takes up and the often contradictory nature of those positionings, and by focusing on the fact that the social world is constantly being constituted through the discursive practices in which individuals engage, we are able to see individuals not as . . . unitary beings but as the complex, changing, contradictory creatures that we each experience ourselves being. (p. xi)

Western discursive practices teach children the absolute dualism of gender—that individuals are either male or female—and children learn to position themselves as males or females. The data of this study indicate the importance for each child to "get its gender right" in order to be "seen as normal and acceptable within the terms of the culture" (Davies, 1989, p. 20). In spite of what appear to be liberalizing influences in society and school practices, in these young children's play and in their interpretation of feminist tales, traditional expectations for differential male–female power relations and role expectations were taken for granted. Davies explains: "Children cannot both be required to position themselves as identifiably male or female and at the same time be deprived of the means of signifying maleness and femaleness" (p. x). Davies proposes a new discourse of gender in which the male–female duality is challenged: "[Children] need the freedom to position themselves in multiple ways, some of which will be recognisably 'feminine', some 'masculine' as we currently understand these terms, and some totally unrelated to current discursive practices" (p. 141).

Other Qualitative Approaches

My classification of the qualitative studies found in the literature search conducted for this chapter indicated a much larger variety of types of studies than can be described here. In addition to the types above, the following were identified: ethnographies, collaborative studies, sociolinguistic studies, microethnographies, policy studies, action research projects, teacher research projects, historical studies, case studies, art criticism, grounded theory, and symbolic interactionist studies. This listing indicates the breadth of the emerging field of early childhood qualitative research.

THE PLACE OF THEORY

The role of theory is the subject of some friendly disagreement among qualitative researchers, again demonstrating the complexity of the field. Depending on methodological stance, qualitative researchers range from those who recommend an extensive literature search and thorough understanding of relevant substantive theory prior to entering the field (e.g., Yin, 1994) to those who see the generation of theory as an outcome of research and prefer to delay references to extant theoretical literature until late in the research process (e.g., Glaser & Strauss, 1967). Such differences make generalizing about the place of theory difficult.

I advise graduate students to first be clear about distinctions between methodological and substantive theories. As they go about designing, implementing, and writing up qualitative work, no matter what the methodological tools to be applied, it is essential that novice researchers have a firm handle on the theoretical roots of their approach. Books designed to introduce researchers to particular qualitative approaches virtually always include a "theory chapter" that provides a good starting place for helping new researchers articulate methodological theory (for a list of such books, see Browning & Hatch, 1995, pp. 113–114).

The place of theory related to the substance of the research is more difficult to explain. For starters, I like Wolcott's (1995) head-on statement: "Theory is supposed to help researchers of any persuasion clarify what they are up to and to help them explain to others what they are up to" (p. 189). Graduate students going into a research setting with a well-defined research focus find themselves in different relation to substantive theory than those taking a more holistic-exploratory orientation. Researchers who begin with specific questions they hope to answer or particular social phenomena they want to examine need to "clarify what they are up to" by connecting what they are doing with related theory and previous work. Researchers who begin with a more wide-angled lens are likely to search out theory later in the inquiry process, depending on the literature to help them explain to others "what they have been up to." In either case, my scholarly sensibilities lead me to require students to write final reports that locate their findings within appropriate literatures in the same ways as is done in more traditional quantitative studies.

The theoretical development of one of my own studies is an example of the flexible application of methodological and substantive theory. The first study I undertook, after my dissertation, was billed (to the funding agency) as an analysis of child-to-child social behavior in a kindergarten. I called my methodology "naturalistic" after Blumer (1969) and Lincoln and Guba (1985), and utilized constructivism (e.g., Berger & Luckmann, 1966) and symbolic interactionism (Blumer, 1969) as methodological theory bases. At the outset of the study, my substantive interest in social interaction was guided by the theoretical work of Goffman (1959, 1967). Goffman's notions of self-presentation and ceremonial communication fit nicely with the methodological theories I was applying. As the study progressed, I became interested in the social relations of a particular child who appeared to be treated as "an outsider" by his kindergarten peers (Hatch, 1988). I began to focus more attention on the social interactions of this child in my data collection (participant observation, interviewing, and artifact gathering). Trying to understand this emergent area of investigation led me to search for theoretical insights from literature related to the "sociology of deviance" (e.g., Becker, 1963; Goffman, 1963; Pfuhl, 1980), which gave me ways to explain this child's social behavior within the context of the norms and values of the peer culture of his classroom.

The point of the example is that both methodological and substantive theory are important in qualitative studies; however, providing a uniform prescription for what ought to be included, and when, is difficult. The same can be said of the tension between adopting a rigid qualitative design before beginning a study and starting with a more open design and planning for alterations as concerns and interests emerge. As with theory, the "completeness" of the initial design is tied directly to the focus of the study. For novices, I recommend going into the field with well-developed plans. If changes are necessary, it is easier to make adjustments to an existing plan than to generate one from scratch. In any qualitative study, it is incumbent on the researcher to (a) detail for the reader the theoretical bases of the study and how they developed, and (b) spell out explicitly the design of the study and how it evolved. Judgments about the worth of a qualitative study rely on the researcher's careful descriptions of the place of theory and the execution of a systematic research process.

ISSUES IN EARLY CHILDHOOD QUALITATIVE RESEARCH

My experience is that the kinds of people attracted to early childhood education are often strong advocates for harmony and uncomfortable with conflict. But early childhood education and early childhood research are conflicted territories at the moment. I see parallels between the controversies within the early childhood education field and the "paradigm wars" in early childhood research.

The critique of developmentally appropriate practice (DAP) (Bredekamp, 1987) symbolizes conflicts across the early childhood terrain. On one side are fundamentalist, right-wing political groups (Cohen, 1996) and behavioristically oriented scholars (e.g., Fowell & Lawton, 1992) who challenge DAP on grounds that it limits what children are supposed to learn and appropriate ways for them to learn it. On the other are advocates for a reconceptualization of early childhood education (e.g., Fleer, 1995; Swadener & Kessler, 1991), which includes challenging DAP as overly dependent on the narrow precepts of developmental psychology at the expense of theory and knowledge from other perspectives such as feminist studies, critical theory, cultural studies, curriculum studies, and poststructuralism. Individuals responsible for revising the DAP guidelines (Bredekamp & Copple, 1997) were trapped between two armies, fighting separate forces on opposite fronts.

Although the political positioning of the combatants is different, the pattern of conflict is the same for qualitative researchers in early childhood education. On one flank, qualitative researchers are struggling to find acceptance and publication sources for their work in a discipline dominated by quantitatively oriented scholars and editors. Most qualitative researchers I know believe they continue to be marginalized within the early childhood research community. On the other flank, qualitative researchers are being accosted with postmodern, poststructuralist critiques that challenge the empiricist assumptions at the core of traditional qualitative methods (see Hatch, 1995b; Tobin, 1995). Qualitative researchers who already see themselves as outsiders in the research community of their content specialty are being chided for being too mainstream by scholars experimenting with the radical fringes of science.

In spite of the strong pull to bring everyone together and to "make whole" early childhood education and early childhood research, the solution to the conflicts described is that there is no solution. Conflict is inevitable and should be seen as healthy. Recognizing that smart, caring, reasonable people can have vastly different notions of what constitutes "appropriate" practice does not make it easy to put together guidelines for an influential early childhood organization; but denying the efficacy of reasonable differences flies in the face of what we know about the complexity of knowledge and how people operate in postmodern life. Bringing early childhood researchers under one big, happy umbrella is neither possible nor advantageous. The assumptions at the core of positivism, postpositivism, and poststructuralism make an unproblematic union impossible (Hatch, 1985, 1995c); and there is energy and creative power in the conflicts themselves. Beating ourselves up over the fact that we have differences keeps us from moving forward as a complex, dynamic field.

ETHICS

Early childhood qualitative research seeks to reveal for inspection the life worlds of participants in settings where young children have a central place. Young children are vulnerable to all kinds of adult exploitation because of their lack of experience and power; and, unfortunately, adults who teach and care for children are also at a disadvantage because of relatively weak status and power in Western society. When qualitative researchers are given access to the intimate details of day-to-day life in early childhood settings, they have an ethical and moral obligation not to exploit the children and adults they are studying.

The kind of exploitation I am referring to is more than just the injunction to "do no harm" that is the basis for most university human subjects requirements. I mean simply that some researchers (qualitative and quantitative) "use" young children and early childhood teachers to advance their own ends. Research participants are "used" when they are "objectified" (Schroeder, 1984, p. 176) in our analyses, when they become codified as voiceless "Others" (Fine, 1994, p. 74) in our reports, and when their participation in our studies does not benefit them in any particular way. I agree with Tripp's (1994) assertion that "for others to gain more professionally from teacher [research] than the teachers themselves is an appropriation I believe to be socially unjust." It is hard to think of early childhood researchers as a privileged, powerful group, but when I find myself listening to (or reporting) research findings at conferences held in world-class hotels in far-away cities, I make myself wonder what the teachers and children being described in the studies are doing at that moment. As researchers, we have power and we are privileged. With that power and privilege comes responsibility.

As my own research agenda has evolved, I have re-examined my ethical and moral responsibilities to those participating in my research (see Hatch, 1995a). As part of that effort, I have developed a set of questions that go beyond the ethical-legal issues usually covered in human subjects safeguards and codes of research ethics:

> Why am I doing this study?
> Why am I doing it at this site?
> What is my relationship to the participants?
> What are the participants' roles in the design, data
>   collection, analysis, and authorship of the study?
> Who owns the study?
> Who benefits from this study?
> How do I benefit?
> How do the participants benefit?
> Who benefits most?
> Who may be at risk in the contexts I am studying?
> Should I intervene on behalf of those at risk? (Hatch,
>   1995a, p. 221)

In an effort to practice what I was preaching and more closely align the power relations and benefits of my work, I collaborated with four early childhood teachers who worked in inner-city schools on a year-long study of the "appropriateness" of developmentally appropriate practice in the settings where they worked. The five of us designed the study, generated the data, completed the analysis, wrote the paper, and presented the findings at a national conference

(Hatch, Brice, Kidwell, Mason, & McCarthy, 1994). Although it will never be published because the final report looks nothing like what editors and reviewers think of as real research, the paper has found a small but influential audience. Moreover, the work demonstrates that genuine collaboration is one way to make researcher–participant relations more equitable and to distribute credit and benefits more evenly.

CAVEATS FOR NEW QUALITATIVE RESEARCHERS

This section includes a series of warnings similar to those I might give a graduate student inexperienced in qualitative research who is considering doing a qualitative dissertation. In some ways, it is a reaction to what I see as several misconceptions about doing qualitative research at the doctoral level. My framework is personal and particular to my own experiences, but researchers new to qualitative approaches and professors responsible for guiding doctoral students may find these comments useful.

Just because you hate statistics does not mean you will love qualitative research. Similarly, just because you are not good at statistics does not mean you will be good at qualitative research. I am not arguing that there are not dispositions and personality types that are better fitted to one research approach or another; indeed, I believe individual ways of conceptualizing and understanding how the world is put together ought to lead logically to one paradigm or the other (see Hatch, 1985, 1995c). But I see too many students whose primary interest in qualitative work seems to be as a way to avoid the statistics block required in most graduate programs. The intellectual rigor required of the two tracks certainly is different, but good preparation in qualitative research is just as challenging as the quantitative route. Students (and professors) who think qualitative research is easier have never done qualitative research. Novice researchers must have a solid preparation in qualitative methods *before* starting a qualitative study. I have met students who, with no formal preparation, wanted to do qualitative studies, and I consistently have refused to serve on their committees. In our college, we now require coursework in qualitative and quantitative perspectives for all doctoral students; I see this as beneficial to everyone concerned.

Qualitative dissertations take longer than quantitative studies. Many graduate students are living on next to nothing and working harder than they ever have. They are understandably anxious to get out from under the high expectations of doctoral committees and to have a real job, salary, and life. Students with strict timelines for finishing their doctoral programs are bad candidates for qualitative dissertations. As mentioned above, it takes a great deal of time to do this kind of research well. It certainly takes longer to collect data, but data analysis and writing require extensive commitments of time and labor as well. It is a mistake to believe one can do "quick and dirty" qualitative research. When I switched from a quantitative to a qualitative study in my doctoral program, I added 18 months to my studies.

It takes strong writing skills to do qualitative work well. I often repeat what Rod Webb told me during my doctoral studies at the University of Florida: "If you want to be a qualitative researcher you better enjoy writing or, at least, enjoy having written." Qualitative reports rely on the researcher's ability to give readers a sense of the richness and complexity of the social contexts being described. Findings seldom are reduced to tables and figures or presented in terms of statistically significant relationships. Data (excerpts, interview transcriptions, field notes) usually are displayed in an effort to support the descriptions, analyses, and interpretations of the researcher. This means that the ability to construct clearly argued, convincing narratives is key. Those who hate to write will hate writing up qualitative research even more than writing traditional quantitative dissertations.

The ability to deal with ambiguity is essential to qualitative work. If everything has to fit for you to feel comfortable, if all the loose ends need to be tied together for you to sleep at night, if you have to have "the answer" before you're satisfied, then qualitative research is not for you. The inductive nature of this work means that researchers gather as many particulars as they can, then try to put together wholes that make sense of those particulars. This sometimes means that long periods of data collection and/or intense data analysis sessions can lead down roads that split in unexpected ways or run the researcher into what seems like a dead end. Qualitative researchers always have more data than they could ever analyze fully; they always paint an incomplete picture of the phenomena or context they are studying; and they never have the sense of security provided by a computer-generated statistical analysis. Qualitative researchers resist the idea that the world can be broken down into its components and studied one piece at a time. That makes the world a much more complex thing to know, and the ways of knowing it much more ambiguous, than some individuals can handle.

Qualitative research is not for everyone. It is certainly not a dumping ground for would-be scholars with math anxiety. It is difficult to do and even more difficult to publish. It is time-, labor-, and mind-intensive work. It requires special talents, dispositions, skills, and knowledge. While its acceptability as legitimate scholarship has increased, it remains the antithesis of science in the eyes of many. Qualitative research is not for everyone.

USEFULNESS

To return to where we began, *verstehen* (understanding) has been the purpose of qualitative research since its beginnings. When it is done well, early childhood qualitative research helps readers understand social phenomena in new and enriched ways. It helps them look with different eyes at participants in social settings like those described and analyzed. It gives educators alternative perspectives from which to examine their own settings and try to understand the perspectives of those who participate in those contexts.

From a pragmatic point of view, if research of any type is to be useful, it must help individuals make better decisions. These individuals may be policy makers whose decisions affect the lives of thousands of children, or a group of kindergarten children learning to make better decisions about interacting with one of their peers; but if the research does not lead someone somewhere to think differently about alternative actions, it has no real usefulness. My view is that the understandings generated from high-quality qualitative studies are invaluable to the processes of thoughtful decision making.

By way of example, I have constructed brief scenarios in which the understandings generated from the studies reviewed in this chapter might make a powerful difference for decision makers in real early childhood contexts:

- A teacher having read Holmes's (1995) description of how young children perceive race may react and respond differently to a preschooler's declaration that "Black people are ugly," because she understands that young children do not apply generalizations concerning groups to their classmates who belong to those groups.
- A primary supervisor trying to influence district-level retention policy might decide on different strategies after becoming aware of Smith's (1989) taxonomy of teacher beliefs and the finding that, paradoxically, teachers across the board endorsed retention.
- The members of a district kindergarten report card committee might think more carefully about the social and curricular implications of their decisions about what to include and how to structure report cards based on their study of the analysis provided by Freeman and Hatch (1989).
- A person contemplating a career path in early childhood education or someone thinking about leaving the field may find insight and inspiration in the life stories of the six teachers portrayed in Ayers's (1989) narrative work.
- A government official responsible for Head Start policy nationwide might think more broadly about the material and symbolic effects of low salaries on Head Start teachers and programs after having seen Ceglowski's (1994) report.
- After a teacher has worked to initiate new ways of talking and thinking about gender identity, as suggested by Davies (1989), a young child might decide to play with peers in ways that do not reflect the fear of being caught in roles that do not fit traditional stereotypes.

I have oversimplified both the findings and the decision-making processes involved, but the point stands that understandings generated from qualitative research can be invaluable to personal and professional decision making. Although they come in many forms and represent a variety of theoretical and political perspectives, well-planned, well-executed, and well-written qualitative studies are powerful tools for revealing the real worlds of real people. Information from those worlds can help make possible clearer understandings of and better decisions about our own worlds.

Acknowledgments. I am grateful for the assistance of Laura Corden, Iris Lamon, Angela Lowry, and Amy McFarlin in completing the literature searches and collecting the studies analyzed for this chapter. Thank you to faculty and student members of the University of Tennessee Early Childhood Research Group for their support and suggestions on earlier drafts of this chapter. Thanks also to the reviewers and editors of this volume and to Charlotte Duncan for her editorial assistance.

REFERENCES

Ayers, W. (1989). *The good preschool teacher: Six teachers reflect on their lives*. New York: Teachers College Press.

Becker, H. S. (1963). *Outsiders: Studies in the sociology of deviance*. New York: Free Press.

Belenky, M., Clichy, B., Goldberger, N., & Tarule, J. (1987). *Women's ways of knowing*. New York: Basic Books.

Berger, P. L., & Luckmann, T. (1966). *The social construction of reality: A treatise in the sociology of knowledge*. Garden City, NY: Anchor.

Blumer, H. (1969). *Symbolic interactionism: Perspective and method*. Englewood Cliffs, NJ: Prentice-Hall.

Bogdan, R. C., & Biklen, S. K. (1982). *Qualitative research for education: An introduction to theory and methods*. Boston: Allyn & Bacon.

Bredekamp, S. (Ed.). (1987). *Developmentally appropriate practice in early childhood programs serving children from birth through age 8*. Washington, DC: National Association for the Education of Young Children.

Bredekamp, S., & Copple, C. (Eds.). (1997). *Developmentally appropriate practice in early childhood programs* (rev. ed.). Washington, DC: National Association for the Education of Young Children.

Browning, P., & Hatch, J. A. (1995). Qualitative research in early childhood: A review. In J. A. Hatch (Ed.), *Qualitative research in early childhood settings* (pp. 99–114). Westport, CT: Praeger.

Bruner, J. (1986). *Actual minds, possible worlds*. Cambridge, MA: Harvard University Press.

Ceglowski, D. (1994). Conversations about Head Start salaries: A feminist analysis. *Early Childhood Research Quarterly, 9*, 367–386.

Clandinin, D. J., & Connelly, F. M. (1994). Personal experience methods. In N. K. Denzin

& Y. S. Lincoln (Eds.), *Handbook of qualitative research* (pp. 413–427). Thousand Oaks, CA: Sage.

Cohen, D. L. (1996, February 14). Georgia chief takes aim at NAEYC materials. *Education Week*, p. 14.

Davies, B. (1989). *Frogs and snails and feminist tales: Preschool children and gender.* Sydney, NSW: Allen & Unwin.

Denzin, N. K., & Lincoln, Y. S. (1994). Introduction: Entering the field of qualitative research. In N. K. Denzin & Y. S. Lincoln (Eds.), *Handbook of qualitative research* (pp. 1–18). Thousand Oaks, CA: Sage.

Donmoyer, R. (1996). Educational research in a era of paradigm proliferation: What's a journal editor to do? *Educational Researcher, 25,* 19–25.

Elkind, D. (1994). *Ties that stress: The new family imbalance.* Cambridge, MA: Harvard University Press.

Erickson, F. (1986). Qualitative methods in research on teaching. In M. C. Wittrock (Ed.), *Handbook of research on teaching* (3rd ed.; pp. 119–161). New York: Macmillan.

Fine, M. (1994). Working with hyphens: Reinventing self and other in qualitative research. In N. K. Denzin & Y. S. Lincoln (Eds.), *Handbook of qualitative research* (pp. 70–82). Thousand Oaks, CA: Sage.

Flax, J. (1987). Postmodernism and gender relations in feminist theory. *Signs, 14,* 621–643.

Fleer, M. (Ed.). (1995). *DAPcentrism: Challenging developmentally appropriate practice.* Watson, ACT: Australian Early Childhood Association.

Fowell, N., & Lawton, J. (1992). An alternative view of appropriate practice in early childhood education. *Early Childhood Research Quarterly, 7,* 53–73.

Freeman, E. B., & Hatch, J. A. (1989). What schools expect young children to know and do: An analysis of kindergarten report cards. *Elementary School Journal, 89,* 595–605.

Glaser, B. G., & Strauss, A. (1967). *The discovery of grounded theory.* New York: Aldine.

Goffman, E. (1959). *The presentation of self in everyday life.* Garden City, NY: Anchor.

Goffman, E. (1963). *Stigma.* Englewood Cliffs, NJ: Prentice- Hall.

Goffman, E. (1967). *Interaction ritual: Essays on face-to-face behavior.* New York: Pantheon.

Hamilton, D. (1994). Traditions, preferences, and postures in applied qualitative research. In N. K Denzin & Y. S. Lincoln (Eds.), *Handbook of qualitative research* (pp. 60–69). Thousand Oaks, CA: Sage.

Hammersley, M., & Atkinson, P. (1983). *Ethnography: Principles and practices.* London: Tavistock.

Hatch, J. A. (1985). The quantoids versus the smooshes: Struggling with methodological rapprochement. *Issues in Education, 3,* 158–167.

Hatch, J. A. (1988). Learning to be an outsider: Peer stigmatization in kindergarten. *Urban Review, 20,* 59– 72.

Hatch, J. A. (1995a). Ethical conflicts in classroom research. In J. A. Hatch (Ed.), *Qualitative research in early childhood settings* (pp. 213–222). Westport, CT: Praeger.

Hatch, J. A. (1995b). Introduction: Qualitative research in early childhood settings. In J. A. Hatch (Ed.), *Qualitative research in early childhood settings* (pp. xi–xvii). Westport, CT: Praeger.

Hatch, J. A. (1995c). Studying childhood as a cultural invention. In J. A. Hatch (Ed.), *Qualitative research in early childhood settings* (pp. 117–134). Westport, CT: Praeger.

Hatch, J. A., Brice, D., Kidwell, M., Mason, M., & McCarthy, B. (1994, November). *Developmentally appropriate for whom? Perspectives of inner-city early childhood educators.* Paper presented at the annual meeting of the National Association for the Education of Young Children, Atlanta.

Hatch, J. A., & Wisniewski, R. (1995). Life history and narrative: Questions, issues, and exemplary works. In J. A. Hatch & R. Wisniewski (Eds.), *Life history and narrative* (pp. 113–136). London: Falmer Press.

Henwood, K. L. (1996). Qualitative inquiry: Perspectives, methods, and psychology. In J. T. E. Richardson (Ed.), *Handbook of qualitative research methods for psychology and the social sciences* (pp. 25–40). Leicester, UK: British Psychological Society.

Hodder, I. (1994). The interpretation of documents and material culture. In N. K. Denzin & Y. S. Lincoln (Eds.), *Handbook of qualitative research* (pp. 393–402). Thousand Oaks, CA: Sage.

Holmes, R. M. (1995). *How young children perceive race.* Thousand Oaks, CA: Sage.

Hymes, D. (1982). What is ethnography? In P. Gilmore & A. A. Glatthorn (Eds.), *Children in and out of school: Ethnography and education* (pp. 22–32). Washington, DC: Center for Applied Linguistics.

Jacob, E. (1987). Qualitative research traditions: A review. *Review of Educational Research, 57,* 1–50.

Jacob, E. (1988). Clarifying qualitative research: A focus on traditions. *Educational Researcher, 17,* 16–24.

King, E. (1996). The use of self in qualitative research. In J. T. E. Richardson (Ed.), *Handbook of qualitative research methods for psychology and the social sciences* (pp. 175–188). Leicester, UK: British Psychological Society.

Lincoln, Y. S., & Guba, E. G. (1985). *Naturalistic inquiry.* Beverly Hills, CA: Sage.

Neilsen, J. M. (Ed.). (1990). *Feminist research methods: Exemplary readings in the social sciences.* Boulder, CO: Westview Press.

Olesen, V. (1994). Feminisms and models of qualitative research. In N. K. Denzin & Y. S. Lincoln (Eds.), *Handbook of qualitative research* (pp. 158–174). Thousand Oaks, CA: Sage.

Patton, M. Q. (1990). *Qualitative evaluation and research methods.* Newbury Park, CA: Sage.

Peshkin, A. (1988). Understanding complexity: A gift of qualitative inquiry. *Anthropology and Education Quarterly, 19,* 416–424.

Pfuhl, E. H. (1980). *The deviance process.* New York: Van Nostrand Reinhold.

Polkinghorne, D. E. (1995). Narrative configuration in qualitative analysis. In J. A. Hatch & R. Wisniewski (Eds.), *Life history and narrative* (pp. 5–24). London: Falmer Press.

Reinharz, S. (1992). *Feminist methods in social research.* New York: Oxford University Press.

Rist, R. C. (1980). Blitzkrieg ethnography: On the transformation of a method into a movement. *Educational Researcher, 9,* 8–10.

Schroeder, W. R. (1984). *Sartre and his predecessors.* London: Routledge & Kegan Paul.

Schwartz, H., & Jacobs, J. (1979). *Qualitative sociology*. New York: Free Press.

Smith, M. L. (1989). Teachers' beliefs about retention. In L. A. Shepard & M. L. Smith (Eds.), *Flunking grades: Research and policies on retention* (pp. 132–150). London: Falmer Press.

Spindler, G. D. (Ed.). (1982). *Doing the ethnography of schooling: Educational ethnography in action*. New York: Holt, Rinehart & Winston.

Spodek, B. (Ed.). (1993). *Handbook of research on the education of young children*. New York: Macmillan.

Spradley, J. P. (1979). *The ethnographic interview*. New York: Holt, Rinehart & Winston.

Spradley, J. P. (1980). *Participant observation*. New York: Holt, Rinehart & Winston.

Swadener, B. B., & Kessler, S. (Eds.). (1991). Reconceptualizing early childhood education [Special issue]. *Early Education and Development*, 2(2).

Tesch, R. (1990). *Qualitative research: Analysis types and software tools*. New York: Falmer Press.

Tobin, J. (1995). Post-structural research in early childhood education. In J. A. Hatch (Ed.), *Qualitative research in early childhood settings* (pp. 223–243). Westport, CT: Praeger.

Tomm, W. (Ed.). (1989). *Effects of feminist approaches on research methodologies*. Waterloo, ON: Wilfrid Laurier University Press.

Tripp, D. (1994). Teachers' lives, critical incidents, and professional practice. *International Journal of Qualitative Studies in Education*, 7, 65–76.

Vidich, A. J., & Lyman, S. M. (1994). Qualitative methods: Their history in sociology and anthropology. In N. K. Denzin & Y. S. Lincoln (Eds.), *Handbook of qualitative research* (pp. 23–59). Thousand Oaks, CA: Sage.

Walsh, D. J., Tobin, J. J., & Graue, M. E. (1993). The interpretive voice: Qualitative research in early childhood education. In B. Spodek (Ed.), *Handbook of research on the education of young children* (pp. 464–476). New York: Macmillan.

Wolcott, H. F. (1992). Posturing in qualitative inquiry. In M. D. LeCompte, W. L. Millroy, & J. Preissle (Eds.), *The handbook of qualitative research in education* (pp. 3–52). San Diego: Academic Press.

Wolcott, H. F. (1994). *Transforming qualitative data: Description, analysis, and interpretation*. Thousand Oaks, CA: Sage.

Wolcott, H. F. (1995). *The art of fieldwork*. Walnut Creek, CA: AltaMira Press.

Yin, R. (1994). *Case study research: Design and methods*. Thousand Oaks, CA: Sage.

CHAPTER 4

Observational Methods in Early Childhood Educational Research

Anthony D. Pellegrini

In this chapter I will be concerned with using observational methods, or methods that are based on direct observations of behavior, with children and families. A goal of these methods is to provide a verbal picture of behaviors as they unfold in time. These descriptions are very useful for a number of important ventures, such as studying children and families at home and in school.

An indispensable part of all description of behavior is a thorough explication of aspects of the contexts in which the behavior is embedded. Behaviors are rendered understandable when they are considered in their context. Context, most generally, refers to the physical (e.g., spatial arrangements of desks in a classroom) and social dimensions (e.g., number and composition of the group being observed) of the observational setting.

While this is a very general definition of context, it is useful in understanding the interrelations between individuals' behaviors and the situation in which the behaviors are embedded. (See Hinde, 1976, for an exhaustive description of context.) Two behaviors that have similar features may have very different meaning, depending on context. For example, the *gentle push* of a child during a play episode (a dimension of the social context) typically is interpreted as playful, not aggressive. On the other hand, exactly the same behavior typically is interpreted as aggressive when it follows a provocative comment from a peer. Thus, the meanings of the behaviors are influenced by the context in which they are embedded (see Chapter 5 in this volume for a related discussion).

While the methods discussed in this chapter are generic, that is, they can be applied to the observations of rhesus monkeys, shoppers in a market, or children on playgrounds, I will be concerned primarily with children embedded in the context of schools and families.

THE OVERTURE

The major focus of this chapter will be on using observational methods with children. I follow the child study tradition (see Pellegrini & Bjorklund, 1998) whereby good descriptions of children are the bases for designing educational, as well as other sorts of intervention, programs. Thus, my basic assumption is that we must understand children before we can intervene. Observational methods are an important family of tools we use in understanding children.

There is a crucial need for good (that is, reliable and valid) descriptions of children in settings where they spend substantial portions of their time. We as researchers know very little about what children do after school. Descriptions of this sort, as well as descriptions of children in more traditional settings such as schools, are useful in a number of ways. They should provide bases for programs for children and families. For examples, models of successful adult–child and child–child interaction, derived from descriptive work, can be used to design programs for teacher–child and peer interaction in schools.

This assumption that programs for children and families should be based on good descriptions of children and their families is an old one, and is basic to the child study movement (see Pellegrini & Bjorklund, 1998). The child study movement assumes that children and their families are at the center of any educational program in which they are enrolled. Dimensions of the program, such as curriculum materials and teacher strategies, as well as evaluation of the program are based on these descriptions.

I advocate using observations to describe children in various stages of their educational experiences. Observations provide the bases for generating curriculum and instruction as well as evaluation procedures. Descriptions of children in their everyday context, that is, school and nonschool settings, are particularly useful here. The importance of using children's relevant, everyday experiences for educational programs has been recognized at least since Dewey and more recently by Cole (1993).

Activities that are important in children's communities and family lives need to be identified and described so that they can be included in educational programs. For example, certain groups of children may experience specific interaction styles of reading and mathematics activities as important aspects of their culture (Pellegrini & Stanic, 1993). These specific activities, rather than others, are often motivating for children. The inclusion of such indigenous strategies and materials in educational curricula is important, particularly when the children in those programs come from culturally diverse communities. Thus, observational methods form an important part of the curriculum planning cycle.

Evaluation of children and programs is another part of the curriculum cycle for which observational methods can be very useful. By evaluation I mean the documenting of the operation and impact of the program and the adults and children involved. Traditionally, children and teachers have been evaluated with various forms of paper-and-pencil tests.

Use of tests is particularly problematic with young children, as we have known for many years (see Messick, 1983, for a thorough discussion, as well as Chapter 2 in this volume). One reason for this limitation is that tests are strange and sometimes anxiety-producing events; this combination of factors, as well as numerous factors related to the design of tests per se, adversely affects children's test-taking behavior. The effect of these extraneous factors on children is probably responsible for the well-known fact that children are unreliable test takers (Messick, 1983). That is, their scores on different days tend to vary. Similarly, when children and adults are placed in anxiety-producing situations, they tend to exhibit lower, rather than higher, levels of competence. This may be because they are unwilling to offer new or novel solutions in a threatening situation. With such unreliability, we have no chance for validity.

In light of these many limitations of testing, the educational community has begun to consider alternative forms of assessment, such as "authentic assessment" and "portfolio assessment." Observational methods fit quite nicely into this movement in that they are excellent for gathering information on children and teachers in "authentic" situations.

Observational methods are useful for evaluation of children and teachers to the extent that they do not put them in anxiety-producing situations; thus, we have a higher likelihood of getting a more reliable measure of their competence. An added benefit of observational methods relates to the fact that we do not have to generalize from an indirect measure of performance, like a test score, to performance in a "real-world setting," such as a classroom. More specifically, reliable and valid test scores are indicators of how children and teachers might perform in the contexts from which the test items were generated. Thus, the scores should generalize or transfer to a real setting. Observational methods have the benefit of documenting competence in those relevant situations from the start. So, if we are interested in making inferences about teachers' ability to teach literacy lessons, we can observe them directly in those sorts of lessons. We do not have to test them on subject and instructional materials related to literacy and then make inferences about their teaching ability.

In order to use observational techniques effectively, however, observers must be careful to choose, or sample, behaviors and events that they see as important. A sure guide here is to observe those aspects of the program that are specified in the program goals and objectives. Based on specified program goals and objectives, the observer, first, can document the degree to which these program components actually are being implemented. Descriptions of program implementation are very important because there is often a mismatch between educational programs as they are stated in a policy manual and the actual implementation of the programs. Thus, we first must describe the actual process and the degree to which it relates to the formal (or written) program. A second step in the evaluation process is for the observer to document the degree to which these program components relate to children's development. Thus, by matching specific program components with specific child outcomes, we can design effective programs.

"MERE DESCRIPTION"?

Descriptive research, in which observational methods play an indispensable part, sometimes are considered "merely" descriptive, implying that description is either unimportant or a theoretical enterprise. "Mere" descriptions often are contrasted with research designs that are "explanatory"; the latter proffer causal statements for the interrelation among variables, while the former describe the nature of those variables. I, along with others (e.g., Blurton Jones, 1972; Hinde, 1980), believe that thorough descriptions are a necessary and very important first step in conducting research that aims to explain. Indeed, Chomsky (1965) considered both descriptive and explanatory adequacy necessary in theory specification. Good descriptions are indispensable to the scientific enterprise, we argue. Adequate descriptions of a phenomenon, especially in complex organisms like humans, require theoretical guidance, however.

The complexity of the human organism interacting, even in the most routine ways, with others necessitates that observers make theoretically guided choices about who, what, and when to observe. For example, take the seemingly simple issue of classifying participants' roles. Kagan's (1994) simple but informative example clearly points to the importance of theory in guiding one aspect of description, classification: "Zoologists classify cows as mammals, economists classify them as commodities, and some cultures regard these animals as sacred symbols" (p. 11). So theory not only informs us what to observe but also provides guidance for categorization of those behaviors.

Further, theory guides us in terms of the levels of specificity of our categories. If we had a biological orientation, we might examine relations between heart rate and social behavior. If, on the other hand, we had a cultural-anthropological perspective, we might examine the match/mismatch between the culture of school tasks and those indigenous to children's homes.

Given the complexity of the phenomena that can be observed, it is important to make explicit those decisions we make when we observe. It is naive and unrealistic for observers to think or state that they enter an observational field with no biases in terms of what they will observe and/or how the phenomena will be observed and categorized. Human observers have too many "schema," or concepts about the ways in which the world works, in their heads to take such a stance. The best we can hope for is to make our biases explicit and to try to minimize them. Similarly, observers cannot go out and observe "everything," for there is clearly too much to observe. With this in mind, we then should make explicit our theory and what it is we are interested in (that is, our theoretically guided "question"). With an explicit question and theory in mind, we can begin to consider what it is specifically that we will observe.

In this chapter I will discuss two important considerations that help observers systematize the ways in which they observe. First, I will discuss ways in which observational categories are formed. Second, I will discuss ways in which these categories can be measured quantitatively, as well as rules that should be followed in sampling and recording the occurrence of those categories. While there are certainly other important issues in observational research, these are two that I consider important and interesting. Readers interested in more thorough treatments of observational methods are referred to a number of excellent books on the topic: Bakeman and Gottman (1989); Martin and Bateson (1993), Pellegrini (1996), and Suen and Ary (1989).

COMING UP WITH A CATEGORY SYSTEM

Category Choice as a Theoretical Act

A coding, or category, system reflects the ways in which those aspects of the "stream of behavior" that we choose to study are organized. As I have noted, interaction between and among individuals is very complicated; there are lots of things going on at many different levels. So some level of theoretically guided choice is imperative. To illustrate the levels of complexity, we will take, for example, the case of a mother and baby interacting around a storybook at bedtime. At a micro level, we could be concerned with the gaze coordination of the mother and baby, and develop a coding system that extracts aspects of the interaction that relate specifically to this issue, for example, the heart rates and facial expressions of each participant at different points of the interaction. At a more macro level, we might develop a coding system that captures the ways in which mothers end the stories and say good-night to their children.

Three points are immediately relevant here. First, interactions are immensely complex; for example, there are lots of behaviors occurring simultaneously. Second, because of this complexity, we must choose specific aspects of the interaction to study; one simply can not describe "everything." Third, and as a direct consequence of the first two points, all coding systems abstract aspects of interaction. That is, by taking behaviors from the context in which they occur and putting them into some coding/category system, we lose some information. We should be aware of what is lost and that the loss is irrelevant to the questions we asked.

We may choose to develop our own coding system, to reflect a unique set of questions and/or research context, or we may choose to use/adapt an extant coding system. If we choose someone else's system, we should recognize that it may not fit. As already noted, a coding system is a theoretical statement; thus, to choose someone else's coding system assumes that we, too, share that orientation. Because of the implications of such a choice, it makes ultimate sense to choose a system only after we have determined the match between our specific research questions and those specified in extant coding systems.

Levels of Category Specificity

The level of category specificity is a basic issue in category definition. There are at least three levels of description that we can consider in developing a coding scheme: physical descriptions, descriptions of consequence, and relational descriptions (Martin & Bateson, 1993). In each case we aspire to group together those behaviors that belong together in some reasonable way. What is "reasonable," however, may be specific to a certain theory, so (again) theoretical assumptions continue to exercise influence.

Physical descriptions are descriptions of muscular contractions and usually are expressed in terms of degree, strength, and patterning (Hinde, 1980). For example, we could describe certain vigorous motor behaviors in terms of patterns of "rough play." Physical descriptions usually are grouped together, or classified in terms of their co-occurrence in space and time. The procedure by which they are grouped should be based on some theory and objective processes, such as factor analysis or Q-sorts. For example, we would group together under the heading of rough-and-tumble play all physical behaviors (e.g., smile, open-hand beat, run, jump, kick at) that co-occur during vigorous outdoor play.

Descriptions of consequence, on the other hand, involve the orientation of a specific set of behaviors toward a certain outcome, or consequence (Hinde, 1980). So rather than looking at the co-occurrence of individual behaviors, we choose a specific outcome and look at the behaviors leading to it; thus, behaviors that lead to the same consequence belong in the same category. For example, we might look at the specific behaviors that lead to a certain form of interaction, like affiliating with peers. It may be that gentle push, run, and smile are grouped under the label of affiliative chase. Similarly, behaviors categorized as aggressive might include peer-directed behaviors leading to a child crying and separating from his or her peer.

When choosing between these two specific levels of categorization, researchers should be aware of the costs and benefits associated with each. The use of physical descriptions originally was proposed in child study by a group of ethologists (e.g., Blurton Jones, 1972) who considered categories typically used in the child development literature to be too subjective, being rooted in introspection, not in observations of children's behaviors. The proposed remedy was to use physical descriptions. These descriptions, however, are often too cumbersome. There are often too many details to attend to.

Correspondingly, such micro-level analyses may miss patterns that are more conspicuous at a more macro level of analysis. We know, for example, that interactions are rife with "miscues" to the extent that we try something then change in mid-stream. Conversational analyses provide particularly good examples of miscues; for example, we may observe lots of self-corrections (at the micro level), but they are all in the service of mutual understanding (at the macro level). Thus, only by attending to more macro levels are we able to make sense of the pattern of the interaction.

In descriptions of consequence, behaviors are grouped into meaningful (rather macro-level) categories that imply some motives, or intent, for the antecedent behaviors. That children hit at and then run with others implies that they are engaging in chase. This level of explanation is very nice to aspire to. The downside of consequential grouping is equally obvious: Consequential considerations have biases. We may be considering a specific consequence as the goal of a set of behaviors, such as playful affiliation being the consequence of wrestling, when in fact there is another goal to which the behavior is directed, such as dominance exhibition: The same affiliative behaviors would be observed but with a very different interpretation. By way of possible remedy, preliminary observations should utilize relatively "objective terms" (like physical descriptions) to describe behaviors and their consequences. The use of relatively objective language enables reconsideration of original intent.

The last level of categorization involves describing individuals in relation to their environment (Martin & Bateson, 1993). In this case individuals are described in terms of where they are and/or with whom they are interacting, rather than being described by their motor activities or consequences of behavior. Relational descriptions of children might consider all behavior observed on the playground at recess to be categorized as play, simply because of where it is observed, or categorizing all acts of children as play, simply because they were exhibited by children.

At this point we should have a general idea of the level of categories that we will use. We should enter the field to test the category system. Categories should be field tested in preliminary observations (see Pellegrini, 1996) before they are used. Often categories need to be adjusted, depending on specific children and locations observed.

Technical Properties of Categories

Categories should be homogeneous and mutually exclusive, and sometimes exhaustive (Bakeman & Gottman, 1989; Martin & Bateson, 1993). By *homogeneous* I mean that all subcomponents of a category should be related to the same construct. That is, they should provide different exemplars of the same phenomenon; there should not be any "lumps," or outliers. For example, a homogeneous category for rough-and-tumble play (R&T) might include smile, hit at, and run. All these behaviors co-occur and represent different dimensions of the same category. A nonhomogeneous (heterogeneous?) category would include the components already noted as well as outliers, like bite and punch. Category homogeneity can be established empirically (that is, by the degree to which they actually co-occur) and theoretically (that is, by whether they can be related for some plausible reasons). If categories are not homogeneous, they are confusing; by aggregating across dissimilar components of categories, we may hide systematic patterns in the data.

Categories also should be mutually exclusive; that is, behaviors should fit into one and only one category. Thus, a behavior cannot be coded simultaneously as both R&T and aggression. Take the case of two categories: social interaction and conversation. They are certainly conceptually, and probably empirically, interrelated to the extent that conversation is a subset of social interaction. In this case, we would need new codes. Either we would collapse conversation into social interaction or have two social interaction categories: verbal and nonverbal. That categories are mutually exclusive is particularly important for data analyses. If different categories measure the same, or related, behaviors, we are limited in our ability to say anything about the separate categories.

Often, however, one set of behaviors can be coded in a number of different ways. For example, R&T also can be categorized as vigorous behavior, cooperative interaction, or (with preschool boys) social fantasy play. That we choose to categorize it as R&T, rather than the alternatives, is a theoretical matter. In terms of mutual exclusivity of categories, by extension, we should not define vigorous behavior or cooperative interaction categories such that R&T could fit into either.

Lastly, category systems could be exhaustive. By exhaustive I mean that there are categories that can account for all of the behavior that occurs in our particular setting. I say categories "could be," rather than "must be," because it is really optional. It is "nice" to have an exhaustive system if we want to construct an ethogram of a particular context to the extent that we have a full index of behavior in that area. Exhaustive systems are necessary, however, if we want to look at sequences of behavior. Specifically, if we want to look at the probability of one behavior following another, we must have categories for all possible behaviors that could be observed. A shortcut here could involve having a "dust bin" category, such as Other Behavior, that accounts for less relevant behavior. Alternatively, observers could note unusual behaviors that occur but are not coded.

RULES FOR MEASURING, SAMPLING, AND RECORDING CATEGORIES

Measuring Behavior

I will discuss five ways in which behavior can be measured: duration, frequency, pattern, latency, and intensity (Martin & Bateson, 1993; Suen & Ary, 1989). Although there are variations on these measures of behavior, they are a sound basis by which to measure behavior and develop more refined measures.

To begin with, observers should note the time period during which the observations occur. This session length is an important qualifier of the measures we generate. If we sample children's behavior across a 20-minute recess period, 20 minutes is the session length.

Duration is a measure of the length of a behavior during a specific session, and it usually is measured in terms of seconds (and parts thereof), minutes, and hours. Duration can refer to the interval from the onset (or beginning) of a behavior to the offset (or termination) of that behavior. Taking a hypothetical 20-minute session length, we might say that for a specific child the duration of "drawing" was 4 minutes. This could be expressed as 4 mins. per 20 mins., and defined as total duration.

Mean durations are averages of total durations, across individuals or within individuals, across sessions. Let's say that we observed four children whose total durations of drawing were 3, 2, 5, and 10 mins. The mean duration would be the sum of these four durations (20 mins.) divided by 4, or 5 mins.

Relative or proportional duration is the duration divided by the session length: 4/20 or .20. While the relative measure is a "timeless" index of specific behavior, the total and mean durations are stated explicitly in terms of time (Martin & Bateson, 1993).

A complement to duration measures is the measurement of frequency. Frequency is a measure of the occurrence of specific behaviors within an observational session. Let's say during our hypothetical 20-minute session, we observed 6 R&T bouts. Discussion of frequency in relation to the session length becomes very clear. Without consideration of the session length, the number 6 is almost meaningless. Were the six bouts observed 6 times in 1 minute, 5 minutes, 30 minutes, or 3 hours? Obviously, the number 6 has a very different meaning in each of the above cases. Frequency, then, should be discussed in terms relative to the session length; thus, frequency could be expressed as a rate to the extent that we measure frequency/time unit. In the above examples, we would have different rates of R&T/minute.

Frequency and duration are very common measures of behavior. Indeed, it is often interesting to collect both types of measures on behavioral categories. Obviously, the nature of one's questions should drive the type of measures used, but frequency and duration sometimes can provide complementary information for specific behaviors. Both, for example, are excellent measures of what individuals spend their time doing and, correspondingly, the degree to which individuals expend resources. Frequency tells us something about the rate of expenditure, while duration tells us the extent to which the expenditure is sustained. It may be, for example, that children frequently, in the course of recess, "run," but the duration of each bout is brief. Longer durations may be exhibited in other types of behaviors, such as "games."

Patterns of behavior are measures of specific categories of behavior across time. These patterns may not, however, be expressed in terms of a specific time interval; their order of occurrence may be noted, with no mention of time between acts. For example, during our 20-minute observation session, we may observe that children's play is patterned in the following way: chase, push, chased, hit at, chase. While we note that this took place during a 20-minute session, we may choose not to note the actual duration of the individual components of the pattern. If we chose to add a temporal dimension, we could add the duration of each of the individual play components and to the total play bout. The time dimension may be useful, and with the use of computerized recording devices it is increasingly easy to record time. By tying patterns to a temporal dimension we come closer to representing the actual occurrence of behaviors.

Latency, like duration, is specifically a measure of time. With latency, we measure the time from when the focal individual is exposed to a relevant stimulus to his or her behavioral response. Some very common examples of latency measures include "wait time" and "reaction time." Wait time is the latency between when an instructor asks a question of a student and when the teacher talks again, assuming that the student does not talk in the interval. The latency in this case is a matter of a few seconds. Reaction time is a measure of the latency between the presentation of a stimulus, such as a word to be read, and the child's reading of the word. Reaction time is usually expressed in terms of micro-seconds.

Intensity is the last measure to be discussed, and it is probably the most difficult to measure. Intensity is a measure of degree or amplitude, rather than frequency (Martin & Bateson, 1993). Following the R&T example, intensity could be measured as high, medium, and low. Because such judgments can be very subjective, and consequently unreliable, it is important to specify the ways in which we differentiate levels of intensity. Martin and Bateson (1993) suggest using *local rates* as one measure of intensity. By local rates they mean the number of components of a behavior that occur within a certain time interval. Take the case of R&T again, where it is defined as having 10 components (e.g., tease, hit/kick at, chase, poke, sneak up, carry child, pile on, play fight, hold/push). A local rate could be the number of those components that occur within a certain period, say 2 minutes. More intense ratings would have more components than less intense ratings. Of course, this type of measure (implicitly) assumes that individual components are equal in terms of intensity. That is, by adding together different units, we treat them as if they were all equally intense and made an equal contribution to the whole. This may be problematic, however, where individual components are not equal; for example, if we had run and walk as components of chase, we could not treat them as equal because run is more intense (e.g., evidenced by a higher heart rate) than walking.

One way to address this issue is to measure intensity by consequence (Martin & Bateson, 1993). Take the running–walking example from above: We could measure the distance covered during an interval, the number of calories burned, or heart rate as consequential measures. While some of these measures may be problematic and obtrusive to use (e.g., taking heart rate), others, such as distance, are not. Distance can be measured, for example, by dividing the observation area into matrix-like plots and noting the number of plots covered during a specified time. A bit more difficult, and obtrusive, is the use of actometers (Pellegrini, Horvat, & Hubertly, 1998). Actometers are mechanical devices attached to a foot or hand that record level of activity. Such measures may, however, be both impractical and undesirable to use, thus compounding the problem of objectively measuring intensity.

In the next section I will discuss the sampling and recording strategies used to extract behaviors from their stream so that they can be measured.

Sampling Rules

Sampling generally refers to the degree to which we choose to observe all that can be observed and is crucial to understanding one specific way in which behavior can be studied. All possible behavior is referred to as the universe of behavior. We sample behavior because it is neither practical nor necessary to observe all behavior. Obviously, the more we sample, the more we approximate the universe; therefore, larger samples are generally more accurate representations of the universe than smaller samples. A large sample, however, is not enough to guarantee an accurate, or representative, sample.

Systematic rules of sampling must be followed to ensure a representative sample. Following Martin and Bateson (1993), I will separate sampling rules, or those rules followed to extract behavior from its ongoing stream, from recording rules, or how the behaviors are recorded (see also Altmann, 1974, for another, often cited discussion of these issues).

Sampling, like the measures discussed earlier, generally can be classified as behavior or time sampling. Behavior, or event, sampling involves observing all occurrences of a specific behavior within a certain observational period. Thus, we become concerned with a specific behavior occurring or not occurring. Behavior/event sampling is most useful when we are interested in a relatively infrequently occurring behavior; thus, we look for it and only it and record it when it occurs. Aggression commonly is studied with event sampling because it does not occur frequently (at least in some contexts). Further, event sampling is useful when we are interested in the structure of the event itself so we want to record it from beginning to end.

Time-oriented methods are concerned with dividing the observational period into time units and making observations (or sampling) within those units. The motivation for time orientation is simple: It is often impractical, and indeed unnecessary, to conduct observations for long, uninterrupted periods of time. Thus, time-oriented sampling involves extracting bits of behavior from their temporal stream. As a result of our taking behaviors out of ongoing behavioral streams, it becomes very important to make systematic decisions about the ways in which it will be done. After all, it is this sample of behavior that will be used to make inferences about the universe of behavior. If we choose an "unrepresentative" sample of behavior, it will yield information that does not represent the universe of behavior. Following specific sampling rules minimizes sampling problems.

I will discuss four sampling rules: *ad libitum*, focal person, scan, and event sampling (Martin & Bateson, 1993). *Ad libitum* sampling is not systematic to the extent that the observer does not follow a prespecified set of rules. He or she observes what, whom, and when he or she sees fit to observe. This method may be useful in the initial stages of observational work to the extent that it helps the observer get a very general picture of what exists in the observational field. That is, it gives the observer some "flavor" of the context. The problem with *ad libitum* sampling is that observers tend to see the most obvious and most visible sets of individuals and behaviors. They also tend to see those behaviors that confirm their biases. Consequently, this procedure is extremely susceptible to the influence of observer bias.

Focal person sampling involves choosing one individual and observing him/her for a specified period. For example, in my R&T research I use focal person (child) sampling for 3-minute intervals, so that during a 20-minute recess period I observe in predetermined random order at least six separate children. During the 3-minute interval for each child, I record all relevant behaviors of the focal child, as well as those of other children and adults with whom the focal child is interacting; this form of recording is known as continuous recording and will be discussed later in this chapter. Focal sampling, especially when tied to continuous recording, is very useful in constructing thorough descriptions of the sample. With this method, as will be seen later, we can derive numerous quantitative measures and accurately reconstruct the behavior of focal participants.

The downside of focal sampling is that it is time-consuming (Sackett, 1978). In observing a large number of individuals, use of focal sampling involves a number of discrete observations for each focal child. This problem may, however, be minimized with numerous observers and video-recording equipment (Sackett, 1978). With numerous observers, separate observers can be assigned to separate focal children. With videotapes, more than one child can be recorded simultaneously, *if* they are in very close proximity, such as in an experimental playroom. Both of these options, however, have associated expenses. Numerous, experienced observers are both expensive and hard to come by. Further, repeated viewing of videotapes is very time-consuming. It is often more time-consuming to code videotapes of behavior than to code it live.

Scan sampling is less time-consuming. In this procedure a whole group, such as a classroom, is sampled very rapidly at predetermined intervals. For example, if we were interested in observing children's attention during various parts of the school day, we could utilize scan sampling: We would observe separate individuals and record their behavior instantaneously. It might take 60 seconds to record the attention of a classroom of 30 children. We would conduct a number of separate scans, varying the order in which each child was observed, across the relevant period.

In this case, all observations for each child during the observation period should be aggregated and treated as one score. Scores for specific individuals taken within a short observational period generally *should not* be treated as separate scores because they are not independent of each other. By aggregating across the individual observations, we get a whole (and reliable) picture of what individuals do during a certain period. By looking only at specific points, we learn only what they are doing at a specific instant.

Event/behavior sampling, as noted above, involves choosing a specific event, or behavior, and recording it either continuously or as having occurred or not. Behavior sampling typically is used where the target behavior does not occur with great frequency, and therefore one does not want to rely on time-oriented sampling because of the risk of missing the behavior. Instead, the observer looks for the target behavior to occur and then records it. When recording an event, observers should make note of the specific end point, or consequence, of the behavior. Typically, an event recording is terminated when behaviors from another behavioral category are observed. For example, if we are observing aggression, we record those behaviors that fall into the aggression category. When the nature of the behavior changes, such as when one child comforts the other, the event recording should be terminated, but we should note the behavior that immediately succeeds the target behavior. These consequences of target behaviors, as noted earlier, provide insight into possible functions of the behavior.

Some basic sampling issues apply to behavior sampling. As noted at the beginning of this section, sampling is an attempt to gather information that is representative of larger bodies of information. To maximize the likelihood of gathering representative information, a few guidelines should be followed. First, we should observe the same individual at different points within the same day. By observing individuals at different points of the day, we get a more representative picture. People do different things at 8 a.m. than at 2 p.m.! Similarly, by observing the same individual on different days, we gain representativeness; Child behavior is probably different on Saturday morning than on mornings before the child goes to school.

By extension, the specific order in which people are observed should be considered (e.g., counterbalanced or randomized) so that the order does not affect, or confound, our measures. In the case of counterbalancing we may have a total of 25 observational sampling slots in an observational period, say 1/30 secs. Order of observation is counterbalanced when each child is observed in each of the 25 observational slots. So on day 1 John would be observed in slot 1 and Joan in slot 2. On day 2 John would be observed in slot 2 and Joan in slot 3, and so on. In the case of randomized order, the sampling slot (1–25) for each child on each day would be determined by randomly assigning him or her to a slot. Thus, to ensure representative and nonconfounded data, the order in which we sample behavior should be either randomized or counterbalanced.

Recording Rules

Specific recording rules correspond to certain sampling rules. This correspondence is displayed in Table 4.1. Continuous recording rules can be used with focal person and event sampling strategies. With this form of recording, the observer records all behaviors of interest for the duration of the observational interval. As noted above, in my R&T studies I recorded continuously all social behavior and social interactants of the focal child for a full 3 minutes. The quantitative measures that can be derived from continuous recording are: frequency, latency, duration, intensity, and pattern if the whole behavioral sequence of interest is observed during the specified interval. In addition to the behaviors of the focal child, it is also useful to record the identity of other children with whom the target child is interacting. For example, we could note the behaviors the focal child aims at other specific children and the behaviors others direct at the focal child.

Rather than coding behavior continuously, across time, we might choose to sample discontinuously, or at different time intervals. The recording rules

Table 4.1. Sampling and Recording Rules

	Recording Rules		
	Continuous	0/1	Instantaneous
Sampling rules			
Ad libitum			
Focal	✓	✓	✓
Scan			✓
Event	✓		✓
Quantitative measures			
Frequency	✓		
Duration	✓		
Latency	✓		
Pattern	✓		
Intensity	✓	✓	✓

based on time intervals include instantaneous sampling and 0/1 sampling. Before discussing these recording strategies, I must diverge to discuss the choice of a sample interval (Martin & Bateson, 1993). By sample interval I mean that duration that will be used to determine the interval at which behavior is recorded. The observation period is divided into specific time intervals; the sample intervals are those points at which behavior is sampled. The point at the end of the sample interval is the sample point. Take the example given above where we were interested in studying classroom attention. We could choose a sampling interval of 5, 10, or 15 seconds in a 10-minute lesson. In the case of the 10-second interval, we have a total of 60 sample points. Obviously the shorter the duration, the more the sample will resemble the universe of behavior and thus contain less sampling error. The logistics of conducting observations, however, often preclude a short duration. For example, we easily could implement a 5-second sample interval to record classroom behavior if children were all seated; this short interval would be less practical if children were moving around the classroom or outdoors. Additionally, the degree of detail in a coding system affects the sample interval to the extent that more complex codes require more time than less complex codes. Lastly, repeated observations within a restricted time range bring into question the independence of the separate observations.

With all this in mind, let's discuss the particulars of 0/1 and instantaneous sampling. With either of these methods, the observer should make clear to the reader the intervals at which behaviors were sampled. While we may have a specific sampling interval, say 10 secs, the exact moment at which we record the behavior may vary according to the rules followed. This section will make clear the way in which we should explicate this process.

For simplicity, let's say that our sample interval is 10 seconds. The observer would need some mechanical timer, such as a series of recorded beeps heard through an earphone, to cue him/her when to record. Beepers on digital watches are also useful, but may be too loud for some locations, such as classrooms. With instantaneous recording (also called point sampling), the observer notes the occurrence/nonoccurrence or level of intensity of the behavior(s) of interest at the instant that the beeper goes off. Instantaneous recording is used with scan sampling. Obviously, complicated decisions about intensity ratings would have an impact on the sample interval; longer intervals are required for more complex ratings. Instantaneous recording can yield intensity scores. It also can yield scores that indicate the proportion of intervals during which specific behaviors were observed. It does not yield true frequencies because behavior is not recorded continuously.

The 0/1 sampling strategy (also labeled interval sampling) is similar to instantaneous sampling to the extent that a sample interval determines when we record. Unlike instantaneous sampling, however, 0/1 sampling simply records whether the behavior occurred (1) or did not (0) during the 10-second interval, not at a specified instant. If a behavior occurred 1 time or 10 times during the 10-second interval, a 1 would be scored in each instance. Like instantaneous sampling, 0/1 sampling can tell us the occurrence/nonoccurrence of a behavior/number of recording intervals. Consequentially, true frequency scores cannot be derived from 0/1 sampling. The advantage of 0/1 over instantaneous sampling is that it is easier for the observer; the observer has more time to process information. Indeed, if the sample interval is short enough, 0/1 and instantaneous sampling rules yield very similar measures (Smith, 1985).

Further, 0/1 and instantaneous sampling rules can be used to derive intensity scores. Given the fact that intensity is more difficult to gauge than occurrence or nonoccurrence, it may be measured more practically with 0/1 than with instantaneous sampling. Specifically, the time needed for observers to gauge intensity may preclude the use of instantaneous sampling, especially where sampling intervals are short.

CONCLUSION

In this chapter we have outlined some of the basic tenets of the observational methods commonly used in anthropology, psychology, and ethology. While these methods can be used in either laboratory or naturalistic settings, they are particularly useful in providing descriptions of children as they interact in various niches. Our primary aim in this chapter was to provide an introduction to the systematic process of categorizing, sampling, recording, and measuring behavior in different situations. Hopefully, the inductive and context-sensitive approaches outline here will be useful to researchers from many different orientations.

Acknowledgments. I acknowledge the comments of an anonymous reviewer. Support for the writing of this chapter was provided, partially, by the W. T. Grant Foundation.

REFERENCES

Altmann, J. (1974). Observational study of behavior. *Behavior*, pp. 227–265.

Bakeman, R., & Gottman, J. (1989). *Observing behavior*. New York: Cambridge University Press.

Blurton Jones, N. (1972). Characteristics of ethological studies of human behavior. In N. Blurton Jones (Ed.), *Ethological studies of child behaviour* (pp. 3–36). London: Cambridge University Press.

Chomsky, N. (1965). *Aspects of a theory of syntax*. Cambridge, MA: MIT Press.

Cole, M. (1993, March). *A cultural-historical goal for developmental research: Create sustainable model systems of diversity*. Paper presented at the biennial meetings of the Society for Research in Child Development, New Orleans.

Hinde, R. (1976). On describing relationships. *Journal of Child Psychology and Psychiatry*, *17*, 1–19.

Hinde, R. (1980). *Ethology*. London: Fontana.

Kagan, J. (1994). On the nature of emotion. In N. Fox (Ed.), The development of emotion regulation. *Monographs of the Society for Research in Child Development*, 59 (2–3, Serial No. 240).

Martin, P., & Bateson, P. (1993). *Measuring behaviour: An introductory guide* (2nd ed.). London: Cambridge University Press.

Messick, S. (1983). Assessment of children. In W. Kessen (Ed.), *Handbook of child psychology* (Vol. 1, pp. 477–526). New York: Wiley.

Pellegrini, A. D. (1996). *Observing children in their natural worlds*. Hillsdale, NJ: Erlbaum.

Pellegrini, A. D., & Bjorklund, D. J. (1998). *Applied child study: A developmental approach* (3rd ed.). Hillsdale, NJ: Erlbaum.

Pellegrini, A. D., Horvat, M., & Huberty, P. D. (1998). The relative cost of children's physical play. *Animal Behaviour*, *55*.

Pellegrini, A. D., & Stanic, G. M. A. (1993). Locating children's mathematical competence: Application of the developmental niche. *Journal of Applied Developmental Psychology*, *14*, 501–520.

Sackett, G. (1978). Measurement in observational research. In G. Sackett (Ed.), *Observing behavior* (Vol. 1, pp. 25–43). Baltimore: University Park Press.

Smith, P. K. (1985). The reliability and validity of 1/0 sampling: Misconceived criticisms and unacknowledged assumptions. *British Journal of Educational Research*, *11*, 17–22.

Suen, H., & Ary, D. (1989). *Analyzing quantitative behavioral observational data*. Hillsdale, NJ: Erlbaum.

CHAPTER 5

Ethological Methods in Early Childhood Education

Peter K. Smith

In this chapter I first will discuss what ethological methods are. Then, I will describe some of the main areas where ethological methods have been used in early childhood education—in nursery schools, kindergartens, and play groups. Primarily, these are studies of social behavior: of affiliation, aggression, rough-and-tumble play, dominance, showing off, attention structure, and settling in the group. Finally, I will consider the potential of ethological methods for continuing to be of relevance to early childhood educators and summarize some practical applications of these findings.

WHAT ARE ETHOLOGICAL METHODS?

Ethology normally refers to the study of behavior in nonhuman species. I use the term "ethological approach" to refer to studies that satisfy three criteria. First, they primarily rely on direct, nonparticipant observation of behavior. Second, such data are gathered in natural settings. Third, there is some interest in the functional and the comparative evolutionary significance of the behavior.

"Direct" observation means that no "indirect" measures (such as tests or interviews) stand between the observer and the observed, and that records are compiled immediately, not retrospectively; "nonparticipant" means that the observer stands apart from the persons being observed, interacting minimally if at all. When we are studying behavior in, say, herring gulls, or macaques, direct nonparticipant observation in natural settings is an obvious methodology to adopt.

We cannot be participant observers, or interview our subjects. We can, of course, do experiments with animals, and many researchers might combine observation in natural settings with experimental approaches and still call themselves "ethologists." For example, Tinbergen used many experimental manipulations in his pioneering ethological text, *The Study of Instinct* (1951), and studied the reactions of animals to test objects and stimuli. Thus, to some extent, equating ethology purely with study in natural settings is misplaced.

However, direct observation in natural settings does have a special place in the study of animal behavior for another reason: Many zoologists, from Lorenz and Tinbergen onwards, have felt that unobtrusive recording of what goes on in the animal's natural environment is an essential first step if we want to get a clear idea of the animal's behavioral repertoire, and if we want to have any reasonable chance of understanding the functional significance of such behavior. Whereas psychologists as much as ethologists have been interested in understanding the causation and development of behavior, it has been a more distinctive concern of ethologists to understand the adaptive value of behavior for the individual, and the evolutionary history of how natural selection has favored this mode of behavioral adaptation. Tinbergen (1951), in fact, suggested that ethologists should be interested in four types of questions about behavior, the "4 Why's":

1. Why is this behavior happening now? (immediate causation or mechanism)
2. Why has this behavior developed in this individual? (causation in ontogenetic perspective)
3. Why is this behavior adaptive? (immediate function)
4. What is the evolutionary history by which this behavior has come to be selected for? (function in evolutionary perspective).

For example, consider a boy pushing another boy out of the way to get to a desired piece of playground equipment. *Why* does he do it? At the first level, because he wants to get to the equipment. At the second level, because he has learned in the past that pushing is one way of getting what he wants. At the third level, because his behavior may help him become dominant over the other child in this and future encounters. At the fourth level, social dominance is one important feature of social groups that has been selected for in humans, as in other primates and many other species, because of its payoff (ultimately, in terms of reproductive success).

A number of researchers, often called human ethologists, have felt that these techniques and interests could be applied to the study of human behavior. The first two criteria of ethology referred to earlier—direct, nonparticipant observation and the use of natural settings—have tended to be the most characteristic of this approach. Clearly, there are problems. Can observation really be unobtrusive? What is a natural setting for the human species, anyway? Nevertheless, the ethological approach to human behavior has had a distinctive impact. Most such research has been carried out with young children. This is probably because it has been felt that it is difficult to get useful information from interviewing children (especially very young ones), because they are relatively easy to observe unobtrusively, and because researchers have felt reasonably comfortable considering a play group or school playground as a natural setting, at least in comparison to the setting of a typical psychological laboratory.

Nonparticipant observational studies of children have, in fact, occurred in two main phases during the twentieth century. The first was in the 1930s, uninfluenced by animal research. The second was in the 1970s, substantially influenced by animal ethology. The 1930s work developed many of the main aspects of observational methodology—category systems, sampling methods, and reliability checks—that are of importance to this day (see Chapter 4 in this volume). However, these studies lacked a comparative and evolutionary perspective (Smith & Connolly, 1972), and, as we shall see, adopting such a perspective has led to research in what otherwise might have been rather neglected areas. The emphasis on comparative and evolutionary aspects of behavior also has been taken up by human sociobiologists and behavioral ecologists (e.g., Barkow, Cosmides, & Tooby, 1992). Generally, human sociobiologists do not feel constrained to use nonparticipant observation in natural settings and indeed often conduct experiments in the laboratory or use questionnaires! This work, however, generally has been with adults.

It is some of the work with young children since the 1970s that has been paradigmatic of human ethology; I will survey the main areas of research with young children in the preschool or early school period. I will not deal with research involving very young infants in the first 18 months of life, which I consider outside the scope of this volume.

ETHOLOGICAL METHODS, OBSERVATION, AND ETHNOGRAPHY

It will be clear that ethological approaches share much in common with other approaches: notably, observational methods and ethnography. Let's briefly look at the commonalities and differences.

Observational methodology is a key feature of the ethological approach; usually, ethologists use observation in natural settings as a first stage in their research. However, they may continue by doing experiments in laboratories or more constrained settings. Thus, ethology provides a broad perspective on a topic, which may use various specific methods, of which observation is a very important one.

Ethologists use the initial observation phase to get insight into the nature of the phenomenon, without imposing preconceived categories. In this sense, it shares a similar aim with ethnography and grounded theory in the social sciences. Ethnographers also may spend time getting to know the situation before trying to interpret it.

An important difference between ethology and ethnography is that ethologists use nonparticipant observation; consequently, they do not try to talk to or interrogate those they are observing. They may record verbalizations, and interpret them at a first-order level as "play invitation," "threat," and so forth, but they do not discuss possible deeper meanings in these utterances or question anyone further. In contrast, ethnographers usually engage in participant observation; they see themselves as part of the social situation. They are likely to look for key informants and question them at some length about the meaning of what is going on. They compare different informants' accounts and attempt to arrive at an interpretation of the meaning of events. Ethologists, most of whom work with nonverbal animal species, prefer to rely on the actual behaviors (including vocal and verbal behaviors) in interpreting what is happening; they are more skeptical that people say what they really mean or think.

My own view is that both ethology and ethnography have much to offer in understanding human social behavior. It is important to both watch what people do, and record what people say they do, and why (including different informants). There is no absolute truth, but the more information we get from different sources, the more reliable the conclusions we can reach (Smith & Sluckin, 1979).

MAIN AREAS OF ETHOLOGICAL RESEARCH
WITH YOUNG CHILDREN

Despite the 1930s work, direct observational methods largely fell into disuse in the 1950s and 1960s. Most research, including that in early childhood, used tests and tightly controlled laboratory situations. This began to change in the late 1960s, and the impetus for change first came from ethology. Ethological methodology had been developed through the preceding decades, initially, at least, largely independent from psychological research on animal behavior. Lorenz and Tinbergen, the two great pioneers of modern ethology, both advocated the application of ethology to the study of human behavior. By the late 1960s, examples of such application were appearing in both Britain and Germany.

In Britain, Blurton Jones (having completed a doctorate with Tinbergen) started studying the social behavior of children in nursery school. His first published work in this area (Blurton Jones, 1967) was in a book titled *Primate Ethology*. Another pioneer of the application of ethological methods to humans was Hutt. The 1970 volume by Hutt and Hutt, *Direct Observation and Mea-*

surement of Behavior, helped to revive interest in observational methodology generally, as well as arguing the benefits of drawing on the work of animal ethologists. McGrew (1972) and Hutt and Hutt (1970) published work on the behavior patterns seen in aggression, the existence of a dominance hierarchy in preschool children, and the influence of the physical environment, especially density, on social and aggressive behavior.

These and other researchers in Britain formed a lively nucleus of human ethologists who formed links with researchers in Germany (e.g., Eibl-Eibesfeldt, 1967) and soon with researchers in the United States, such as Charlesworth and Hartup. By the mid-1970s, human ethology was being strongly influenced by the theoretical ideas of sociobiology, brought to the attention of the general scientific community by Wilson (1975). This resulted in some rethinking and regrouping in the human ethology movement. A journal was started in 1979 entitled *Ethology and Sociobiology* (retitled *Evolution and Human Behavior* in 1997). This movement combines ethological work, still much of it observational research on children, with sociobiological work, much of it based on anthropological research, that examines the adaptive value, or fitness, of human behavior in different cultural contexts. The links between the two strands exist, in terms of an overall interest in the functional aspects of behavior and its evolutionary context, but in practice they are rather tenuous.

Ethograms and the Structure of Behavior in Preschool Groups

Some of the early work in the ethological tradition (Blurton Jones, 1972; McGrew, 1972; Smith, 1973) attempted to devise ethograms of preschool children's behavior. An ethogram is a comprehensive catalogue of behaviors for a species. For preschool children, these could include facial expressions, body postures, motor activity, actions with objects, nonverbal and verbal communications, and social exchanges. On the basis of co-occurring categories at a micro level, it was possible to describe higher-level, or macro, categories. For example, Blurton Jones (1972) arrived at three main categories in a study of 2- to 4-year-olds in an English nursery:

Social. Point, give, receive, talk, smile
Aggression. Fixate, frown, hit, push, take-tug-grab
Rough-and-tumble play. Laugh, play face, run, jump, hit at, wrestle

The Blurton Jones findings were replicated in finer detail by Appleton (1980).

Studies by Smith and Connolly (1972) and Smith (1973) examined individual differences among children in terms of macro-factors; the main factor was social maturity, which correlated with age, talking, and social play. A second factor was whether play was with toys or without toys (e.g., rough-and-tumble). The relationship between these and other studies is discussed by Pellegrini (1992).

The majority of ethological work has gone on to examine especially these aspects of social behavior: affiliation and alliance; aggression, particularly how dominance comes to mediate overt aggression; and rough-and-tumble play as a behavior that may seem aggressive but is usually friendly.

Affiliation and Prosocial Behavior

An example of an ethological study of prosocial, or altruistic, behavior is that of Strayer, Wareing, and Rushton (1979) in a Canadian early childhood center. They observed four main categories of prosocial behavior: *cooperative activities* (task or play cooperation); *object related activities* (giving and sharing objects); *helping activities* (help in task, or play); and *empathic activities* (looking at, approaching, or comforting an upset peer).

These authors found some degree of consistency across these types of prosocial behavior, especially for peer-related behavior. That is, some children were consistently more prosocial than others; this consistency showed some stability over time. An exception to this pattern of consistency was empathic behavior, which related negatively to the other prosocial categories; however, the definition of empathic behavior was perhaps too broad, since *looking at an upset peer* and even *approaching an upset peer* may not involve any intent to help or feeling of empathy as such.

Friendship, or affiliation, was measured separately, in terms of approaches to play or interaction with other children. The pattern of prosocial behavior matched closely the pattern of affiliation. Also, these relationships tended to be reciprocal. The authors interpreted this as meaning that prosocial behaviors function for young children to learn about and maintain reciprocal friendships.

Although prosocial behavior is fundamental to social groups, individuals often disagree with each other. Possibly the largest body of ethological work has been on aggressive behavior.

Types and Typologies of Aggressive Behavior

Many researchers have used "aggressive behavior" broadly in terms of intentional behavior that causes distress or harm to another person. However, there are many types of aggressive behavior, and it may be important to distinguish among them. Indeed, it often is argued that a distinctive advantage of an observational/ethological approach is that it enables valid distinctions to be made between different types of aggression (e.g., Attili, 1985).

There are a number of ways in which distinctions can be drawn. These include *verbal* and *nonverbal* aggression (based on the presence or absence of verbal threats or insults); *instrumental* or *hostile* aggression (based on whether the distress or harm is inferred to be the primary intent of the act); and *individual* or *group* aggression (depending on whether more than one child attacks another).

The distinction based on intent was elaborated by Manning, Heron, and Marshall (1978). They proposed a three-way classification of hostile incidents, based on observations of children in nursery school. They defined *specific hostility* as that which occurs in a specific situation that annoys or frustrates the aggressor. Hostility is used as a tool enabling the aggressor to get his or her own way or assert his or her opinion; the victim is often incidental. They distinguished six subcategories of this: property or territorial disputes, exclusion of another child from a group or game, ordering about, precedence, organization-ordering, and judgment.

In contrast, *harassment* appears unprovoked (at least in the immediate situation) and is directed at a person. The aggressor gains nothing tangible from the act; the reward appears to be the victim's reaction. They distinguished three subcategories of this: physical harassment, teasing, and threat. Finally, *games hostility* is seen as rough, intimidating, or restrictive activities that occur in a rough-and-tumble or fantasy game; for example, very rough variants of rough-and-tumble, or bullying, intimidating or imprisoning the victim against his or her will in a fantasy game.

Attili and Hinde (1986) built on this threefold distinction and included a fourth, *defensive or reactive hostility*, provoked by the action of others. This might, however, link to specific hostility where the dispute is over objects or space, or to harassment if the response to provocation is particularly strong.

Some construct validity for these distinctions has been found by a number of researchers. For example, boys seem to score higher than girls in harassment but not in specific hostility (Manning et al., 1978; Smith & Connolly, 1980). Provoked aggression (e.g., defensive hostility) is correlated with popularity in schoolchildren, whereas unprovoked aggression (e.g., harassment) is correlated with sociometric rejection (Lesser, 1959). Different kinds of aggression may show a characteristic ontogenetic sequence of appearance in the first few years of life (Szegal, 1985).

These distinctions ultimately are based on inferences of the intent of the actors, although the observer uses aspects such as the context of the incident, its temporal structure, and the facial expressions and vocalizations of the participants as the observable cues for such inferences. Nevertheless, the full complexity of how such inferences are based on observable phenomena has not been spelled out. Thus, these distinctions are somewhat different from those of Blurton Jones, for example, which apparently are based only on the occurrence of actions defined in physical rather than motivational terms.

Hinde (1985) and Attili and Hinde (1986) have taken the issue of intent a step further. They have postulated two distinct motivational factors. *Aggressive-*

ness is seen as a general propensity toward violence. *Assertiveness* is seen as a motivation to elevate one's position or push oneself forward, whether in general terms or in relation to particular objects or goals (as in *acquisitiveness* with regard to specific objects or situations). These motivations are postulated to underlie observer behavior in a systematic way, with *aggressiveness* leading primarily to harassment/teasing or to specific hostility, and *assertiveness* leading primarily to specific hostility or to showing off. Thus, showing-off behavior (to be discussed later) is an example of an assertive but not an aggressive behavior.

Another related development has been the attempt to categorize children into certain types according to their characteristic patterns of aggression. Manning and associates (1978) distinguished among *specific specialists, harassment specialists, games specialists,* and *teaser-specifics* (who showed a considerable amount of both specific hostility and harassment). These types of children, determined at nursery school, were linked to family communication patterns and to social adjustment both in nursery school and later in school at age 7 to 8. *Specific specialists* appeared well adapted at both home and school, whereas other types of children exhibited some maladjustment in one or other context. This interesting report is limited by the small number ($N = 17$) of children studied.

An independent typology has been developed by Montagner, based on observations of preschool children in daycare centers (see Montagner, Restoin, & Henry, 1982). This more obviously includes elements of dominance than does Manning's categorization. Montagner's six types of children are *leaders* (who frequently compete, impose themselves on others, and show appeasement); *dominated with leader mechanisms* (who compete less often); *dominant-aggressive* (who frequently compete and impose themselves on others, but do not frequently show appeasement); *dominated-aggressive* (who compete less often); *dominant-fearful* (who do not impose themselves and are often targets of aggression by others); and *dominant-isolated* (who seldom interact with other children). These types were related to family profiles and also to biological rhythms based on measurements of corticosteroid excretion in urine samples.

Discussion of possible links between the typologies of Manning and Montagner can be found in Sluckin (1981) and Attili and Hinde (1986).

Aggression and Rough-and-Tumble Play

A particularly important outcome of the ethological approach to aggression has been the distinction made between aggressive behavior and rough-and-tumble play. Blurton Jones (1967) took the term *rough-and-tumble* from Harlow's descriptions of play in rhesus monkeys. Blurton Jones first described explicitly the behaviors involved in rough-and-tumble, and showed that they occurred in behavior sequences separate from aggression in his observations of preschool children. However, the general types of fighting play had been described at least as far back as Groos (1901).

Subsequent research on rough-and-tumble has confirmed that it can be distinguished from aggressive behavior in terms of the specific behaviors present (e.g., open rather than closed hand when making beating or hitting movements; play face rather than frown and fixate), and the context (e.g., participants tend to stay together rather than separate) (Smith & Lewis, 1985). Also, children who often are seen in aggression are not necessarily often seen in rough-and-tumble (Blurton Jones, 1972). Through the preschool and middle school years, sociometric assessments show that children tend to like their rough-and-tumble play partners (Humphreys & Smith, 1987; Smith & Lewis, 1985). Even at age 4, some children can articulate the ways in which rough-and-tumble play and real fighting can be distinguished (Smith & Lewis, 1985).

Nevertheless, the distinction has not always been observed in more traditional psychological research. As Blurton Jones (1972) pointed out, studies of the imitation of aggression in children (e.g., Bandura, Ross, & Ross, 1961; Nelson, Gelfand, & Hartmann, 1969) confounded the two. Measures such as punching a doll could be, and illustrations showed sometimes were, associated with rough-and-tumble indicators such as a play face, while measures such as gun play or fantasy aggression clearly implicated rough-and-tumble. Thus, one cannot conclude from these studies that watching aggression makes children more aggressive. Studies such as Huston-Stein, Fox, Greer, Watkins, and Whitaker (1981) and Potts, Huston, and Wright (1986) included hitting an inflated clown or bobo doll as aggressive, and thus continued this confound.

These studies on aggression, imitation, and the mass media are not the only examples. In a study of the effects of density on aggression, Loo (1972) did not distinguish rough-and-tumble from real fighting. Her finding that reduced space led to reduced aggression in boys (but not girls) is probably artifactual because of this confound (as noted later, it was not confirmed by the research of Smith & Connolly, 1980). In a study of children's social networks, Ladd (1983) defined rough-and-tumble as "unorganised agonistic activity with others, e.g. fights or mock-fights, wrestling, pushing/shoving" (p. 291). Again, this means that his substantive finding, that rough-and-tumble play is more frequent in sociometrically rejected than in popular or average children, may reflect the effects of (unprovoked?) aggression rather than rough-and-tumble play per se.

Teachers also appear to have some misconceptions about rough-and-tumble play. Although most recognize that the two forms of behavior are distinct, Schäfer and Smith (1996), in a study of 30 English infant school teachers, found evidence for two misconceptions. Teachers overestimated the relative proportion of rough-and-tumble play to real fighting (2:1) compared with the observational evidence (4:1 or greater); and they overestimated the likelihood that rough-and-tumble play will turn into real fighting (29%) compare with findings from observational studies (about 1%). Possibly, teachers are basing their judgments on the small number of aggressive and sociometrically rejected children for whom this really is true (Pellegrini, 1994; Smith, 1997).

Up to around age 9 or 10, the consensus of the evidence is that rough-and-tumble and aggression are clearly distinct. There is no excuse for continuing to confound them in observational studies. The situation is different as children approach adolescence and the relationship between these two classes of behaviors becomes more complex (Pellegrini, 1994; Smith, 1997).

Dominance Relationships

Several researchers in the ethological tradition have examined groups of children or adolescents to see whether dominance has the same salience or predictive characteristics as have been found in groups of primates and other species. While some of the research has involved asking children for their rankings of peers for toughness or dominance, or strength, much of it has relied on direct observation of which individuals win conflicts in (usually) dyadic encounters. An edited volume by Omark, Strayer, and Freedman (1980) is a sourcebook for a great deal of this research.

Although Blurton Jones (1967) initially doubted whether a linear dominance hierarchy would be useful in describing the social behavior or organization of children as young as preschool age, subsequent researchers clearly have shown its value. For example, McGrew (1972) found a nearly linear hierarchy of dominance, based on naturalistic observation of wins and loses during conflict over the possession of preferred objects. The most systematic program of research in this area has been that of Strayer and his associates.

Strayer and Strayer (1976), observing 18 children in a preschool, delineated three kinds of measures: *threat-gesture* (comprising intention hit, intention kick, intention bite, and face/body posture); *physical attack* (comprising bite, chase, hit, kick, push-pull, and wrestle); and *object/position struggles* (with or without physical contact). They also classified responses to these as *submission, object/position loss, help seeking, counterattack,* and *no response*. They then examined the usefulness of a dominance hierarchy based on the three mean measures of initiated behavior, when the response was either *submission* or *object/position loss,* that is, when there was a clear winner or loser.

Observations were made using a matrix-completion method, with the aim of filling as many dyadic cells of the matrix as possible; that is, of observing encounters between as many different dyads of children as possible. The most dominant children are placed at the top of the list on the left-hand vertical of the matrix. This order of children maximizes the number of entries above the upper-left/lower-right diagonal of the matrix. Matrix entries represent incidents with a clear win by the child higher in dominance (above diagonal) or lower in dominance (below diagonal).

Strayer and Trudel (1984) examined both affiliation and social dominance in a number of preschool groups, with children aged 8 to 66 months. Although affiliative actions are much more common than dominance actions (by at least 4:1), the authors argue that dominance emerges as a very early characteristic of relationships, before affiliation. This study, as do several others (e.g., LaFreniere & Charlesworth, 1983), suggests that frequencies of overt conflict decrease with age; this can be interpreted as being due to dominance signals allowing resolution of competition without overt conflict being necessary.

A more critical view of the applicability of dominance hierarchies to preschool children's groups is provided by Archer (1992); he feels that the dyadic concept generally has been applied too narrowly and that at times even random ordering may give the appearance of a hierarchy. Strayer and Noel (1986) have broadened the dyadic examination of dominance to look at triadic conflicts, in which one child may intervene to help another, or a child may solicit another's help. This further links the concept of dominance to that of affiliation and crucially to the idea of alliance. Camras (1984) has analyzed strategies of both verbal and nonverbal communication in resolving conflicts. Recently, there has been some interest in looking at reconciliation behavior in preschoolers after conflicts, following the example of deWaal (1989) and others in nonhuman primates.

Attention Structure

A concept related to that of social dominance, has been that of attention structure. This refers to the amount of visual attention (looking) directed to individuals by others in a group. A volume edited by Chance and Larsen (1976) contains a collection of both primate and human studies on this. Several studies have examined the relationships between dominance and attention structure in preschool groups. The correlations are generally high, but not so substantial that the two constructs can be considered as interchangeable.

One example of such a study is that by LaFreniere and Charlesworth (1983), on a class of 20 four- and five-year-olds. Dominance was calculated in a manner similar to that used by Strayer and Strayer (1976), while attention was based on observations of looking behavior. In addition, affiliation was assessed by observations of interactive play with other children. Besides confirming a highly linear and rigid hierarchy in their group, LaFreniere and Charlesworth found that it was reasonably stable over a 9-month period of observations, as was the attention structure. Dominance and attention ranks correlated together quite highly. The correlations of dominance with affiliation and also with sociometric popularity were smaller and nonsignificant; however, attention structure correlated with these latter measures. Thus, it seems that attention structure may be picking up aspects both of dominance (children monitoring what highly dominant children are up to) and of affiliation (children watching their friends or children they are playing with).

Showing-off Behavior

Related to attention structure is the phenomenon of showing-off behavior, discussed by Hold-Cavell (1985). The most frequent items of showing off observed in a group of 25 German kindergarten children were *attracting attention verbally* (e.g., calling someone), *intensity of voice or noise* (e.g., singing loudly), *aggrandizement of body size* (e.g., climbing on a chair), *obvious body movement* (e.g., jumping around in the room), and *seeking attention with an object* (e.g., wearing unusual headgear). Both showing-off behavior and threat displays were found to correlate significantly with attention structure and with physical aggression. Looking also at the temporal patterns of these behaviors over a school year, Hold-Cavell has suggested that both showing off and threat display may serve as strategies for getting high regard in the group. Koyama and Smith (1991) replicated some of Hold-Cavell's findings, in an English nursery. However, they found showing-off behavior to be independent of any measures of aggression, a finding they consider in relation to the motivational theories of Hinde (1985) and Attili and Hinde (1986) discussed earlier.

Environmental Effects on Behavior

Most ethological work with children has been nonexperimental. An example of a combination of observational/ethological methods with systematic experimentation is a series of studies on the play-group environment by Smith and Connolly (1980). They carried out systematic environmental variations on two preschool play groups over a 3-year period and made observations of the children's behavior.

One study was on the effects of a free-play nursery regime, compared with a structured activities nursery regime. One play group in each condition was observed over an 8-month period. In the structured activities condition, the attention span of children at activities increased. However, unexpected findings were obtained for aggression; frequencies of aggression did not differ between the two groups initially and did not change significantly in the children experiencing the free-play regime. But all categories of aggression increased steadily for the children in the structured activities regime, especially when the children were allowed back into free play in a final baseline assessment period. The authors concluded that the decreased peer interaction that characterized the structured activities condition might have decreased the ability of the children to manage their own conflict situations without escalation.

Other studies by Smith and Connolly (1980) examined the effects of numbers of children, spatial density, and resource density. Within a range of 10 to 30 children in the group, numbers of children had a major impact on friendship patterns. In small groups, children tended to play with everyone else, and cross-sex pairings were common. In larger groups, there was a more fragmented sociometric structure and fewer cross-sex pairings, but more chance of very close dyadic relationships. Group size did not affect the incidence of aggression, provided that space and resources were varied commensurately.

Variations in spatial density, within a range of 75–25 square feet per child, mainly affected physical activity (a decrease at higher densities, partly compensated for by more climbing rather than running). Spatial density did not affect affiliation or aggression; but a further reduction to 15 square feet per child did increase aggression, suggesting a threshold effect and leading to a recommendation that 25 square feet per child should be a minimum provision in preschool facilities. Finally, providing more toys per child systematically reduced the frequency of aggression between children, although it also reduced the frequency of sharing and of children being together in large subgroups, due to the greater dispersal of the children among the available items of toys and equipment.

Settling in to the Group

Several studies have used ethological methods to examine the process of settling in at a nursery school or play group. For example, McGrew (1972) observed children from day 1 to day 65 of starting at a group, as well as changes through a particular morning. At the beginning of a particular day, or during the first few days, children were much more often immobile and showed more automanipulative behaviors such as scratching, rubbing, or fingering—probably signs of anxiety or fearfulness.

Bensel (1992) discriminated between behaviors shown by young children on arrival at a German kindergarten, those at leave-taking from the parent, and those shown subsequently. While many children went to play with others on arrival and left their parents without fuss, a clear minority of children clung to their parents and protested at leave-taking. Such children were more likely subsequently to show what Bensel called *aside-behavior*, including sucking fingers or objects, stroking the body, using comfort objects, and just staring into space. Bensel comments on the possible unnaturalness of a new play-group experience for young children and the need to form a bond with an adult in the nursery to ease the leave-taking experience.

USING ETHOLOGICAL METHODS

This final section starts by indicating how one might actually set about doing an ethological study. Then it attempts to summarize some of the pros and cons of the various methodological aspects that often are associated with the ethological approach: direct nonparticipant observation; study in natural settings; and explicit adherence to a functional and comparative/evolutionary perspective.

Doing an Ethological Study

A lot of ethologically based research has been carried out with young children, so a first step is to be aware of this. However, there is still more to be learned—both about well-studied areas such as aggression and also about new areas. For example, a few studies are beginning to be done about reconciliation after conflicts, following similar work in nonhuman primates (deWaal, 1989; Kappeler & van Schaik, 1992; Sackin & Thelen, 1984).

Having selected a topic, it would be important to do the preliminary period of natural observation; first, acclimatizing the children to the researcher's presence, and then recording on paper, audiotape, or videotape examples of the behavior of interest, initially as diary records. Even in a well-worked area, one should verify that previous studies match with one's own observations.

Then, a category list or ethogram will need to be constructed; an existing list may be used or adapted, or one may be developed. However, there are a lot of issues to bear in mind in developing one's own categories; guidance can be found in any good handbook of observational methods, such as Colgan (1978); Martin and Bateson (1993); or Pellegrini (1991; Chapter 4 in this volume). These issues include reliability of observations, validity issues, and issues of what time sampling procedures to use.

One then can use the category scheme to make systematic observations and address the problem of interest; this might be a general issue of what behaviors occur in certain situations, or it might involve sequential analysis (Bakeman & Gottman, 1986), or it might involve comparing children of different age, sex, or personality, or in different environments.

However, to conduct an ethological study rather than just an observational study, the researcher would need to keep in mind issues such as the adaptive value of behavior; whether useful comparisons can be drawn with nonhuman species (e.g., monkeys and apes); whether theorizing in sociobiology or evolutionary psychology may lead to certain predictions (e.g., Barkow, Cosmides, & Tooby, 1992); and whether the findings from the observational work might lead to testing these predictions further, perhaps in a less natural setting and using experiments or interviews.

Pros and Cons of the Ethological Approach

Direct Nonparticipant Observation. As compared with interviews, questionnaires, or rating scales, direct observation has the advantage that the investigator can record what "really" happens, rather than what someone says happens or has an impression of happening. In this sense, direct observation appears to yield more valid data, or at least data whose validity we can be more confident of, than other methods of data gathering. In particular, interview or questionnaire data may draw out socially desirable responses.

It is, of course, true that the act of observing may itself induce socially desirable behavior to be produced for the observer, or socially undesirable behavior to be inhibited. This can be partly overcome by making concealed observations, or by making observations over such extensive periods that habituation to the observer occurs and/or the observations cover most of the time in the setting under consideration (e.g., Smith & Connolly, 1980). Nevertheless, certain phenomena, such as bullying in schools, may remain more tractable to interviews or rating scales than to direct observation (e.g., Olweus, 1978). It is also true that what people say happens may be as interesting as what "really" happens. In fact, many of the studies cited have combined observational data with other kinds of data such as sociometric data based on interviews or responses to video material. Few, if any, current researchers would want to argue that direct observation is the only useful way of getting data (although many might wish to advocate it as the most useful way, for certain purposes).

Another advantage of direct observation is that, following a period of relatively unstructured watching, the investigator may come up with behavioral categories or distinctions that were not previously conceived but that turn out to be useful or have some construct validity. The examples of aggressive types (e.g., Manning et al., 1978) and of rough-and-tumble play (e.g., Blurton Jones, 1967) support this consideration. This line of argument traditionally has been advanced by ethologists, and it characterizes the 1970s phase of observational research more than that of the 1930s (Fassnacht, 1982; Smith & Connolly, 1972).

Natural Settings. Studies in both the 1930s and 1970s phases generally have been carried out in natural settings such as daycare centers, play groups, schools, or homes. This has been seen as an advantage in terms of the ecological validity of the studies and hence the confidence with which results can be taken to be representative of real life, compared with studies carried out in contrived or laboratory situations. A contrived situation has some clear disadvantages. By simplifying the environment, certain behaviors are excluded and certain hypotheses will not be generated or tested from the resulting data. For example, effects of third-party interventions in fights cannot be assessed by watching dyads in a laboratory. In addition, contrived situations may introduce unwanted behaviors, such as responses to a novel situation, or behavior directed to the experimenter. Hence, unwanted hypotheses (such as experimenter effects or response to novelty) may confound the testing of the hypotheses supposedly under study.

The use of natural settings does not necessarily exclude some experimental control. For example, Smith and Connolly (1980) carried out experimental manipulations of the environment of their play groups in a reasonably ecologically valid way. Also, few researchers would disagree that some more contrived studies can supplement those in natural settings.

At a deeper level of meaning, no setting is totally "natural" for humans in the way that certain settings can be seen as "natural" for particular nonhuman species in terms of the ecological niche to which that species' behavior is adapted. As cultural animals, we have changed our environment too much; it can be argued that even the home of a nuclear family, or the large peer groups of a school, are somewhat "unnatural" in these terms. Indeed, Bensel (1992) made this point explicitly about toddler play groups. Thus, it would be wrong to be too dogmatic about the naturalness of settings in studying human behavior. The basic points at issue are to which range of settings the investigator wishes to be able to generalize results, and how important and feasible it is, at the current level of knowledge, to include or exclude certain hypotheses from testing.

Functional and Comparative/Evolutionary Significance of Behavior. A number of researchers have been inspired by comparative work, especially methodologies and concepts used in the study of nonhuman primates. Examples include nonverbal communication signals for threat, appeasement, and reconciliation; rough-and-tumble play; and attention structure and dominance hierarchies. There has been some interest in at least considering the function of behavior. Sociobiological theorizing has had an imput in this, encouraging a shift from thinking about functional significance of behavior for the group, to its significance for the individual. It also has encouraged interest in more specific hypotheses, such as the extent of reciprocation for aid-giving behavior.

The functional and evolutionary aspect probably has been strongest in the research on dominance relationships and attention structure. Distinctively, it leads to questions as to why individuals should seek high regard or high dominance rank, and hence encourages a longer time perspective. Also, it emphasizes alternative strategies that individuals may pursue toward the same functional ends. This may have interesting implications for the traditional developmental distinctions between normal and maladaptive behavior (cf. Manning et al., 1978). As yet, however, the functional and evolutionary perspective has had relatively little impact on the observational research with children. Functional questions are notoriously difficult to address, perhaps especially so for children, since function ultimately is related to adult survival and reproductive success. Children remain among the easiest populations to observe in natural settings.

Practical Implications

Ethological approaches can help preschool teachers and educators approach the domain with a new perspective—that of the child, and why (in various ways) the child behaves as he or she does. The studies we have considered highlight such aspects as the importance of reciprocation in friendship; the role of social dominance in resolving conflicts, and perhaps facilitating the reduction of overt conflicts, with age and experience, in a play group; the abilities of young children to signal dominance and appeasement, and engage in reconciliation; the distinction between real fighting and play fighting or rough-and-tumble, and the primarily friendly nature of the latter; the role of showing off and attention structure in the development of leadership; the effects of environmental constraints and opportunities; and the process of settling in to an established social group and the signs of distress shown by some children during this process.

Such knowledge can broaden the perspective of adults. Knowing the significance of play fighting can lead to a different attitude to such behaviors; knowing the role of dominance and children's own conflict-resolution strategies can lead to working with these rather than imposing alien standards of resolving conflicts; knowing signs of distress, even subtle ones, can lead to more effective comforting. In these and other ways, ethological methods have much to offer early childhood educators.

REFERENCES

Appleton, P. (1980). A factor analytic study of behavior groupings in young children. *Ethology and Sociobiology, 1,* 93–97.

Archer, J. (1992). *Ethology and human development.* New York and London: Harvester Wheatsheaf.

Attili, G. (1985). Aggression in young children—Introduction: Some methodological issues related to the nature of aggression. *Aggressive Behavior, 11,* 279–281.

Attili, G., & Hinde, R. A. (1986). Categories of aggression and their motivational heterogeneity. *Ethology and Sociobiology, 7,* 17–27.

Bakeman, R., & Gottman, J. (1986). *Observing interaction: An introduction to sequential analysis.* New York and Cambridge: Cambridge University Press.

Bandura, A., Ross, D., & Ross, S. A. (1961). Transmission of aggression through imitation of aggressive models. *Journal of Abnormal and Social Psychology, 63,* 575–582.

Barkow, J. H., Cosmides, L., & Tooby, J. (Eds.). (1992). *The adapted mind: Evolutionary psychology and the generation of culture.* Oxford: Oxford University Press.

Bensel, J. (1992). Behavior of toddlers during daily leave-taking and separation from their parents. *Ethology and Sociobiology, 13,* 229–252.

Blurton Jones, N. (1967). An ethological study of some aspects of social behaviour of children in nursery school. In D. Morris (Ed.), *Primate ethology* (pp. 347–368). London: Weidenfeld & Nicolson.

Blurton Jones, N. (1972). Categories of child–child interaction. In N. Blurton Jones (Ed.), *Ethological studies of child behaviour* (pp. 97–127). Cambridge: Cambridge University Press.

Camras, L. (1984). Children's verbal and nonverbal communication in a conflict situation. *Ethology and Sociobiology, 5,* 257–268.

Chance, M. R. A., & Larsen, R. R. (Eds.). (1976). *The social structure of attention.* London: Wiley.

Colgan, P. W. (Ed.). (1978). *Quantitative ethology.* New York: Wiley.

deWaal, F. B. M. (1989). *Peacemaking among primates.* Cambridge, MA: Harvard University Press.

Eibl-Eibesfeldt, I. (1967). Concepts of ethology and their significance in the study of human behavior. In H. W. Stevenson, E. H. Hess, & H. L. Rheingold (Eds.), *Early behavior: Comparative and developmental approaches* (127–146). New York: Wiley.

Fassnacht, G. (1982). *Theory and practice of observing behaviour.* London: Academic Press.

Groos, K. (1901). *The play of man.* London: W. Heinemann.

Hinde, R. A. (1985). Categories of behavior and ontogeny of aggression. *Aggressive Behavior, 11,* 333–335.

Hold-Cavell, B. C. L. (1985). Showing-off and aggression in young children. *Aggressive Behavior, 11,* 303–314.

Humphreys, A. P., & Smith, P. K. (1987). Rough and tumble, friendship, and dominance in schoolchildren: Evidence for continuity and change with age. *Child Development, 58,* 201–212.

Huston-Stein, A., Fox, S., Greer, D., Watkins, B. A., & Whitaker, J. (1981). The effects of TV action and violence on children's social behavior. *Journal of Genetic Psychology, 138,* 183–191.

Hutt, S. J., & Hutt, C. (1970). *Direct observation and measurement of behavior.* Springfield, IL: C.C. Thomas.

Kappeler, P. M., & van Schaik, C. P. (1992). Methodological and evolutionary aspects of reconciliation among primates. *Ethology, 92,* 51–69.

Koyama, T., & Smith, P. K. (1991). Showing-off behaviour of nursery children. *Aggressive Behavior, 17,* 1–10.

Ladd, G. W. (1983). Social networks of popular, average and rejected children in school settings. *Merrill–Palmer Quarterly, 29,* 283–307.

LaFreniere, P., & Charlesworth, W. R. (1983). Dominance, attention, and affiliation in a preschool group: A nine-month longitudinal study. *Ethology and Sociobiology, 4,* 55–67.

Lesser, G. S. (1959). The relationship between various forms of aggression and popularity among lower-class children. *Journal of Educational Psychology, 50,* 20–25.

Loo, C. M. (1972). The effects of spatial density on the social behavior of children. *Journal of Applied Social Psychology, 2,* 372–381.

Manning, M., Heron, J., & Marshall, T. (1978). Styles of hostility and social interactions at nursery, at school, and at home: An extended study of children. In L. A. Hersov, M. Berger, & D. Shaffer (Eds.), *Aggression and anti-social behaviour in childhood and adolescence* (pp. 29–58). Oxford: Pergamon Press.

Martin, P., & Bateson, P. (1993). *Measuring behaviour: An introductory guide* (2nd ed.). Cambridge: Cambridge University Press.

McGrew, W. C. (1972). *An ethological study of children's behaviour.* London: Academic Press.

Montagner, H., Restoin, A., & Henry, J. C. (1982). Biological defense rhythms, stress, and communication in children. In W. W. Hartup (Ed.), *Review of child development research* (Vol. 6, pp. 291–319). Chicago and London: University of Chicago Press.

Nelson, J. D., Gelfand, D. M., & Hartmann, D. P. (1969). Children's aggression following competition and exposure to an aggressive model. *Child Development, 40,* 1085–1099.

Olweus, D. (1978). *Aggression in the schools: Bullies and whipping boys.* New York: Wiley.

Omark, D. R., Strayer, F. F., & Freedman, D. G. (Eds.). (1980). *Dominance relations: An ethological view of human conflict and social interaction.* New York: Garland.

Pellegrini, A. D. (1991). *Applied child study: A developmental approach.* Hillsdale, NJ: Erlbaum.

Pellegrini, A. D. (1992). Ethological studies of the categorization of children's social behavior in preschool: A review. *Early Education and Development, 3,* 284–297.

Pellegrini, A. D. (1994). The rough play of adolescent boys of differing sociometric status. *International Journal of Behavioral Development, 17,* 525–540.

Potts, R., Huston, A. C., & Wright, J. C. (1986). The effects of television form and violent content on boys' attention and social behavior. *Journal of Experimental Child Psychology, 41,* 1–17.

Sackin, S., & Thelen, E. (1984). An ethological study of peaceful associative outcomes to conflict in preschool children. *Child Development, 55,* 1098–1102.

Schåfer, M., & Smith, P. K. (1996). Teacher perceptions of playfighting and real fighting in primary school. *Educational Research, 38,* 173–181.

Sluckin, A. (1981). *Growing up in the playground: The social development of children.* London: Routledge & Kegan Paul.

Smith, P. K. (1973). Temporal clusters and individual differences in the behaviour of pre-school children. In R. P. Michael & J. H. Crook (Eds.), *Comparative ecology and behaviour of primates* (pp. 751–798). London and New York: Academic Press.

Smith, P. K. (1997). Play fighting and real fighting: Perspectives on their relationship. In A. Schmitt, K. Atzwanger, K. Grammer, & K. Schåfer (Eds.), *New aspects of ethology* (pp. 47–66). New York: Plenum Press.

Smith, P. K., & Connolly, K. (1972). Patterns of play and social interaction in pre-school children. In N. Blurton Jones (Ed.), *Ethological studies of child behaviour* (pp. 65–95). Cambridge: Cambridge University Press.

Smith, P. K., & Connolly, K. J. (1980). *The ecology of preschool behaviour.* Cambridge: Cambridge University Press.

Smith, P. K., & Lewis, K. (1985). Rough-and-tumble play, fighting and chasing in nursery school children. *Ethology and Sociology, 6,* 175–181.

Smith, P. K., & Sluckin, A. M. (1979). Ethology, ethogeny, etics, emics, biology, culture: On the limitations of dichotomies. *European Journal of Social Psychology, 9,* 397–415.

Strayer, F. F., & Noel, J. M. (1986). The prosocial and antisocial functions of preschool aggression: An ethological study of triadic conflict among young children. In C. Zahn-Waxler, E. M. Cummings, & R. Iannotti (Eds.), *Altruism and aggression: Biological and social origins* (pp. 107–131). Cambridge and New York: Cambridge University Press.

Strayer, F. F., & Strayer, J. (1976). An ethological analysis of social agonism and domi-
    nance relations among preschool children. *Child Development*, 47, 980–989.
Strayer, F., & Trudel, M. (1984). Developmental changes in the nature and function of
    social dominance among young children. *Ethology and Sociobiology*, 5, 279–295.
Strayer, F. F., Wareing, S., & Rushton, J. P. (1979). Social constraints on naturally oc-
    curring preschool altruism. *Ethology and Sociobiology*, 1, 3–11.
Szegal, B. (1985). Stages in the development of aggressive behavior in early childhood.
    Aggressive Behavior, 11, 315–321.
Tinbergen, N. (1951). *The study of instinct*. London: Oxford University Press.
Wilson, E. O. (1975). *Sociobiology: The new synthesis*. Cambridge, MA: Belknap Press.

CHAPTER 6

Assumptions and Features of Longitudinal Designs: Implications for Early Childhood Education

Richard M. Lerner, Penny Hauser-Cram, and Erez C. Miller

Whether a longitudinal design is used to study aspects of early childhood education depends on the metatheoretical and theoretical conceptions of an investigator and on the purposes of the investigation. Although the traditions of cross-sectional studies and longitudinal investigations both have their place in furthering knowledge about early childhood, researchers gain different types of information from the two approaches. McCall (1990) emphasizes a critical distinction: Cross-sectional studies enable us to understand developmental distinctions (i.e., differences in groups), whereas longitudinal investigations promote the understanding of intraindividual differences. As investigators in early childhood education, we benefit from both types of information. For example, we want to know how 4-year-old boys and girls differ in social skills, but to determine possible points of intervention, we also want to know how 4-year-old children with poorly developed social skills progress throughout their school years. The pattern of intraindividual differences in growth trajectories can be studied only through a longitudinal design.

Longitudinal designs are also well suited to studies of the emergence of a developmental or educational process, such as language development or literacy. For example, Brown and Bellugi (1964) followed two children longitudinally and documented the emergence of two-word utterances and simple sentences. In another study, Sulzby (1985) documented the changes over a year in the emergence of oral reading ability in kindergartners and 2- to 4-year-old children.

Those in the field of early childhood are familiar with the advantages of longitudinal designs in studying the effects of early education programs on children and families. Hundreds of investigations have been conducted on the effects of early childhood programs (Barnett, 1995); two of the best-known early childhood projects for children from low-income families are the Carolina Abecedarian program (Campbell & Ramey, 1994) and the Perry Preschool Project (Weikart & Schweinhart, 1992). The results of these projects have been influential in program development, early childhood education, and public policy arenas. The Perry Preschool Project, in particular, exemplifies the benefits of conducting a longitudinal study of participants that spans from their early childhood years to adult life. Advantages for children participating in that project (and, indeed, many similar ones) gained "social currency" as children became adolescents and young adults, and demonstrated lower rates of delinquency, adolescent pregnancy, and school dropout in comparison to nonparticipants (Yoshikawa, 1995).

Longitudinal designs are necessary to study the interrelation between the child and the context in which that child is developing, learning, and affecting the environment over time. Just as we cannot assume that a measure of the child at one time is sufficient, we also cannot assume that the context in which the child is learning and growing remains stable. Indeed, much research is emerging that suggests the assumption of acontextual development is faulty and instead we should focus our attention on understanding the range of contexts in which children develop (Bronfenbrenner, 1993), the transactions that occur within these contexts (Sameroff & Chandler, 1975), and how they vary over time (Lerner, 1995). For example, in discussing the effects of Head Start programs, Zigler (1990) describes how the programs affect parents, who in turn are influenced by multiple changing systems such as the world of work, school, the media, and health care systems.

The opportunity to conduct contextualized research should be used not only by scientists, but also by teachers (and other early childhood practitioners). The very nature of their work requires teachers to spend several hours a day over a year with the children in their class. Hence, teachers' unique position provides them the opportunity—which "visiting researchers" do not always have—to study longitudinally developmental and educational processes as they emerge, evolve, and change (Fleischer, 1994).

The decision to employ a longitudinal design is a purposeful one. If an investigator determines that the phenomena being studied are best understood by employing a longitudinal design, a range of other conceptual issues arise that influence the type of longitudinal design eventually selected. It is the researcher's stances on these issues, and not the use of a longitudinal design per se, that will shape the qualities of the data provided by a particular study. The investigator's assumptions about continuity, stability, universality, and embeddedness of human behavior, to a large extent, will determine the timing and nature of assessments. In this way, the investigator's prior beliefs about development determine the frame within which a study constructs understanding of early childhood. Recognizing the importance of the influence of such prior beliefs on the knowledge generated by research is as important as understanding the benefits of the design employed.

Whether the study shows linkages within or among levels of analysis, or displays evidence for the historical variability of program influences, depends on premethodological decisions about issues of units and levels of analysis and of cross-cohort generalizability. Accordingly, assessment of the metatheoretical and theoretical perspectives involved in designing a given longitudinal investigation must be coupled with an appraisal of the data derived from the study, in order to fully evaluate how the study contributes to a more comprehensive understanding of the nature and outcomes of early childhood education.

CONCEPTUAL PRESUPPOSITIONS
AND METHODOLOGICAL CHOICES

A researcher's decision to use a longitudinal design to study or evaluate programs in early intervention and early childhood education is not a choice based exclusively, or perhaps even primarily, on empirical considerations. A researcher's choice of a research method or design is derived from his or her implicit or explicit presuppositions and assumptions about the character of the phenomena to be studied (Kagan, 1980; Lerner, 1976, 1986; Overton & Reese, 1973). Simply, researchers' methodological choices—including their decisions about whether to use a longitudinal design—rest on their philosophical and derivative theoretical conceptions about the character and bases of development.

The purposes of this chapter are (1) to discuss the assumptive bases—the philosophical and theoretical ideas—that lead researchers to adopt particular methodological approaches regarding research design, measurement, and data analysis, and (2) to illustrate how deciding to adopt longitudinal methods may enhance scholarship about child development, early childhood education, and early intervention. A key point is that researchers' pre-empirical ideas shape the nature of understanding of early childhood development–program linkages as much as does information "residing" in data. Different methods provide contrasting sensitivities for the behaviors selected for study, and both screen in and screen out particular behaviors. If the researchers' choice of a specific method has been predicated, even in part, on pre-empirical presuppositions, philosophical assumptions, or theoretical prescriptions and proscriptions, then part of the

variance in the available research information about development, early childhood education, and early intervention may be due to these non- (or at least
pre-) empirical orientations.

A number of philosophical models, or world views, have informed the study
of development. For instance, several scholars have discussed this connection
by presenting an evaluation of the role in developmental science of organismic,
mechanistic, and developmental contextual world views (e.g., Lerner, 1986;
Reese & Overton, 1970). To discuss the connections between philosophy and
methodology, other scholars have drawn on issues of continuity–discontinuity
(e.g., Block, 1971; Brim & Kagan, 1980) and/or on the related issues of the universality versus the temporality of the human developmental trajectory (e.g.,
Baltes, Reese, & Nesselroade, 1977; Lerner, 1986; Lerner & Nesselroade, 1991;
Nesselroade & Baltes, 1979; Wohlwill, 1991). Although any of these approaches
may allow the same points to be illustrated, continuity–discontinuity and universality versus temporality are the focus of this discussion because of their more
ready connection to ideas about longitudinal methods.

DEVELOPMENT AS A CONTINUOUS
AND A UNIVERSAL PHENOMENON

Within the study of human development, debates about the role of, on the
one hand, implicit presuppositions or explicit philosophical world views and, on
the other hand, theory and method have centrally engaged scholars for at least
20 years (e.g., Dixon, Lerner, & Hultsch, 1991; Kagan, 1980; Lerner, 1976, 1986,
1991; Lerner & Nesselroade, 1991; Overton & Reese, 1973, 1981; Reese &
Overton, 1970; Wohlwill, 1991). One of the somewhat surprising conclusions to
be drawn from this literature is that scholars who share an interest in studying
"development" differ in the extent to which they believe that their task involves
the conceptualization and study of change.

Conceptually, some scholars believe that the task of developmental analysis is to ascertain the connectivity that exists across life periods; that is, they believe
that the identification of continuity, constancy, or stability is the major task of
the developmental scholar (e.g., see Brim & Kagan, 1980; Clarke & Clarke, 1976;
and Lerner, 1984, for a discussion of this point of view). From this perspective,
there is a universal, or generic, developmental trajectory; any variation around
this purported trajectory that is empirically discovered is interpreted as "noise
in the system," that is, as error variance (e.g., Wohlwill, 1973). Indeed, some
scholars claim that variation around a universal trajectory is not even a pertinent topic to study within a psychological science aimed at describing and explaining "basic" developmental processes (e.g., see Baltes, 1987). They argue,
albeit tautologically, that basic processes are universal, generic ones.

Those who have put this assumption of continuity of development to a test have provided some advancement in understanding the intricacy of development, but some findings have been unexpected. For example, Pasamanick and Knobloch (1961) hypothesized that a range of birth complications, termed the "continuum of reproductive casualty," related directly to children's later development, and speculated that infants who experienced abnormal births would display atypical development. In empirically testing this hypothesis, however, Sameroff and Chandler (1975) found little evidence to support the direct relation between reproductive risk and later development. To better understand why development was compromised in some cases, but not others, Sameroff and Chandler (1975) constructed a complex model of development that contrasts with the linear direct model previously proposed and, in doing so, took into account the transactions that occur between infants and features of their environment, including interactions with caregivers.

Another set of findings that runs counter to expectations based on the belief in continuity of development has emerged in studies of children born prematurely. Many, although not all, preterm infants display evidence of "catching up" with their chronological age peers by around age 2 (e.g., Friedman & Sigman, 1980; Greenberg & Crnic, 1988). If theorists operate from a position of belief in continuity of development, they would not anticipate that some children would "catch up." Instead, they would predict that these children would display some form of delay, albeit perhaps increasingly small, across the early childhood period.

Thus, tests of the assumptions of continuity of development have served an important function in furthering more complex and ecologically valid models of development during the early childhood period. When researchers assume continuity by dismissing variation and failing to test their assumptions, however, they unknowingly can construct insufficiently articulated models. For example, researchers holding this view have had to marshal conceptual inventions such as "sleeper effects" or "heterotypic versus homotypic continuity" to maintain the stance of developmental continuity in the face of descriptively disparate time-ordered empirical observations (Kagan & Moss, 1962).

Effects of Assumptions on Methods

Methodologically, if a researcher believes that the basic character of behavioral, psychological, or social phenomena is stability or constancy across time, methods and designs that provide valid and reliable assessments at any given single occasion of measurement suffice as adequate science (cf. Baltes, Reese, & Nesselroade, 1977; Nesselroade & Baltes, 1979). From this methodological perspective, then, designs that involve the appraisal of intraindividual change (i.e., repeated measurement, or longitudinal, designs) have no conceptual advantage over designs that appraise only interindividual differences (presumably, but not necessarily, in intraindividual change, i.e., cross-sectional designs). Issues of availability, efficiency, and economy are the only important determinants, then, of whether one or the other design is used.

Temporality. Several research literatures in the general field of early childhood education provide illustrations of this emphasis on atemporality. In early childhood, much research on temperament assumes it to be a stable and basic early-emerging characteristic of an individual's personality (Buss & Plomin, 1984; Rutter, 1964). Empirical elaboration of the construct of temperament has evolved from the pioneering work of Thomas and Chess (1977) and Kagan and Moss (1962). From these studies emerged a typology of temperament by which infants could be classified as "easy," "difficult," or "slow-to-warm-up." Since then, much empirical work has centered on using early indicators of temperament as predictors of later behavior. For example, Caspi and Silva (1995) report that dimensions of temperament measured during early childhood predicted aspects of personality during the adult years. The assumption of stability in temperament at least within developmental periods (Goldsmith, Bradshaw, & Riesser-Danner, 1986) predominates in research investigations, and the measurement of temperament during only one time point, therefore, often is considered sufficient (precisely because stability is assumed).

Moreover, the issue of whether change-sensitive measures (i.e., assessments psychometrically developed to be able to detect change in a developmentally continuous construct) are employed in a "developmental" design is essentially irrelevant to a scholar who believes in continuity and universality. Indeed, to such a scholar the purpose of measurement is to identify that which does not change (e.g., Costa & McCrae, 1980), that is, to identify that which remains "still stable after all the years" (p. 65). Thus, the researcher may select measures that were developed to be insensitive to age-associated variation. Similarly, the issue of measurement equivalence—the concern with whether the use of different measures at distinct age periods index the qualitatively same underlying construct—does not arise from a universalistic, continuity perspective that emphasizes the identification of cross-time (i.e., age-general) constancy.

Type of Measures. If researchers assume continuity and universality in measuring outcomes during early childhood years, they will be likely to think that standard cognitive performance measures administered at any ontogenetic time often suffice. Scales such as the Bayley Scales of Infant Development (Bayley, 1993), the Stanford–Binet Fourth Edition (Thorndike, Hagen, & Sattler, 1986), or the Wechsler Preschool and Primary Scale of Intelligence (Wechsler, 1967) frequently are used to measure infant, toddler, and early childhood cognitive functioning. Underlying the use of these instruments is the assumption that a measure of a child's cognitive performance during the infant years will be an adequate predictor of later performance.

Despite the widespread use of such measures, empirical evidence suggests that these standardized tests fail to demonstrate high levels of continuity in cognitive performance across the infant and early childhood period (Kopp & McCall, 1982). The tests themselves have different types of items for the infant and the toddler assessments. Infant test items are based largely on psychomotor skills, whereas toddler and preschool items often include assessment of language and other symbolic functions. Thus, although the same test may yield an identical standard score for an infant and a toddler, the meaning of the score changes with age, a point that often gets lost in the search for universal continuity.

Occasions of Measurement Finally, even if issues of convenience, efficiency, or economy lead a scholar working from a universalistic perspective to employ a longitudinal design, the particular occasions of measurement used in this context are completely arbitrary, if not irrelevant, features of the research design (Lerner & Tubman, 1989). Just as issues of convenience, economy, and efficiency are the essential basis for the choice of a longitudinal design, these issues are the primary, indeed the exclusive, concern in regard to the choice of which ontogenetic times within the life-span one "samples" in the study of development. Since the goal of such sampling is to identify the constancies—the connections that exist—across the course of life, and since such research employs, almost without exception, change-insensitive measures for which no information exists about cross-time measurement equivalence, there is little, if any, compelling theoretical reason to select one ontogenetic time of measurement over another.

Examples of the roles of convenience, economy, and efficiency in the selection of occasions of measurement abound in evaluations of early childhood intervention programs. Child assessment points often are chosen to maximize the efficiency and practicality of evaluation efforts rather than being derived from theoretically driven models of development. Thus, frequently children are assessed when they enter a program (which could be at various ages), at one or more time intervals during the program, and finally when they leave the program (again, often at various ages). For example, Gardner and her colleagues (Gardner, Grantham-McGregor, Chang, Himes, & Powel, 1995) studied the effects of nutritional supplementation and psychosocial stimulation on the activity level and development of young Jamaican children over a 12-month period. The children first were assessed when they enrolled in the program, and subsequently twice more at intervals of 6 months, in the middle and at the conclusion of the program. Similarly, Wasik and her colleagues selected intervals of 6 months for assessing the cognitive performance of young children who were at risk for developing cognitive difficulties (Wasik, Ramey, Bryant, & Sparling, 1990). Thus, it is not uncommon for researchers to designate times for measurement based on programmatic factors rather than on children's individual developmental trajectories or more general developmental milestones.

Cross-Sectional Designs. Designs using comparisons of interindividual differences in intraindividual change in order to study development still predominate in the field of early childhood. That is, cross-sectional designs, involving either different birth cohorts (e.g., Sophian, Wood, & Vong, 1995) or different groups compared on a variable other than age assessed at a common time of measurement (e.g., Merriman, Marazita, Jarvis, Evey-Burkey, & Biggins, 1995), have been the most frequently used in the field of child development. A review of all the empirical studies published in four major journals in developmental psychology (*Child Development, Developmental Psychology, Merrill–Palmer Quarterly*, and *Early Childhood Research Quarterly*) in 1995 shows that cross-sectional designs are still in the majority. Only studies that focused on some aspect of development in early childhood and that had at least one group of participants younger than 8 years were included in the review. Studies categorized as "longitudinal studies" had at least two measurement points that were at least 1 month apart on the same participants. As Figure 6.1 illustrates, nonlongitudinal studies in early childhood development constituted 68% of the studies published in the reviewed journals in 1995.

Figure 6.1. Longitudinal versus nonlongitudinal designs for early childhood studies reported in four developmental psychology journals in 1995.

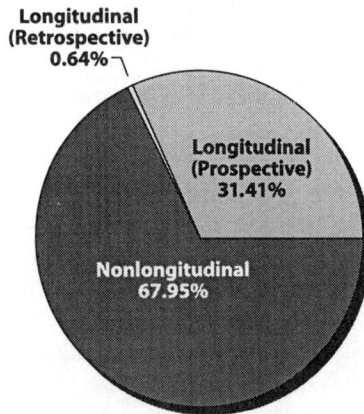

Cross-sectional designs involving the comparison of groups (e.g., males and females, or children with and without a disability) have provided important bases of the description of children's behavior and learning. For instance, such studies described the role of imitation in aggressive behavior (Bandura, Ross, & Ross, 1961), gender differences in social and play behavior of young children (Jacklin & Maccoby, 1978), and preschoolers' understanding of numerical concepts (Gelman & Meck, 1983). These studies can, however, only suggest critical markers of the potentially numerous, multiply determined pathways that lead to similar or strikingly disparate outcomes during childhood. Cross-sectional studies serve as inadequate proxies of longitudinal designs for describing developmental trajectories.

The absence of theoretical bases for the selection of ontogenetic measurement points (i.e., for the selection of the ages or stages within the life-span that are assessed), and the use instead of arbitrary or adventitious criteria for selecting times of measurement, provide an inadequate means to identify change trajectories. It should be noted that this is a concern that may be raised in regard to all developmental designs, including longitudinal and sequential ones. However, in cross-sectional designs this problem is coupled with several others. That is, even if there were a rationale in a given cross-sectional study for the use of particular ontogenetic observation points, the problems that cross-sectional designs pose for the valid identification of developmental change trajectories are such that these designs remain inadequate for the analysis of developmental pathways. These shortcomings arise because, depending on the particular ontogenetic observation points that happen to be used for the set of cohorts involved in a cross-sectional study, it is possible to find "evidence" for almost any form of developmental trajectory. Yet, because each cohort is observed only once (thus confounding age-associated variation with cohort-associated variation) (Baltes et al., 1977; Schaie, 1965), this evidence may not provide a veridical depiction of the developmental trajectory for that cohort.

Sher (1991), writing about the study of vulnerability to alcoholism and to related disorders, has discussed in some detail the limitations of cross-sectional studies. Cross-sectional studies, comparing individuals with positive and negative family histories for alcoholism, can only identify potential mediators of risk. That is, variables for which significant differences in levels exist by group are likely to be correlated with, or to be the consequences of, a risk factor, rather than being risk factors themselves (McNeill & Kaij, 1979). Etiological relevance is more likely to be established in a longitudinal prospective design, within which description of temporal ordering, prospective prediction, and the logical exclusion of third-variable explanations may be accomplished more readily.

The extensive use of cross-sectional designs to identify correlates of, or actual mediators of, risk has tended to influence the conceptualization of vulnerability to the development of alcoholism (Sher, 1991). Finally, this design typically has been associated with an emphasis on analyses of group means highlighting between-group differences among risk groups; this work has minimized within-group heterogeneity and overlap in levels of functioning between groups (Sher, 1991). This approach has resulted in a reification of the risk groups initially proposed in these cross-sectional studies.

Moreover, there is no way in which a change trajectory can be identified through one time of measurement. Nevertheless, this limited observation is all that is (ordinarily) available. Thus, the lack of veridicality between an "observed" and an actual trajectory cannot be identified. As such, results of cross-sectional studies provide an inadequate and necessarily erroneous representation of the developmental change trajectory of any cohort involved in a study; in addition, the data from such studies may not even provide a depiction of development pertinent to some "overall" or "composite" trajectory for the cohorts involved in the study.

Several figures may be used to illustrate these points. First, consider the change trajectories of the three cohorts depicted in Figure 6.2. For Cohort 1 an inverted U-shaped function characterizes the developmental change trajectory for variable Y. For Cohort 2 the scores for this variable decrease linearly from birth. Finally, for Cohort 3 the scores for variable Y increase linearly from birth.

Figure 6.3 illustrates the developmental change trajectory identified from a cross-sectional study involving these three cohorts and using the ontogenetic observation points labeled "1A," "2A," and "3A." In this figure a "composite"

Figure 6.2. Three possible development trajectories.

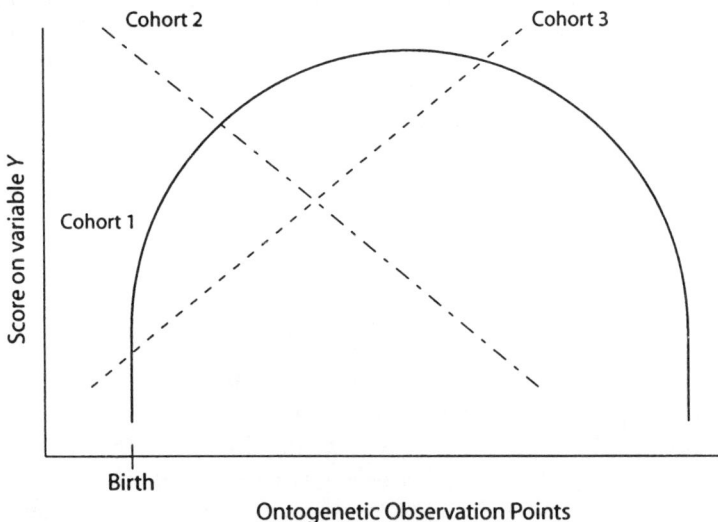

Figure 6.3. "Composite" trajectory involving linear increase.

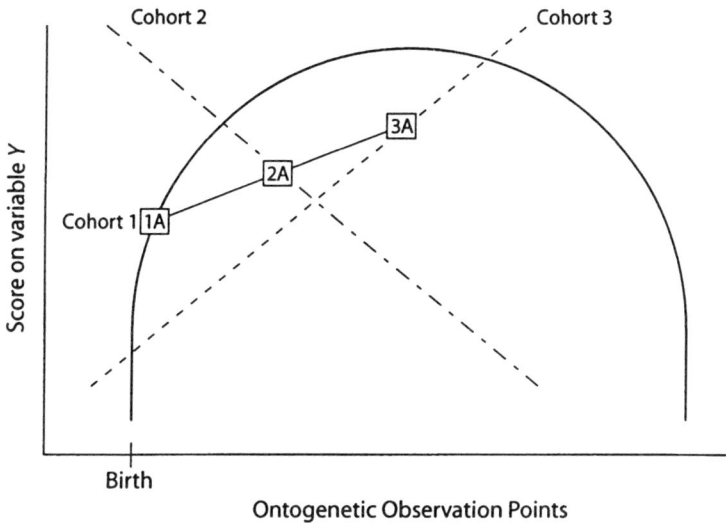

trajectory involving a linear increase is seen. However, this trajectory exists at a slope different from the one actually involved in the linear increase trajectory for Cohort 3. Moreover, the composite trajectory is not at all an adequate representation of the change patterns found for the other two cohorts. Finally, that the composite trajectory displayed in Figure 6.3 is primarily a product of the particular ontogenetic observation points that happen to have been used, can be seen by reference to Figures 6.4 and 6.5.

In Figure 6.4 the same three cohorts are used, but a set of ontogenetic observation points different from the ones in Figure 6.3 are employed: "1B," "2B," and "3B." Here a composite trajectory reflecting linearly decreasing changes is seen. Once again, however, the slope of this trajectory is not the same at that seen in regard to the cohort (No. 2) that displays a linear decrease; similarly, the composite trajectory displayed in Figure 6.4 is not reflective of the change patterns seen for the other two cohorts in the study.

Finally, Figure 6.5 illustrates that a composite trajectory derived from a cross-sectional design may not be representative of the change patterns of any of the cohorts in the study. The ontogenetic observation points ("1C," "2C," and "3C") in Figure 6.5 depict a pattern of constancy, of neither increases nor decreases in the scores for variable Y, across the times of measurement. This pattern is not representative of the change trajectories associated with any of the three cohorts involved in the illustration.

Figure 6.4. "Composite" trajectory involving linear decrease.

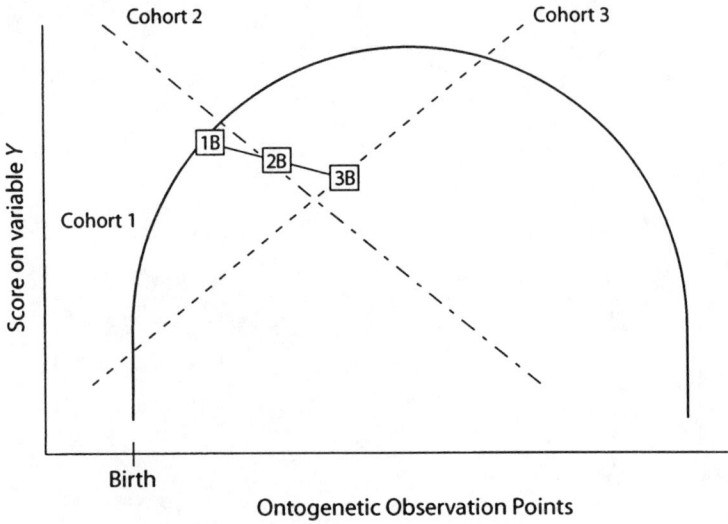

Figure 6.5. "Composite" trajectory reflecting constancy.

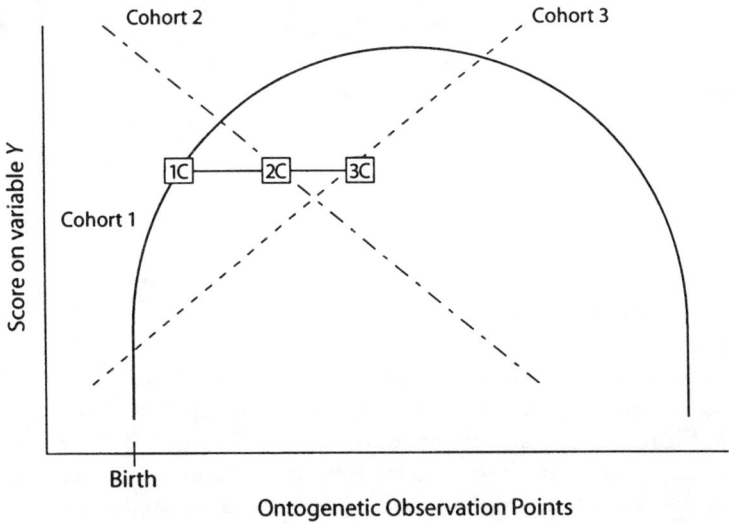

In sum, cross-sectional designs, despite their widespread use in the study of human development, cannot accurately depict patterns of intraindividual change. Indeed, the ontogenetic observation points used in such designs may not even reflect variance associated uniquely with age-associated functions. Accordingly, in order to appraise temporal linkages across the life-spans of individuals, only longitudinal designs should be employed.

However, not all studies of intraindividual change use the exact same longitudinal design. The variation that exists in the type of longitudinal methods employed is linked also to contrasts in the philosophical and theoretical views of researchers.

TEMPORALITY AND THE POSSIBILITY OF DISCONTINUITY

If researchers believe that temporality is a core part of the fabric of human development, then changes—at any one or several levels of organization ranging from the individual through the sociocultural and historical—may be seen to alter the course of the life of individuals, groups, or entire cohorts (e.g., Baltes, 1987; also see Dixon & Lerner, 1988, for a discussion of the history of the emergence of the conceptual linkage between ideas of development and of temporality). In other words, these researchers subscribe to the view that human life inextricably involves change (Dixon & Lerner, 1988). They may differ, however, in regard to the levels of organization they see as involved in changes in human development. Some scholars consider only individual or social levels of organization in their models of temporality (e.g., Block, 1971), while others include additional levels, ones involving institutional and, most centrally, historical influences (e.g., Tobach, 1981). Indeed, for these scholars intraindividual change trajectories are inextricably linked with historical change, and, in fact, the scope of such variation includes evolution (e.g., Gould, 1977; Lewontin, 1981). Thus, this range of perspectives regarding temporality means that individuals or cohorts differ because they live in distinct historical periods and/or because one individual or group experiences a set of dyadic, familial, or institutional life events that is not encountered by another individual or group.

Because temporal variation (e.g., historical change) is not the same, then, for all individuals, this view posits that there is no one universal life course or generic developmental trajectory. Individual differences, arising from the connections between the developing person and the temporally changing context, are figure—not ground. That is, interindividual differences in intraindividual change are not error variance; they are not "noise in the system." Rather, such individual differences become the prime descriptive target and key explanatory objective of developmental science.

Therefore, to test this theoretical view, there is a need for developmental models that can account for the multiple processes that operate over time to influence a range of adaptive and maladaptive outcomes via the interaction of numerous variables at different levels of analysis—that is, there is a need for probabilistic epigenetic, or developmental contextual, models (Lerner, 1984, 1986). In contrast to predetermined epigenetic models, in developmental contextualism the contextual features that serve to influence individuals' developmental trajectories do not simply alter the pace of development of particular outcomes; they may be depicted as qualitatively transforming influences.

From the perspective of such developmental contextual models (Lerner, 1986), and given the definitional constancy of temporal variation, human development is characterized across life by the potential for qualitative discontinuity, by the possible lack of connections between points across ontogeny. Simply, then, this view sees the potential for systemic change or, in other words, plasticity (Lerner, 1984) as a basic characteristic of human developmental phenomena. The potential plasticity of human development has several implications for the methodology of longitudinal research.

Methodological Implications of Plasticity

The potential for plasticity that derives from the temporal embeddedness of human development means that only change-sensitive measures, methods, and designs are adequate in scientific analysis (Baltes et al., 1977; Nesselroade, 1983; Nesselroade & Baltes, 1979). At a minimum, two occasions of measurement must be involved in the research design, since change cannot be detected through measures employed only at one point in time (Baltes et al., 1977; Rogosa, 1988).

The types of developmental processes that can be depicted in analyses are also dependent on the number of occasions of measurement included in the research design (e.g., Windle, 1988). At least two occasions of measurement are needed to model developmental processes with linear trajectories, while nonlinear trajectories require three or more occasions of measurement to model. Bryk and Raudenbush (1987) delineate the value of modeling change over multiple time points in understanding human development. The assumption of linearity can be tested only if data are collected over more than two time points, so that other models (e.g., curvilinear) also can be tested.

Moreover, predictors of status and predictors of growth often differ. For example, in analyses of preschoolers attending Head Start programs, Bryk and Raudenbush (1987) found that while neither home language nor hours of instruction were related to measures of initial status in children's knowledge of natural science, home language was related to later growth in this domain. Ideally, data should be collected at multiple occasions if (1) there is an expectation of discontinuity in behavior over the span of the study; and (2) multiple paths of behavior are possible (e.g., Huttenlocher, Haight, Bryk, Seltzer, & Lyons, 1991; Tubman, Vicary, von Eye, & Lerner, 1990).

Moreover, a principled selection must be made of the occasions of measurement involved in a given design. First, at the least, some consideration must be given to the issue of whether the intermeasurement interval is sufficient for the identification of change in regard to a particular psychosocial phenomenon. In other words, divisions of the X axis are not equivalent for all psychosocial phenomena (Lerner, Skinner, & Sorell, 1980). For example, divisions of a year make sense in the study of the development of psychometric intelligence across the adolescent years (Bloom, 1964); and if cohort or generational change is being indexed (e.g., in regard to cultural values regarding drinking and driving), then divisions no smaller than a decade may make sense. In contrast, assessment of changes in infant psychomotor performance must involve X axis divisions no greater than a few weeks or months. Divisions of a year are too great to provide sensitivity to the changes in this domain of development; indeed, such divisions would result in changes literally "falling through the cracks" of the X axis divisions. In short, the timing of the repetition of measurement in change-oriented research designs is, ultimately, a theoretically and conceptually derived decision (Lerner, 1986; Lerner & Tubman, 1989).

Similarly, the design of research concerning the effects of early childhood education programs requires that attention be paid to the length of time between occasions of measurement. Intervals will vary as a function of the particular aspect of educational programs under investigation, that is, the substantive focus of the program, the level of analysis, and the point in early childhood being assessed. The pace of change may be sufficiently modest that intervals of 1 year between occasions of measurement may be adequate for some early childhood developments, such as the development of children's cognitive schemata related to health issues (e.g., Noll, Zucker, & Greenberg, 1990). Shorter intervals between measurement occasions may be appropriate in periods or in regard to substantive areas in which development is more fast-paced, such as the development of language in young children. For example, in a study of toddlers' vocabulary growth, Huttenlocher and her colleagues (Huttenlocher et al., 1991) found that although most children express their first words at around the age of 12 months and display acceleration in vocabulary through age 5 years, the structure of individual vocabulary growth is not linear. By appraising children's vocabulary growth every 2 months, Huttenlocher and her colleagues were able to display growth trajectories, which they found were best expressed as a quadratic function of age, as well as to analyze the factors that led to early and later growth. If, instead of multiple closely spaced assessment points, vocabulary growth during the early childhood period had been measured at two disparate times (e.g., at 12 months and at 60 months), vocabulary growth would have been inaccurately displayed as linear.

The ontogenetic observation points used in longitudinal research also should be driven by theoretical concerns or, at the least, by empirical generalizations drawn from the extant literature. For example, Seifer and Vaughn (1995) postulate that goal-directed exploration of the environment manifests itself differently at different ontogenetic points. Building on the work of Yarrow and Pederson (1976), Barrett and Morgan (1995) postulate that behavioral shifts occur in the second half of the first year in object mastery-related behaviors. According to their model, during the first 8 months or so of life, the motivated infant displays preference for novelty and engages in a range of well-practiced behaviors that are often unrelated to the task (e.g., banging a puzzle with a stick). They speculate that a shift in the nature of mastery motivation behaviors occurs at around 8 to 9 months of age. Subsequent to that shift the motivated infant engages in purposeful means-to-end activities (e.g., attempts to place a piece in the puzzle). Thus, if we wanted to study mastery motivation in infants, we would need to anticipate that the nature of the tasks and the markers of motivation would differ for older and for younger infants. The point at which the infant is studied therefore needs to be well chosen and based on whether one wants to study motivated behavior in early versus later infancy. The need to consider ontogenetic observation points becomes especially problematic in studies of children with developmental disabilities, whose cognitive skills may be at variance with their chronological ages. Thus, in studying mastery motivation in infants and toddlers with developmental disabilities, the question of whether children have made a shift into means–end behavior is critical to determining the nature of the assessment (e.g., Hauser-Cram, 1996).

However, the choices made in regard to planning repeated measurement (longitudinal) designs are not limited to those pertinent to the intertime spacing and ontogenetic timing of occasions of measurement. Issues of units and levels of analysis, and of generalizability of change patterns, arise as well. As we have noted, all longitudinal designs are not the same, and the variations in design that occur as a consequence of researchers making different methodological choices in regard to these additional issues also rest on contrasts in their philosophically and theoretically based concept of change (Lerner, 1986; Overton & Reese, 1973; Reese & Overton, 1970).

CONCEPTUAL ISSUES AND VARIATION IN THE DESIGNS OF LONGITUDINAL RESEARCH

Researchers differ in regard to the units and levels of analysis thought to be necessary and sufficient to involve in a longitudinal design. These differences arise especially when the longitudinal research is aimed at explaining developmental change, that is, conceptually or statistically modeling causal linkages. The issue here, then, is whether (1) intraindividual developmental change can (or should) be measured (and modeled) through intraindividual units and levels alone; or (2) more molar units and levels (e.g., units of analysis representative of dyads, families, communities, or schools) should be employed—either in conjunction with individual units or *instead* of them (e.g., contrast Featherman & Lerner, 1985, with Dannefer, 1984).

Different stances in regard to decisions about units and levels of analysis typically relate to the theory, and associated concept, of development used by the researcher (Kaplan, 1983; Lerner, 1986; Wohlwill, 1973). Often, the disciplinary focus of the researcher (e.g., compare Dannefer, 1984, with Baltes & Nesselroade, 1984) is involved in these differences as well.

For instance, researchers who wish to provide data about causal linkages across individual development will consider individual-level units as necessary and sufficient, if their theory is one that specifies the bases of development as lying within the person's biological and/or psychological characteristics. In turn, if individual-level developmental phenomena are seen as derivative of more molar (e.g., social institutional) variables (e.g., Dannefer, 1984; Meyer, 1988), then any units employed to model causality will be associated with these more molar levels. Similarly, theories that stress the role of variables from both individual and institutional levels will either use units from both levels or seek to form an interlevel, relational unit of analysis (e.g., Lerner & Lerner, 1989) in order to conduct explanatory longitudinal research.

Thus, if developmental changes—whether normative or atypical, or adjusted or maladjusted—are believed to be caused by phenomena associated primarily, if not exclusively, with one domain of phenomena (e.g., the biological, or the psychological, or the social), then a unilevel (or unidisciplinary) design will be employed (e.g., see Meyer, 1988). In other words, beliefs in the biogenetic basis of developmental change (e.g., Rushton, 1988), in the psychogenic basis of developmental change (Costa & McCrae, 1980), or in the sociogenic basis of developmental change (Dannefer, 1984; Meyer, 1988) ordinarily result in longitudinal designs that focus on variables from one level of analysis, at least insofar as appraisals pertinent to the explanation, cause, or etiology of such change are concerned (e.g., see the Costa & McCrae, 1980, studies of personality development in adulthood).

Examples of these approaches to developmental phenomena are readily apparent in the field of early childhood education when one considers investigations of the effects of programs for young children and their parents. In a review of 31 studies of the effects of early intervention programs for infants and toddlers with developmental disabilities, Shonkoff and Hauser-Cram (1987) found the majority of studies employed child IQ or developmental quotient as the outcome of choice. Only seven studies included any parent-related outcomes (most frequently, parental attitudes toward child rearing), and no study used measures of

family functioning. Thus, outcomes for children were restricted largely to measures of cognition, and information about program effects on families was sparse.

In contrast, in a review of Child Survival/Fair Start programs for adolescent
parents, Larner, Halpern, and Harkavy (1992) reported that programs included a
wide array of outcomes for children in addition to cognitive performance, such as
measures of children's play and of children's health, and for parents, such as measures of interaction with children, use of health care, and the provision of an adequate home environment. The contrast in outcomes presented in these two types
of studies may indeed reflect the contrast in beliefs about the focus of developmental change in these two populations. Studies of children with developmental
disabilities, at least in the past, have focused on creating changes within the child,
based on the belief that the child's biological system was the focal problem. Investigations of programs for adolescent parents have concentrated on changing
parenting outcomes, based on the belief that although the child may be biologi-
cally intact, the parenting system requires revision.

Evaluation studies of both types of programs, however, could more adequately consider the embeddedness of children's development within multiple
contexts. Indeed, the context in which children develop is not a unitary phenomenon. For example, Wachs and Chan (1986) described how different aspects of a child's environment (e.g., the physical environment and the social
environment) have differential effects on communication performance. Further
elaboration of how children's development is interrelated to and embedded
within context is a critical need in research on programs for young children.

The Need for Ecological, Multilevel Research Designs

If developmental changes are believed to result from combinations of variables from multiple layers, or tiers, of phenomena, then multilevel research designs need to be employed (e.g., see Baltes et al., 1977; Schaie, 1965; Schaie &
Strother, 1968). These designs often involve, for instance, the appraisal of biological, psychological, and social variables in the context of analyses directed to
the synthetic, or fused, bases of developmental change (e.g., Brooks-Gunn, 1987;
Elder, 1974; Hetherington, 1988; Lerner & Lerner, 1989; Magnusson, 1988;
Nesselroade & Baltes, 1974; Petersen, 1987; Schaie, 1979; Simmons & Blyth, 1987;
Stattin & Magnusson, 1990; Thomas & Chess, 1977). It should be noted, however, that both unilevel and multilevel longitudinal designs may be multivariate in
character. The difference in these designs is more of a qualitative one; they differ
in regard to the number of distinct levels of organization (one versus two or more)
employed to study and explain developmental change (Baltes et al., 1977).

Finally, there are design differences that are associated with the issue of
the generalizability of change patterns identified within a given longitudinal study.
This generalizabilty issue derives from the level of analysis issue. A researcher

may believe that the developmental trajectories discerned in his or her longitudinal investigation are prototypical of developmental changes characteristic of the species (at least insofar as the portion of the life-span assessed in the study is concerned). In such cases, levels of temporality associated with the individual, and perhaps even the proximal social (e.g., caregiver) and institutional (e.g., familial) context, may be considered in the study. However, the role of historical temporality will be excluded from concern (e.g., Block, 1971). That is, if the researcher believes that the changes discovered are generic, nomothetic ones, then assessment of a single cohort suffices to identify this pattern. In contrast, however, a researcher may believe that human development is embedded in history—that is, that the changes seen in an individual or group are fused with variables associated with the historical level of analysis. In such a situation, then, the study of a single cohort will not provide information necessarily generalizable to people developing in different historical eras (Baltes et al., 1977; Caspi & Elder, 1988; Elder, 1974, 1980; Schaie, 1965). To test for such generalizability, a multicohort design is required.

An example of the potential need for a multicohort longitudinal design, and of the possible shortcomings of a unicohort investigation, may be seen by again referring to Figure 6.2. Consider that only one of the three cohorts depicted in the figure would have been sampled. In such a case, it is probable that any inference about the character of the developmental trajectory for the scores for variable Y that likely would have been drawn would have been quite different from inferences drawn after all three of the depicted cohorts had been studied. In essence, then, a study of any single cohort confounds age-associated variation with time of measurement-associated variation (Baltes, 1968; Schaie, 1965), and only through the longitudinal assessment of multiple cohorts can these patterns of covariation begin to be disentangled.

Birth (or event) cohort becomes, then, an essential parameter of a longitudinal design (Baltes, 1968; Schaie, 1965). A multicohort design is necessary to appraise the degree of generalizability of any given developmental trajectory. In such situations, cohort comparative, or sequential, longitudinal designs must be employed (Baltes et al., 1977; Nesselroade & Baltes, 1979). Although these designs are not free of methodological and interpretive difficulties (Baltes, 1968; Baltes et al., 1977; Lerner, 1986), they offer the best means available to appraise the associations between historical-level temporality and trajectories of intraindividual change. This point leads to some concluding observations.

CONCLUSION

Designing a study of early childhood development and education is based primarily on the investigator's conceptions of development, which may vary from universalistic and constant to temporal and malleable. Adoption of different conceptions from within this range necessarily influences the selection of not only the research design, but also the types of measurements employed (change-sensitive or stable), as well as the times across the developmental trajectory at which the phenomena studied are measured.

Traditionally, cross-sectional designs have been predominant in the study of young children's development. While such designs are important in describing some aspects of children's learning and behavior, they are clearly inadequate in delineating the numerous potential ontogenetic pathways that an individual may follow. Like the shutter of a camera, they offer only a glimpse of the child's development at a certain moment "frozen" in time; such observations are insufficient for describing what happens when the child continues to "move" and change over time. Thus, not only is their scope limited, but they also may mislead us about the character of the individual's behavior and learning.

In contrast, longitudinal designs are more appropriate for examining change across the life-span. The researcher's premethodological assumptions on the nature of development will prescribe the selection of a particular longitudinal design over others. As our understanding of young children's development continues to grow, we realize the necessity of studying intraindividual developmental trajectories as nested in, in interaction with, and as agents of multiple physical, psychological, social, cultural, and historical contexts as they change over time (Bronfenbrenner, 1983; Lerner, 1986; Sameroff & Chandler, 1975).

Multilevel longitudinal designs are particularly well suited to studying the emergence and change in learning and behavior, especially in relation to the teaching, parenting, and socialization of young children. Information from multilevel longitudinal studies can guide the scope, timing, duration, and nature of early child, family, and community interventions. Studies based on such designs also can help educators and administrators in early childhood make more informed decisions regarding effective instruction and curriculum design and their adaptation over time. Professionals in early childhood education also may undertake their own investigations of the children in their care, as children develop over time in the context of their schooling, family, and community. Understanding the effect of implicit and explicit theoretical presuppositions on the type and meaning of the data collected will help guide such professionals to develop and implement appropriate child and program evaluations, and thus develop programs that are responsive to both context and changes in children's lives.

REFERENCES

Baltes, P. B. (1968). Longitudinal and cross-sectional sequences in the study of age and generation effects. *Human Development, 11,* 145–171.

Baltes, P. B. (1987). Theoretical propositions of life-span developmental psychology: On the dynamics between growth and decline. *Developmental Psychology, 23,* 611–626.

Baltes, P. B., & Nesselroade, J. R. (1984). Paradigm lost and paradigm regained: Critique of Dannefer's portrayal of life-span developmental psychology. *American Sociological Review, 49,* 841–846.

Baltes, P. B., Reese, H. W., & Nesselroade, J. R. (1977). *Life-span developmental psychology: Introduction to research methods.* Monterey, CA: Brooks/Cole.

Bandura, A., Ross, D., & Ross, S. A. (1961). Transmission of aggression through imitation of aggressive models. *Journal of Abnormal and Social Psychology, 63,* 575–582.

Barnett, W. S. (1995). Long-term effects of early childhood programs on cognitive and school outcomes. *The Future of Children, 5* (3), 25–50.

Barrett, K. C., & Morgan, G. A. (1995). Continuities and discontinuities in mastery motivation during infancy and toddlerhood: A conceptualization and review. In I. E. Siegel (Series Ed.) & R. H. MacTurk & G. A. Morgan (Vol. Eds.), *Advances in applied developmental psychology: Vol. 12. Mastery motivation: Origins, conceptualizations, and applications* (pp. 57–94). Norwood, NJ: Ablex.

Bayley, N. (1993). *Bayley scales of infant development: Birth to two years.* San Antonio: Psychological Corporation.

Block, J. (1971). *Lives through time.* Berkeley: Bancroft.

Bloom, B. S. (1964). *Stability and change in human characteristics.* New York: Wiley.

Brim, O. G., & Kagan, J. (Eds.). (1980). Constancy and change: A view of the issues. In O. G. Brim & J. Kagan (Eds.), *Constancy and change in human development* (pp. 1–25). Cambridge, MA: Harvard University Press.

Bronfenbrenner, U. (1993). The ecology of cognitive development: Research models and fugitive findings. In R. H. Wozniak & K. W. Fischer (Eds.), *Development in context: Acting and thinking in specific environments* (pp. 3–44). Hillsdale, NJ: Erlbaum.

Brooks-Gunn, J. (1987). Pubertal processes and girls' psychological adaptation. In R. M. Lerner & T. T. Foch (Eds.), *Biological-psychosocial interactions in early adolescence: A life-span perspective* (pp. 123–153). Hillsdale, NJ: Erlbaum.

Brown, R., & Bellugi, U. (1964). Three processes in the child's acquisition of syntax. *Harvard Educational Review, 34,* 133–151.

Bryk, A. S., & Raudenbush, S. W. (1987). Application of hierarchical linear models to assessing change. *Psychological Bulletin, 101*(1), 147–158.

Buss, A. H., & Plomin, R. (1984). *Temperament: Early developing personality traits.* Hillsdale, NJ: Erlbaum.

Campbell, F. A., & Ramey, C. T. (1994). Effects of early intervention on intellectual and academic achievement: A follow-up study of children from low-income families. *Child Development, 65,* 684–698.

Caspi, A., & Elder, G. H. (1988). Childhood precursors of the lifecourse. In E. M. Hetherington, R. M. Lerner, & M. Perlmutter (Eds.), *Child development in life-span perspective* (pp. 115–142). Hillsdale, NJ: Erlbaum.

Caspi, A., & Silva, P. A. (1995). Temperamental qualities at age three predict personality traits in young adulthood: Longitudinal evidence from a birth cohort. *Child Development, 66,* 486–498.

Clarke, A. M., & Clarke, A. D. B. (Eds.). (1976). *Early experience: Myth and evidence.* New York: Free Press.

Costa, P. T., & McCrae, R. R. (1980). Still stable after all these years: Personality as a key to some issues in aging. In P. B. Baltes & O. G. Brim (Eds.), *Life-span development and behavior* (Vol. 3, pp. 65–102). New York: Academic Press.

Dannefer, D. (1984). The role of the social in the life-span psychology, past and future: Rejoinder to Baltes and Nesselroade. Reappraisal. *American Sociological Review*, *49*, 847–850.

Dixon, R. A., & Lerner, R. M. (1988). A history of systems in developmental psychology. In M. H. Bornstein & M. E. Lamb (Eds.), *Developmental psychology: An advanced textbook* (2nd ed.; pp. 3–50). Hillsdale, NJ: Erlbaum.

Dixon, R. A., Lerner, R. M., & Hultsch, D. F. (1991). Maneuvering among models of developmental psychology. In P. V. van Geert & L. P. Mos (Eds.), *Annals of theoretical psychology* (Vol. 7, pp. 357–368). New York: Plenum Press.

Elder, G. H. (1974). *Children of the great depression.* Chicago: University of Chicago Press.

Elder, G. H. (1980). Adolescence in historical perspective. In J. Adelson (Ed.), *Handbook of adolescent psychology* (pp. 3–46). New York: Wiley.

Featherman, D., & Lerner, R. M. (1985). Ontogenesis and sociogenesis: Problematics for theory about development across the life span. *American Sociological Review*, *50*, 659–676.

Fleischer, C. (1994). Researching teacher-research: A practitioner's retrospective. *English Education*, *26*(2), 86–124.

Friedman, S. L., & Sigman, M. (Eds.). (1980). *Preterm birth and psychological development.* New York: Academic Press.

Gardner, J. M. M., Grantham-McGregor, S. M., Chang, S. M., Himes, J. H., & Powel, C. A. (1995). Activity and behavioral development in stunted and nonstunted children and response to nutritional supplementation. *Child Development*, *66*(6), 1785–1797.

Gelman, R., & Meck, E. (1983). Preschoolers' counting: Principles before skill. *Cognition*, *13*, 343–359.

Goldsmith, H. H., Bradshaw, D. L., & Riesser-Danner, L. A. (1986). Temperament as a potential developmental influence on attachment. In J. V. Lerner & R. M. Lerner (Eds.), *Temperament and social interaction in infants and children* (pp. 5–34). San Francisco: Jossey-Bass.

Gould, S. J. (1977). *Ontogeny and phylogeny.* Cambridge, MA: Belknap Press.

Greenberg, M. T., & Crnic, K. A. (1988). Longitudinal predictors of developmental status and social interaction in premature and full-term infants at age two. *Child Development*, *59*(3), 554–570.

Hauser-Cram, P. (1996). Mastery motivation in toddlers with developmental disabilities. *Child Development*, *67*, 236–248.

Hetherington, E. M. (1988). Parents, children and siblings six years after divorce. In R. Hinde & J. Stevenson-Hinde (Eds.), *Relationships within families: Mutual influences* (pp. 311–331). Oxford: Clarendon.

Huttenlocher, J., Haight, W., Bryk, A., Seltzer, M., & Lyons, T. (1991). Early vocabulary growth: Relation to language input and gender. *Developmental Psychology*, 27(2), 236–248.

Jacklin, C. N., & Maccoby, E. E. (1978). Social behavior at thirty-three months in same-sex and mixed-sex dyads. *Child Development*, 49, 557–569.

Kagan, J. (1980). Perspectives on continuity. In O. G. Brim & J. Kagan (Eds.), *Constancy and change in human development* (pp. 26–74). Cambridge, MA: Harvard University Press.

Kagan, J., & Moss, H. (1962). *Birth to maturity*. New York: Wiley.

Kaplan, B. (1983). A trio of trails. In R. M. Lerner (Ed.), *Developmental psychology: Historical and philosophical perspectives* (pp. 185–239). Hillsdale, NJ: Erlbaum.

Kopp, C. B., & McCall, R. B. (1982). Predicting later mental performance for at-risk and handicapped infants. In P. B. Bates & O. G. Brim (Eds.), *Life-span development and behavior* (Vol. 4, pp. 33–61). New York: Academic Press.

Larner, M., Halpern, R., & Harkavy, O. (1992). Realistic expectations: Review of evaluation findings. In M. Larner, R. Halpern, & O. Harkavy (Eds.), *Fair Start for children: Lessons learned from seven demonstration projects* (pp. 218–245). New Haven: Yale University Press.

Lerner, R. M. (1976). *Concepts and theories of human development*. Reading, MA: Addison-Wesley.

Lerner, R. M. (1984). *On the nature of human plasticity*. New York: Cambridge University Press.

Lerner, R. M. (1986). *Concepts and theories of human development* (2nd ed.). New York: Random House.

Lerner, R. M. (1991). Changing organism–context relations as the basic process of development: A developmental contextual perspective. *Developmental Psychology*, 27, 27–32.

Lerner, R. M. (1995). *America's youth in crisis*. Newbury Park, CA: Sage.

Lerner, R. M., & Lerner, J. V. (1989). Organismic and social contextual bases of development: The sample case of early adolescence. In W. Damon (Ed.), *Child development today and tomorrow* (pp. 69–85). San Francisco: Jossey-Bass.

Lerner, R. M., & Nesselroade, J. R. (1991). Theory and method in the study of behavioral development: On the legacy of Joachim F. Wohlwill. In P. V. Geert & L. P. Mos (Eds.), *Annals of theoretical psychology* (Vol. 7, pp. 177–189). New York: Plenum Press.

Lerner, R. M., Skinner, E. A., & Sorell, G. T. (1980). Methodological implications of contextual/dialectic theories of development. *Human Development*, 23, 225–235.

Lerner, R. M., & Tubman, J. (1989). Conceptual issues in studying continuity and discontinuity in personality development across life. *Journal of Personality*, 57, 343–373.

Lewontin, R. C. (1981). On constraints and adaptation. *The Behavioral and Brain Sciences*, 4, 244–245.

Magnusson, D. (1988). *Individual development from an interaction perspective: A longitudinal study*. Hillsdale, NJ: Erlbaum.

McCall, R. B. (1990). Infancy research: Individual differences. In F. D. Horowitz & J. Colombo (Eds.), *Infancy research: A summative evaluation and a look to the future* (pp. 141–157). Detroit: Wayne State University Press.

McNeill, T. F., & Kaij, L. (1979). Etiological relevance of comparisons of high-risk and low-risk groups. *Acta Psychiatrica Scandinavica, 59,* 545–560.

Merriman, W. E., Marazita, J. M., Jarvis, L. H., Evey-Burkey, J. A., & Biggins, M. (1995). What can be learned from something's not being named. *Child Development, 66*(6), 1890–1908.

Meyer, J. W. (1988). The social construction of the psychology of childhood. In E. M. Hetherington, R. M. Lerner, & M. Perlmutter (Eds.), *Child development in life-span perspective* (pp. 47–65). Hillsdale, NJ: Erlbaum.

Nesselroade, J. R. (1983, August). *Implications of trait–state distinction for the study of aging: Still labile after all these years.* Presidential address to Division 20, Ninety-first Annual Convention of the American Psychological Association, Anaheim, CA.

Nesselroade, J. R., & Baltes, P. B. (1974). Adolescent personality development and historical change: 1970–72. *Monographs of the Society for Research in Child Development, 39* (154).

Nesselroade, J. R., & Baltes, P. B. (Eds.). (1979). *Longitudinal research in the study of behavior and development.* New York: Academic Press.

Noll, R. B., Zucker, R. A., & Greenberg, G. S. (1990). Identification of alcohol by smell among preschoolers: Evidence for early socialization about drugs occurring in the home. *Child Development, 61,* 1520–1527.

Overton, W. F., & Reese, H. W. (1973). Models of development: Methodological implications. In J. R. Nesselroade & H. W. Reese (Eds.), *Life-span developmental psychology: Methodological issues* (pp. 65–86). New York: Academic Press.

Overton, W. F., & Reese, H. W. (1981). Conceptual prerequisites for an understanding of stability–change and continuity–discontinuity. *International Journal of Behavioral Development, 4,* 99–123.

Pasamanick, B., & Knobloch, H. (1961). Epidemiologic studies on the complications of pregnancy and the birth process. In G. Caplan (Ed.), *Prevention of mental disorders in children: Initial explorations* (pp. 74–94). New York: Basic Books,.

Petersen, A. C. (1987). The nature of biological psychosocial interactions: The sample case of early adolescence. In R. M. Lerner & T. T. Foch (Eds.), *Biological-psychosocial interactions in early adolescence* (pp. 35–61). Hillsdale, NJ: Erlbaum.

Reese, H. W., & Overton, W. F. (1970). Models of development and theories of development. In L. R. Goulet & P. B. Baltes (Eds.), *Life-span developmental psychology: Research and theory* (pp. 115–145). New York: Academic Press.

Rogosa, D. (1988). Myths about longitudinal research. In K. W. Schaie, R. T. Campbell, W. Meredith, & S. C. Rawlings (Eds.), *Methodological issues in aging research* (pp. 171–209). New York: Springer.

Rushton, J. P. (1988). Do r/K reproductive strategies apply to human differences? *Social Biology, 35,* 337–340.

Rutter, M. (1964). Temperament characteristics in infancy and the later development of behavior disorders. *British Journal of Psychiatry, 110,* 651–661.

Sameroff, A. J., & Chandler, M. J. (1975). Reproductive risk and the continuum of caretaking casualty. In F. D. Horowitz, M. Hetherington, S. Scarr-Salapatek, & G. Siegel (Eds.), *Review of child development research* (Vol. 4, pp. 187–244). Chicago: University of Chicago Press.

Schaie, K. W. (1965). A general model for the study of developmental problems. *Psychological Bulletin, 64*, 92–107.

Schaie, K. W. (1979). The primary mental abilities in adulthood: An exploration in the development of psychometric intelligence. In P. B. Baltes & O. G. Brim (Eds.), *Life-span development and behavior* (Vol. 2, pp. 67–115). New York: Academic Press.

Schaie, K. W., & Strother, C. R. (1968). A cross–sequential study of age changes in cognitive behavior. *Psychological Bulletin, 70*, 671–680.

Seifer, R., & Vaughn, B. E. (1995). Mastery motivation within a general organizational model of competence. In I. E. Siegel (Series Ed.) & R. H. MacTurk & G. A. Morgan (Vol. Eds.), *Advances in applied developmental psychology: Vol. 12. Mastery motivation: Origins, conceptualizations, and applications* (pp. 95–116). Norwood, NJ: Ablex.

Sher, K. J. (1991). *Children of alcoholics: A critical appraisal of theory and research.* Chicago: University of Chicago Press.

Shonkoff, J. P., & Hauser-Cram, P. (1987). Early intervention for disabled infants and their families: A quantitative analysis. *Pediatrics, 80*(5), 650–658.

Simmons, R. G., & Blyth, D. A. (1987). *Moving into adolescence: The impact of pubertal change and school context.* Hawthorne, NJ: Aldine.

Sophian, C., Wood, A. M., & Vong, K. I. (1995). Making numbers count: The early development of numerical inferences. *Developmental Psychology, 31*(2), 263–273.

Stattin, H., & Magnusson, D. (1990). *Pubertal maturation in female development.* Hillsdale, NJ: Erlbaum.

Sulzby, E. (1985). Children's emergent reading of favorite storybooks: A developmental study. *Reading Research Quarterly, 20*(4), 458–481.

Thomas, A., & Chess, S. (1977). *Temperament and development.* New York: Brunner/Mazel.

Thorndike, R. L., Hagen, E. P., & Sattler, J. M. (1986). *Stanford–Binet intelligence scale—fourth edition.* Chicago: Riverside Publishing.

Tobach, E. (1981). Evolutionary aspects of the activity of the organism and its development. In R. M. Lerner & N. A. Busch-Rossnagel (Eds.), *Individuals as producers of their own development* (pp. 37–68). New York: Academic Press.

Tubman, J. G., Vicary, J. R., von Eye, A., & Lerner, J. V. (1990). Longitudinal substance abuse and adult adjustment. *Journal of Substance Abuse, 2*, 317–334.

Wachs, T. D., & Chan, A. (1986). Specificity of environmental action, as seen in environmental correlates of infants' communication performance. *Child Development, 57*, 1464–1474.

Wasik, B. H., Ramey, C. T., Bryant, D. M., & Sparling, J. J. (1990). A longitudinal study of two early intervention strategies: Project CARE. *Child Development, 61*, 1682–1696.

Wechsler, D. (1967). *Manual for the Wechsler preschool and primary scale of intelligence.* San Antonio: Psychological Corporation.

Weikart, D. P., & Schweinhart, L. J. (1992). High/Scope Preschool program outcomes. In J. McCord & R. E. Tremblay (Eds.), *Preventing antisocial behavior: Interventions from birth through adolescence* (pp. 67–86). New York: Guilford.

Windle, M. (1988). Are those adolescent to early adulthood drinking patterns so discontinuous? A response to Temple and Fillmore. *The International Journal of the Addictions, 23,* 907–912.

Wohlwill, J. F. (1973). *The study of behavioral development.* New York: Academic Press.

Wohlwill, J. F. (1991). Relations between method and theory in developmental research: A partial isomorphism view. In P. V. Geert & L. P. Mos (Eds.), *Annals of theoretical psychology* (Vol. 7, pp. 91–138). New York: Plenum Press.

Yarrow, L. J., & Pederson, F. A. (1976). The interplay between cognition and motivation in infancy. In M. Lewis (Ed.), *Origins of intelligence: Infancy and early childhood* (pp. 379–399). New York: Plenum Press.

Yoshikawa, H. (1995). Long-term effects of early childhood program on social outcomes and delinquency. *The Future of Our Children, 5*(3), 51–75.

Zigler, E. (1990). Foreword. In S. J. Meisels & J. P. Shonkoff (Eds.), *Handbook of early childhood interventions* (pp. ix–xvii). New York: Cambridge University Press.

CHAPTER 7

Early Learning and Continued Development for Teachers: Teachers as Researchers

Renee T. Clift and Lillie R. Albert

Those of us who have struggled to find caring and committed teachers for our young children can share stories of excellence in preschool and kindergarten settings, and we can share horror stories. While the importance of skilled, knowledgeable teachers has long been recognized by parents who are able to send their children to particular schools, or who are allowed to request particular teachers, the comparable importance of initial and continuing education for these teachers has not been widely acknowledged. We who study teaching, teacher education, and learning are beginning to accumulate a body of evidence that documents the relationship between education for the teaching profession and success in teaching (National Commission on Teaching and America's Future, 1996). The development of knowledge and skill is no accident. Formal study, reflective analysis of experience, participation in a community of learners, and analysis of one's own practice, combined with a disposition toward caring for children, enable dedicated teachers to begin the profession and to continue to learn while teaching.

In this chapter we discuss issues related to early childhood teachers' learning from their own practice, by drawing from selected action research studies conducted by early childhood teachers. In so doing we explore various ways in which early childhood educators can become more involved in educational research.

We argue that knowledge from current and emergent research is, certainly, one source of information for continuing professional development, but we also argue that early childhood teachers can contribute to the knowledge base through teacher research. Our purpose here is to raise issues that we feel are important topics for further discussion by educational researchers, school administrators, and practicing teachers. We further argue that initial teacher preparation is necessary to prepare novice practitioners, but that such preparation is not sufficient for the professional education of early childhood teachers.

LEARNING FROM RESEARCH AND PRACTICE

Educational research can help us understand the complex interactions that occur as teachers and students meet together in schools, classrooms, centers, play groups, and sports arenas. The three handbooks (soon to be four) sponsored by the American Educational Research Association (Gage, 1963; Richardson, in preparation; Travers, 1973; Wittrock, 1986), the two handbooks sponsored by the Association of Teacher Educators (Houston, 1990; Sikula, Buttery, & Guyton, 1996), the *Handbook of Research on the Education of Young Children* (Spodek, 1993), and the Yearbooks in Early Childhood Education are only a subset of the growing knowledge base we are accumulating. Researchers from different paradigmatic frames, using a wide array of quantitative and qualitative methodologies, are documenting the actions and interaction that enhance or inhibit successful teaching and learning.

As Lee Shulman (1986) noted, "We conduct research in a field to make sense of it, to get smarter about it, perhaps to learn how to perform more adeptly within it" (p. 3). Because these interactions among the factors that influence education are so complex and so dependent on other interactions (Cronbach, 1975), it is almost impossible to search for universal laws in education in the same way that we might search for laws governing the behavior of energy in chemistry. Rather, we can expect to identify important trends that help us to understand successful instructional practices, and we can identify the effects (and side effects) of particular practices.

However, no research conducted by anyone in any country can derive results that will guarantee desirable outcomes with no undesirable side effects for all children in all situations across cultures, across time, and across international boundaries. Researchers can and will strive to make sense of education and educational practice in relation to specific countries and to our particular social, cultural, and political constraints. As we get smarter about more and more educational practices, we can begin to examine practices in specific contexts. Ideas generated by others (whether based on empirical or conceptual analyses) and ideas generated by practice (whether that of others or our own) may help us

improve our own work and may help our students improve as well. We emphasize that there are several sources of important ideas—empirical, conceptual,
practical—and that these ideas can be generated by those who study education,
but do not necessarily teach.

In some cases, research means that one or more trained investigators go
into a school, classroom, or play area as outsiders to describe social interactions,
academic instruction, creativity, and so forth. It also may mean examining possible links between what teacher educators value and model, what practitioners
value and model, and what novice teachers value and act upon once they are in
the field. Some of the findings of such research can be informative or useful to
others, whether teachers, teacher educators, or policy makers.

In other cases, research means looking at one's own classroom, pedagogy,
or values in order to study one's own practice. Most of the findings of this kind
of research are intended to produce locally usable knowledge, but some of these
findings are also useful or informative outside of the local context. Research also
can be generated by those who teach and who study their own teaching.

Outside knowledge often is generated by scholars and researchers who

> have asked what it means to know about teaching: what can be known, how it
> can be known, who has the authority to know, and how knowledge can or
> should be used for theoretical and practical purposes. . . . The epistemology
> embodied in these assumptions, however, is exclusionary and disenfranchis-
> ing. It stipulates that knowing the knowledge base for teaching—what uni-
> versity researchers have discovered—is the privileged way to know about
> teaching. (Cochran-Smith & Lytle, 1993, p. 42)

Cochran-Smith and Lytle argue that inside knowledge is constructed in
ongoing teacher–student interactions: "Essentially, teachers and students nego-
tiate what counts as knowledge in the classroom, who can have knowledge, and
how that knowledge can be generated, challenged, and evaluated" (p. 45). In
many communities teachers are beginning to form inquiry groups to study their
own practice. Cochran-Smith and Lytle present several of these inquiries in their
book. Often, teacher research is local, particularized, unchronicled, and, therefore, unknown to a larger audience. More recently, however, teachers have begun
publishing their work in books, book chapters, and refereed journals.

The point here is that teacher research, often referred to as action research,
is a fundamentally different notion from traditional definitions of educational
research. Teacher research often is conducted by practitioners (in pre-K–12
education and in postsecondary education) for the same three reasons as
Shulman (1986) referred to in his handbook chapter. "To make sense of" becomes a teacher's understanding of the local nature of teaching and learning.
"To get smarter about" becomes a systematic search for practices that interest,

excite, and work for individual students. Finally, "perhaps to learn how to perform more adeptly" becomes our continuing struggle to reach more of the children, more of the time—without unpleasant side effects.

The teacher research model is becoming recognized by an increasing number of educators, like ourselves, and practitioners as having far-reaching implications for what happens in classrooms and why it happens. The idea is to improve educational practices by bridging the gap between teacher and researcher. This model operates under the assumption that teachers know what their problems are and are in positions to investigate those problems. However, teacher research goes far beyond teachers focusing on problematic situations; it requires teachers to observe, think through, and try to understand their practices. Cochran-Smith and Lytle (1993) propose that

> what is missing from the knowledge base of teaching, therefore, are the voices of the teachers themselves, the questions teachers ask, the ways teachers use writing and the interpretive frames teachers use to understand and improve their own classroom practices. (p. 2)

In their desire to improve educational practices, educational researchers and educational practitioners at all learning levels are collaborating to provide more evidence of what happens in classrooms as teachers seek to connect teaching and learning. This research suggests that teacher research can produce some desirable changes in classroom and schools (Florio-Ruane, 1990; Sirotnik & Goodlad, 1988), thus increasing the possibility that the results of the research will be used in practice (Huberman, 1990), in opposition to research that is generated solely by educational researchers outside the margin of collaboration.

An example of this approach is illustrated in the work conducted by the early childhood educator, Vivian Paley, who teaches kindergarten at the Laboratory Schools of the University of Chicago. For more than 15 years Paley has been studying young children in her classroom in a desire to improve her teaching practices. As Paley documents in *White Teacher* (1979), her attempt to help African-American children feel more comfortable in a white environment made her more aware of the discomfort all children experience as they are judged by someone who lacks knowledge of them and their cultural experiences. In Paley's most recent work, *Kwanzaa and Me* (1995), she continues to examine her teaching to gather and explore ways to constructively deal with issues of racial and social differences. Paley's careful documentation of her teaching practices and children's interactions with her and with each other serves as a powerful force in highlighting her awareness of her own "professional reasoning" (Evan, 1991) and professional development. In the Epilogue to *White Teacher*, Paley (1979) writes:

> The more I study this culture the children fashion as they learn to play out the rhythms and meaning of group fantasy, the more I see that the unique-

ness of every person is an accepted premise from the very beginnings of social life. The children know they are each different in style and story; they listen eagerly and identify with one another's separate visions of pleasure and pain, of strength and weakness, of love and loss. In their play, they reveal the intuitive and universal language that binds us all together.

When I began writing *White Teacher*, I thought I knew certain children best because our backgrounds were similar, and that it was my task to open up the classroom, to explore and welcome differences. I have since discovered that all the children have more in common with one another than any one of them has with me. The major source of incongruity is between their thinking and mine.

The children, in fact, already know how to open up a classroom, for play is the original open-ended and integrated curriculum. It is the pathway to learning in which differences are valued and regarded because they enhance the creative potential of the imagination. Children do not ask: Where do you come from? They ask: What role will you play? The children have much to teach us, if we but stop and listen. (pp. 141–142)

In the next section we present three examples of early childhood teachers studying their own practice.

THREE ACTION RESEARCH EXAMPLES

The first example is that of preschool teacher Cindy Ballenger (1992), who worked with predominantly Haitian students. In *Harvard Educational Review*, she describes the way she came to understand her students' culture. Her work also is cited in Anderson, Herr, and Wihlen (1994). They note that through journals and audiotapes of her classroom, Ballenger studied her students' awareness of print, particularly the recognition of letters. One of her field notes reads:

Tiny Tatie, not yet three years old, never says a word and never comes to circle where we read the names and talk a little about letters. I am amazed to discover that she has been walking around all morning with two fingers in the shape of a T. When asked what she's doing, she says, "it's me," and continues silently to parade around the classroom. (Quoted in Anderson et al., 1994, pp. 67–68)

An interpretation of Tatie's multiple understandings of the letter T reads:

Tatie, the youngest in the class, tries to keep all the T's—coloring papers, magnetic T's, and cut out letters—in her cubby. She knows that she shares T at least with Teo, another child in the classroom. She is a very silent child, although obviously aware. In note 4 [a reference to Ballenger's field notes] Tatie has used the S and the T to greet, to make some sort of social connection with Sora's mother at a point where she is still not willing to talk. (Anderson et al., 1994, p. 69)

Ballenger uses her analysis of Tatie's actions in conjunction with her notes on many other children in the class to conclude that print awareness has a social dimension, which leads her to critique prevalent theories of literacy development. Anderson and colleagues (1994) point out:

> It is important to note that, without Ballenger's tacit knowledge of the existing relationships among her children, her meaning making of what she was seeing and hearing could have taken her in extremely different directions; the framing of the data in relational terms pushed her toward theory questioning and expansion. (p. 70)

The second example is a chapter written by Janet Albarado (1994), a first-grade teacher in Louisiana. Janet and her colleagues began to question the reading program for first grade:

> Because the basal reading program treated literacy as though it occurred in a vacuum, it was devoid of any spontaneity and real meaning. Children were bored, and so was I. And to my surprise, so were the three other first-grade teachers at my school. . . .
> Eventually we discovered our common discontent, got together, and decided we had to do something differently. We read Goodman (1986) and Holdaway (1979) and discussed how to apply their ideas in our classrooms. We observed other whole language teachers, attended workshops and conferences, and formed a local support group. . . .
> I realized that the underlying principles supporting whole language were ones I had learned in my teacher preparation program but had lost sight of as a beginning teacher. . . .
> . . . my young readers now make predictions and hypothesize as they try to make sense from text. As writers, they experiment with what they want to say, approximate conventional orthography, and try out punctuation to convey a meaningful message. (Albarado, 1994, p. 51)

Janet's example demonstrates the synthesis of formal reading, formal and informal study groups, and data collection and analysis in teacher research. Teacher research is seldom anti-intellectual; learning about others' work (including that of academics) is often valued and helpful. But teacher research turns the discussion from, "Why don't teachers incorporate the findings of research into their practice?" to, "What resources are available to help me improve practice now?"

The final example is taken from a chapter in Cochran-Smith and Lytle (1993). Eileen Glickman Feldgus, a kindergarten teacher in Philadelphia, also writes about early literacy. In this example, we are able to follow the raising of questions, the execution of methodology, and the formulation of data-driven conclusions:

> I was an "observant participant" (Florio-Ruane, 1986) of six target children whom I selected to represent varying levels of accomplishments in the approximations of the conventions of writing. . . . I investigated three areas:
>
> *Genre.* How were the children using the genres evident in classroom print?
>
> *Language.* How were they incorporating the actual words used in environmental print?
>
> *World knowledge.* How were the children using the topics and information that were in the classroom environment?
>
> Additionally, social interactions were analyzed to see how the children were helping one another through talk and action. Journal data were also analyzed to see whether children "knew" words in the classroom environment; spontaneously sought them out independently; found the words only after the prompting question, "Where can you find that word in our room?"; or were unaware of the presence of the needed words even after the prompting question. . . .
>
> As I analyzed the data, I noted the varying ways that individual children seemed to respond to classroom print. I analyzed six children's writing behavior to discover patterns of usage of classroom environmental print and to discover the meaning that children constructed for themselves of this print-rich environment. (Feldgus, 1993, p. 173)

Feldgus concluded that the children had an overwhelming preference for the genre of writing personal news, which led her to wonder if she was sending messages that influenced this preference. She also concluded that the most accomplished writers ceased to use the words in the classroom environment by the end of the year, while the mid-level writers became the most active users. The most accomplished writers no longer needed the scaffold of having the words in the classroom environment. She concluded, "Rapidly changing the bulletin boards would seem to be counterproductive!" (p. 177).

From these three examples it should be obvious that teachers of young children are also students of children. That is, they learn from their students through careful, systematic documentation of their students' work, social interactions, and individual differences. These teachers are teacher-researchers. They are influenced by theoretical frames, but they also are capable of challenging theory. Their conclusions are contextualized, but they challenge and improve the status quo. They make research a part of their work, and their teaching is enhanced by their learning.

For these teachers, teacher research provides timely, local information that lets them develop more detailed understandings of their students and their own pedagogical practices. One advantage of teacher research over more traditional research is the generation of local knowledge that can be acted upon immediately. Ballenger came to understand the importance of the social context as it affects early literacy. Feldgus's (1993) research enabled her to arrange the visual displays in her classroom to support language learning and the expansion of written vocabulary. Albarado (1994) transformed the teaching of reading and literature in her classroom. For Albarado, in particular, the process of engaging in teacher research also meant participating in a community of teacher colleagues who supported and challenged one another's understandings and interpretations. These three examples provide clear, positive, and powerful illustrations of the potential of teacher research.

But research is seldom a part of an early childhood teacher's job description. Ballenger, Albarado, and Feldgus do not tell us of the time it took to study, collect data, analyze results, and make meaning of it all. They do not tell us what they sacrificed in order to meet or to engage in professional reflective activities with others or by themselves. Indeed, we have some concerns about advocating that all teachers should be researchers and that all teachers should write about their research. As schools and child-care centers presently are structured, there are few, if any, hours (or minutes) allocated for research.

Clift, Veal, Holland, Johnson, and McCarthy (1995) documented teachers and administrators in five schools who worked with university professors to implement and study projects in their schools. The authors found wide variability in teachers' or principals' willingness to collect or analyze data. They also found that, in some instances, the very process of interpreting data produced discomfort, particularly when the data surfaced problems within the school. Although we are advocates of teacher research, we would be dishonest with ourselves and with readers if we did not note that there are downsides to such research. In addition to the time factor, disadvantages include the problems inherent in studying small numbers of students or instances of behavior, and in reflectively analyzing a process or product in which one has invested a good deal of oneself and one's ego.

More traditional quantitative educational research works within parameters that guide sample size, selection of participants, and assignment of participants to settings, procedures, or educational treatments. More traditional qualitative research works within parameters that encourage researchers to actively seek evidence that does not confirm the researchers' working interpretations of meaning within a particular setting. While teacher research can use quantitative or qualitative techniques, it often cannot operate within traditional parameters. Teacher researchers are interested in local, immediate issues that they care about—issues that need resolution this year, not 3 years after a study has been published in a reputable journal. Thus, assisting those who want to become teacher researchers is as important as assisting those who wish to become educational researchers.

Several of us (e.g., Clift, Meng, & Eggerding, 1994; Noffke & Brennan, 1991; Ross, 1990) have advocated that the process of learning to conduct teacher research can begin in preservice programs. We know that preservice teacher education is only a formal beginning of one's professional learning. We know that many times perfectly reasonable adults construct ideas that were never intended by their teacher educators; we know that many times there is miscommunication between university participants, prospective teachers, and field-based teacher educators. In other words, we are beginning to know a great deal about the process of learning to teach.

LEARNING FOR TEACHING

It generally is acknowledged that one of the most powerful influences on an individual's teaching is the experience that he or she has had as a student prior to attending a college or university. The source most often cited for this finding is the analysis of surveys and interviews of elementary and secondary teachers that led Lortie (1975) to identify a phenomenon he labeled "the apprenticeship of observation." Subsequent to Lortie, others (e.g., Weiss, 1989) have argued that prospective teachers remember spending a lot of time sitting passively at desks, completing worksheets, waiting for directions, and learning to please the teacher.

In other words, an "apprenticeship of observation" seldom prepares anyone to teach in ways that are different from their own experience. This might include ways to design, implement, monitor, or evaluate learning centers in preschools. It may include strategies to design, implement, and evaluate curriculum projects that integrate literacy activities with mathematics activities while also promoting prosocial development. An apprenticeship of observation also seldom prepares anyone to study carefully the cultural and linguistic backgrounds that influence the ways in which children understand or to design instruction that complements this background.

Much of the professional preparation of teachers in college coursework is designed to help students transcend or transform their own school experiences. By this we mean that professional preparation is intended to help future teachers see that their experiences as students are not necessarily typical of others' experiences, that there are alternative ways of interpreting information, and that organizing instruction includes learning about how different students react to different pedagogical techniques.

Typically, consideration of alternative forms of instruction and their impact on students has not been a part of prospective teachers' backgrounds. Sometimes, possible alternatives had not even been fully articulated when the prospective teachers were in preschools or kindergartens. Furthermore, few of us can recall our experiences in preschool, kindergarten, or the primary grades—even if they did represent a conception of best practice. While we still have much to learn about how early childhood teachers' biographies influence their conceptions of teaching and leaning, clearly, learning to work effectively with young children requires special preparation that transforms prior experience in typical elementary, secondary, and university settings (Saracho, 1993; Washington, 1996).

In addition, many prospective teachers are, for the first time, encountering students whose cultures, home environments, languages, and abilities are very different from their own (Cunningham, 1996). Ballenger's (1992) study is a reminder that we must learn about students' backgrounds in order to help them learn and that this is particularly important when they and we do not share common life experiences. Thus, it makes sense that university-based teacher educators are also responsible for preparing novice teachers to continue learning. While it is important to provide prospective teachers with access to the growing knowledge base developed by educational researchers, it is equally important to provide them with the experiences to engage in research themselves. Following are four examples of curricula that can help provide those experiences.

Self-Study

Because prior experience is such a powerful filter that influences our understanding of current experiences, individuals are unaware of either the relation of current experiences to prior experiences or how the past acts as a filter for current understanding. One function of teacher education is to enable prospective teachers to understand their own biographies and the impact of those biographies on their views of learning, curriculum, students, and school settings.

There are many versions of self-study that are already incorporated into existing teacher education programs, such as journals, reflective logs, and biographical reflections. The continuing popular advocacy incorporated into the term *reflective practice* emphasizes the importance of understanding self as individual and as an agent in the lives of others (Clift, Houston, & Pugach, 1990). One benefit of self-study is that one can examine the influences that one's past has over current actions and interpretations. One downside, however, is that self-study may not suggest alternative interpretations of situations and events and may not lead to action.

Problem-Based Learning

Recently, teacher educators and administrator educators have been adapting the medical model of problem-based learning to their own uses. Bridges (1992) defines problem-based learning as "an instructional strategy that organizes knowledge around administrative problems rather than the disciplines" (p. 20). Central to such learning is the assignment of a project that one is likely to encounter as an administrator (or teacher). Working in groups, students identify, collect, and study resource materials, debate alternative ways to deal with a problem, and present their solution to the problem. Instructors serve as resources, as guides, and as critical friends who seek to challenge the inquiry process and the proposed resolution. Those who write about problem-based curricula usually do not label themselves as action research advocates. They do share the assumption that professional learning entails active inquiry.

What prospective teachers can learn from this is that there are multiple perspectives on educational issues and that there is information available that can inform one's perspective. By working in groups, prospective teachers can learn to rely on one another to think through issues and to challenge opinions in a respectful, collegial manner. In theory, they would be able to transfer both their problem-solving skills and their abilities to work collegially to the classroom.

Interpretive Child Study

In this curriculum students immerse themselves in a setting in which there are young children, and they observe both the setting and the children over a period of time. They describe what they see (field notes); they interpret what they see (a first level of analysis); they read about others' work and discuss their observations and readings with others (a second level of analysis). In other words, they begin to acquire the habits of careful ethnographic researchers. They also learn to be *very* careful about jumping to analytical conclusions without sufficient data.

The study of children can serve as a foundation for early childhood teacher preparation. We can begin by teaching our students how to work with and learn from one child. Then, we can broaden their studies to include children in groups. If desirable, we can observe children in home and community settings, as well as in school. But we also must move beyond observation. In teaching methods classes, we can combine assignments to develop lesson plans with assignments that investigate how these plans operate in classroom settings. We can study different students' successes and struggles as they work through innovative and traditional instructional materials. Such studies might even be conducted in collaboration with classroom teachers, thus merging preservice teacher education with teacher research.

Collaborative Study of Teaching and Learning

This approach differs from the problem-centered approach in that prospective teachers work in real classrooms to identify and deal with immediate social, pedagogical, and interpersonal issues. Perhaps the best example of collaborative study is found in an experimental teacher education program that was pilot tested at the University of Calgary in Canada (Clandinin, Davies, Hogan, & Kennard, 1993).

Teachers and teacher educators designed and implemented a program called the Alternative Program. They also met together on a regular basis to discuss their work with one another and to analyze their experiences. All participants kept journals throughout the experience and shared them with one another. Several of these exchanges are included in the book chapters, which were written by teachers, student teachers, and university professors. One chapter (Kennard & Johnston-Kosik, 1993) is composed primarily of poems written between cooperating teacher and student teacher. These records, whether poems, narratives, or analyses, document the experiences of a community of teacher educators working together to understand their own practice. From this, prospective teachers can learn the power and the collegiality inherent in working with other adults in order to understand children and teaching.

Implicit in the ordering of these four teacher education curricula is a transition from an emphasis on self to an emphasis on working with others in action settings. Please note that these four ways of introducing inquiry and teacher research into a teacher education program are not exhaustive, nor are they mutually exclusive.

The assumptions underlying this ordering are that prospective teachers must get beyond a limited focus on, "Who am I and what do I believe?" to a broader focus on, "Who am I working with, children and adults, and how can we best work with one another to our mutual benefit?" The degree to which these curricula support attaining a broader focus among teacher education students is, itself, an open question. The curricula are intended to enable students to view their own learning as an active, constructive process; they seek to provide students with useful skills that can transfer to practice. More important, they emphasize that teaching is always a process of learning—an emphasis we, as teacher educators, also can model.

TEACHER EDUCATORS AS RESEARCHERS

As teacher educators, we too bring our biographies with us into the classroom. We too can benefit from self-study, from problem investigation, from the study of those who are our students, and from collaborative research. As teacher educator researchers, we can find much to investigate about the impacts of any curriculum. A series of guiding questions might be:

- How do individual students respond to different forms of teacher education? What responses are desirable? undesirable?
- How do different instructors respond? What responses are desirable? undesirable?
- Are there any patterns of response that hold across certain groups? genders? educational backgrounds? other characteristics?
- What modifications within forms facilitate more desirable learning from more prospective teachers?

These questions are only a beginning point. We can look at communication and miscommunication, social interactions, the role of frustration in learning, and many other aspects of teacher preparation curriculum. The important point here is that, unless we as teacher educators conduct "inside" research on our own practice, we are not likely to get smarter about what we do. In addition, we are not likely to make the right changes in our programs for the right reasons.

A special interest group of the American Educational Research Association has acknowledged this fact. The annual meeting of the association serves as a forum in which we can discuss our work with other, like-minded teacher educators. In many cases, it is easier to speak within this community than it is in our home institutions. To speak reflectively and honestly about our successes and failures is not the norm in most universities—particularly when our salaries are tied more to demonstrated success than to reflective analyses of failure. This should serve as a challenge, but also as a caution to those who advocate teacher research. As we mentioned earlier, many people feel vulnerable in situations wherein they open their practice to analytical scrutiny.

Still, we advocate that educational research by teachers, whether in early childhood classrooms or university classrooms, can help us all make sense of our work, ourselves, and our students' behaviors. We can get smarter about methods, materials, and the teaching/learning process. We can use this knowledge to try to improve our practice. Some of this knowledge will be generated by people who are outside of the classroom; some we will generate ourselves. From these sources we will construct our own theories of practice, which, if we are careful, we will question and challenge throughout our careers.

In our teacher education programs at the University of Illinois and at Boston College, we are working with other faculty members and with students to collaborate on research and to co-author papers and articles that report on our work together. "Insider" research of teacher education is beginning to be published in numerous journals and books. We also could benefit from "outsider" research that goes beyond large-scale surveys or scathing condemnations based on a series of interviews. One interesting possibility is to invite and support teachers who wish to study universities in general and teacher education in particular. Our point here is that if educational researchers are allowed to study and comment on schools, shouldn't our field-based colleagues be allowed to study and comment on university practice? And, if we think of ourselves as a teacher education learning community, can't we grow and improve our collaborative inquiries? Can't we come to a better understanding of schools, children, and one another?

SUMMARY

Early childhood educators have long written about the ways children construct knowledge from their environment, formal instruction, and prior experiences. For those who adopt a constructivist view (as we do), knowing (learning) is a process of attending to one's environment (sights, sounds, smells, words, print, people) and creating an understanding of how people behave and the possible causes of such behavior, how objects behave and the possible causes of such behavior, how one works with people, how one works with objects, one's efficacy, and so forth. Input from texts, other people's views, and the media influence our constructions, but they do not control them. Early childhood educators have long been accustomed to thinking about curriculum and experiences that enable young children to grow and develop into competent, caring adults.

For equal attention to be given to curriculum and experiences that enable young educators to grow and develop into competent and caring teachers of young children, we must attend to their early professional education and to the contexts in which we and they work. What can, and should, be modified to encourage us to talk, work, and even inquire as a community of learners, should be a major topic for discussion and for action. The discussion, at least, is beginning. In September 1996, the National Commission on Teaching and America's Future issued a thoughtful series of recommendations concerning the changes needed in schools, in universities, and in the profession so that all children can be well served by highly qualified teachers who are also learners. The report makes five recommendations that serve as organizers for changing current practice in the ways we enable teachers to learn:

1. Get serious about standards for both students and teachers.
2. Reinvent teacher preparation and professional development.
3. Fix teacher recruitment and put qualified teachers in every classroom.
4. Encourage and reward teacher knowledge and skill.
5. Create schools that are organized for student and teacher success.

Recommendations 2 and 5 are especially relevant to this chapter. We would argue that any "reinvention" and "reorganization" must enable teachers, teacher researchers, educational researchers, teacher educators, and teacher educator researchers to work together. This means devising ways to revise the norms of individual and bureaucratic isolation. It also means revising the view that the only "good" research is conducted by trained specialists or that the only "valid" form of knowledge is reliance on one's own experience. In other words, it means listening to, learning from, and respecting one another as educators who are all interested in promoting learning—that of adults as well as of children.

One solid example of how we might create schools that are organized for student and teacher success can be seen in the early childhood curriculum taught in Reggio Emilia, an Italian village that has gained an international reputation for its curriculum, school structure, and recognition of teachers who are students of children (Katz & Cesarone, 1994). The prospect of reorganizing schools has been documented carefully by an American art teacher who has helped several schools in the United States import Italian practice into the context of U. S. early childhood programs (Cadwell, 1997).

Teacher research and action research provide teachers ways to become more involved in the interpretation of research, because it draws upon teachers' expertise as practitioners. "It encourages teachers to give serious attention to their own work and their questions concerning it" (Evan, 1991, p. 11). It also provides teachers with satisfaction and growth in professional knowledge, by providing a medium for building cases and telling stories that include their interpretations about their professional lives and the complex activity of teaching.

REFERENCES

Albarado, J. (1994). You might as well go on home. In G. G. Goffin & D. E. Day (Eds.), *New perspectives in early childhood education: Bringing practitioners into the debate* (pp. 48–58). New York: Teachers College Press.

Anderson, G. L., Herr, K., & Wihlen, A. S. (1994). *Studying your own school: An educator's guide to qualitative research*. Thousand Oaks, CA: Sage.

Ballenger, C. (1992). Because you like us: The language of control. *Harvard Educational Review, 62,* 199–208.

Bridges, E. M. (1992). *Problem based learning for administrators*. Eugene, OR: ERIC Clearinghouse on Educational Management.

Cadwell, L. B. (1997). *Bringing Reggio Emilia home: An innovative approach to early childhood education*. New York: Teachers College Press.

Clandinin, D. J., Davies, A., Hogan, P., & Kennard, B. (Eds.). (1993). *Learning to teach; teaching to learn: Stories of collaboration in teacher education*. New York: Teachers College Press.

Clift, R. T., Houston, W. R., & Pugach, M. C. (1990). *Encouraging reflective practice in education: An analysis of issues and programs*. New York: Teachers College Press.

Clift, R. T., Meng, L., & Eggerding, S. (1994). Mixed messages in learning to teach English. *Teacher and Teacher Education, 10*, 265–279.

Clift, R., Veal, M. L., Holland, P., Johnson, M., & McCarthy, J. (1995). *Collaborative leadership and shared decision making: Teachers, principals, and university professors*. New York: Teachers College Press.

Cochran-Smith, M., & Lytle, S. (Eds.). (1993). *Inside/Outside: Teacher research and knowledge*. New York: Teachers College Press.

Cronbach, L. J. (1975). Beyond the two disciplines of scientific psychology. *American Psychologist, 30*, 116–127.

Cunningham, G. (1996). The challenge of responding to individual and cultural differences and meeting the needs of all communities. In S. Bredekamp & B. Willer (Eds.), *NAEYC Accreditation: A decade of learning and the years ahead* (pp. 79–82). Washington DC: National Association for the Education of Young Children.

Evan, C. (1991). Support for teachers studying their own work. *Educational Leadership, 48*, 11–13.

Feldgus, E. G. (1993). Walking to the words. In M. Cochran-Smith & S. Lytle (Eds.), *Inside/Outside: Teacher research and knowledge* (pp. 170–177). New York: Teachers College Press.

Florio-Ruane, S. (1986, April). *Taking a closer look at writing conferences*. Paper presented at the annual meeting of the American Educational Research Association, San Francisco.

Florio-Ruane, S. (1990). The written literacy forum: An analysis of teacher–researcher collaboration. *Journal of Curriculum Studies, 22*, 313–328.

Gage, N. L. (1963). (Ed.). *Handbook of research on teaching*. Chicago: Rand McNally.

Goodman, K. (1986). *The art of teaching writing*. Portsmouth, NH: Heinemann.

Holdaway, D. (1979). *The foundations of literacy*. Portsmouth, NH: Heinemann.

Houston, W. R. (1990). *Handbook of research on teacher education*. New York: Macmillan.

Huberman, M. (1990). Linkage between researcher and practitioners: A qualitative study. *American Educational Research Journal, 27*, 363–391.

Katz, L. G., & Cesarone, B. (Eds.). (1994). *Reflections of the Reggio Emilia approach*. Urbana, IL: ERIC Clearinghouse on Early Childhood Education.

Kennard, B., & Johnston-Kosik, L. (1993). Poetry: An improvised conversation. In D. J. Clandinin, A. Davies, P. Hogan, & B. Kennard (Eds.), *Learning to teach; teaching to learn: Stories of collaboration in teacher education* (pp. 84–94). New York: Teachers College Press.

Lortie, D. (1975). *Schoolteacher*. Chicago: University of Chicago Press.

National Commission on Teaching and America's Future. (1996). *What matters most: Teaching for America's future*. New York: Author.

Noffke, S. E., & Brennan, M. (1991). Student teachers use action research: Issues and examples. In B. R. Tabachnick & K. Zeichner (Eds.), *Issues and practices in inquiry-oriented teacher education* (pp. 186–201). London: Falmer Press.

Paley, V. (1979). *White teacher*. Cambridge, MA: Harvard University Press.

Paley, V. (1995). *Kwanzaa and me: A teacher story*. Cambridge, MA: Harvard University Press.

Richardson, V. (in preparation). *Handbook of research on teaching* (4th ed.). New York: Macmillan.

Ross, D. D. (1990). Programmatic structures for the preparation of reflective teachers. In R. T. Clift, W. R. Houston, & M. C. Pugach (Eds.), *Encouraging reflective practice in education: An analysis of issues and programs* (pp. 97–118). New York: Teachers College Press.

Saracho, O. N. (1993). Preparing teachers for early childhood programs in the United States. In B. Spodek (Ed.), *Handbook of research on the education of young children* (pp. 412–426). New York: Macmillan.

Shulman, L. S. (1986). Paradigms and research programs in the study of teaching: Contemporary perspectives. In M. C. Wittrock (Ed.), *Handbook of research on teaching* (3rd ed.; pp. 3–36). New York: Macmillan.

Sirotnik, K. A., & Goodlad, J. I. (Eds.). (1988). *School–university partnerships in action: Concepts, cases, and concerns.* New York: Teachers College Press.

Sikula, J., Buttery, T., & Guyton, E. (Eds.). (1996). *Handbook of research on teacher education* (2nd ed.). New York: Macmillan.

Spodek, B. (Ed.). (1993). *Handbook of research on the education of young children.* New York: Macmillan.

Travers, R. (1973). *Second handbook of research on teaching.* Chicago: Rand McNally.

Washington, V. (1996). Professional development in context: Leadership at the borders of our democratic, pluralistic society. *Young Children, 52,* 30–34.

Weiss, I. (1989). *Science and mathematics education briefing book.* Chapel Hill, NC: Horizon Research.

Wittrock, M. C. (Ed.). (1986). *Handbook of research on teaching* (3rd ed.). New York: Macmillan.

CHAPTER 8

Meta-Analysis in Early Childhood Education: Progress and Problems

Marinus H. van IJzendoorn

In this chapter, the methodology of meta-analysis and its application to early childhood education is discussed. I argue that meta-analysis is a crucial, quantitative step in the spiral of research efforts; nevertheless, meta-analysis remains embedded in a narrative or hermeneutic context. Four stages in meta-analysis are presented, and new approaches for the formulation of meta-analytical hypotheses as well as the meta-analysis of categorical data are introduced. In early childhood education, more than 25 meta-analyses have been performed during the past few decades.

DEVELOPMENT OF THE USE OF META-ANALYSIS

Meta-analysis is the analysis of primary analyses, that is, the analysis and synthesis of a set of empirical studies, and it focuses on the quantification of the reviewing process. Its history is at the same time quite long and rather brief: Almost a century ago Karl Pearson (1904) reported on the meta-analytical combination of the outcomes of four medical studies on the inoculation for typhoid fever, and during the past few decades the approach became extremely popular in the medical sciences. It was Glass (1976) who only 20 or so years ago introduced the concept of meta-analysis into the educational and behavioral sciences. He provided a controversial example of its application in psychotherapy studies, arguing that in general psychotherapy had considerable effect (combined r = .32), but that no specific treatment modality stood out (Smith & Glass, 1977).

During the past 20 years, meta-analysis has become widely used and hotly disputed in the educational sciences. In fact, it seems that it has been applied on a much wider scale in education than in any other social or behavioral science. The reason may be that educational policy decisions (like medical decisions) are supposed to be based on a firm foundation of empirical data. Every decade the number of scientific papers doubles (Garfield, 1979), and it becomes impossible even for the specialists to keep track of the literature in their own field. Meta-analyses are used increasingly to monitor new developments in all areas of the social and behavioral sciences.

In the past, narrative reviews were considered the royal road to the synthesis of literature, and some narrative reviews indeed were very powerful in shaping the future of a field of inquiry (e.g., Bornstein & Sigman, 1986; Hoffman, 1974; Maccoby & Jacklin, 1980). In a narrative review of high standards, the author tries to make sense of the literature in a systematic and at the same time creative way. In formulating a hypothesis for review in a precise manner, and in collecting systematically the pertinent papers to address the issue, the narrative reviewer does not act differently from the meta-analyst. It is in the stage of data analysis that the narrative and meta-analytical reviewers go separate ways. The narrative reviewers rely somewhat more on their intuition, whereas the meta-analysts proceed in a statistically rigorous way.

Cooper and Rosenthal (1980) showed experimentally that narrative reviewers are more inclined to commit Type II errors, that is, they do not reject the null hypothesis, although it should be rejected on statistical grounds. The authors asked 41 graduate students and senior researchers to review a set of seven studies on the association between sex and persistence in performing rather dull tasks. Half of the reviewers were assigned randomly to a course on meta-analysis. Seventy-three percent of the untrained narrative reviewers found no association; only 32% of the meta-analysts came to this conclusion. The correct outcome was that female participants are significantly more persistent than males in performing boring tasks. Graduate students and senior researchers did not differ in their performance. In particular, in cases in which studies show insignificant trends, the accumulated effect size across these studies tends to be underestimated.

Although narrative reviews and meta-analyses differ in precision and rigor during the stage of data analysis, interpretation of the meta-analytical data requires the same creativity and intuition that narrative reviewers often have used in such an impressively fruitful way. To explore the implications of some average effect size across studies for future research or applications, meta-analysts cannot rely only on algorithms or statistical tests. In this respect a narrative component should always be integrated in the meta-analytical approach. In fact, every meta-analysis seems to be embedded in a narrative context: In searching for a meta-analytical hypothesis, researchers cannot avoid using their creativity and common sense in exploring areas and issues in need of synthesis; in interpreting the meta-analytical outcome, researchers again have to fall back on their "hermeneutic" skills and to make creative sense of its implications. The embeddedness of meta-analysis in a narrative context is analogous to Habermas's (1981) theory of the hermeneutic context of empirical science.

Furthermore, in some areas the set of studies to be reviewed is extremely heterogeneous in terms of the quality of the designs and measures. If the number of studies is rather small, it may be impossible to perform a meta-analysis on the material, because the search for homogeneous subsets of studies is obsolete. In that case, the researcher should use the narrative approach to make sense of the data, and formulate an incisive critique on the state of the art in the area under study. An example of this approach is a review of the influence of children's television watching on their fantasies (Valkenburg & Van der Voort, 1994).

Meta-analysis cannot replace narrative reviews. First, meta-analysts have to rely on their narrative skills when they design a meta-analytical study or interpret its results. Second, some areas will remain closed to a meta-analytical effort, and a narrative review will be the only means to synthesize such a field. Lastly, meta-analysis is, of course, dependent on the availability of quantitative primary studies. If qualitative studies dominate a field of inquiry, the meta-analytical approach is not applicable, unless the concept of meta-analysis as quantitative synthesis is stretched (e.g., Noblit & Hare, 1988).

META-ANALYSIS AS A STEP IN A RESEARCH PROGRAM

Meta-analysis can be applied most fruitfully within research programs in which studies with similar designs or measures accumulate over the years to depict an increasingly accurate picture of some dimension of human behavior or development. In the spiral of research efforts, primary studies, secondary analyses, replications, and meta-analyses each play their crucial roles in promoting our understanding (Van IJzendoorn, 1994). In primary studies, data are collected to test a hypothesis derived from a well-articulated theory; the hypothesis often will be stated in the following form: Variable X is associated with variable Y, or X is causally related to Y. In correlational or experimental designs, standard measures for X and Y are used, and the results are therefore comparable across studies. If the results of the first empirical study on the association between X and Y are remarkable because of their effect size or direction, the next step in the spiral of research is secondary analysis of the first study. The secondary analysis uses the data as collected in the primary study, and the original outcome is scrutinized through recoding with a different coding system and re-analyzing the data using different statistical methods.

The re-analysis may lead to falsification of the original outcome, as in Kamin's (1974) re-analysis of some of Burt's data on the heredity of intelligence in twins. In some cases it may be difficult, however, to make the original data available for further study (Craig & Reese, 1973; Wolins, 1962). Replication studies should then be performed to test the same hypothesis with new data collected in a different sample, and with different designs or measures. If the number of replications increases, and if characteristics of replication studies vary, the meta-analytical approach is feasible to synthesize the extant literature and to test the effects of variations in study characteristics on the outcome of the studies.

For example, in 18 experimental studies on the teacher expectancy effect, Raudenbush (1984) found that the prediction of academic success in a random group of pupils led to increased IQ scores compared with a random control group without such prediction, if the teacher was acquainted with the pupils for only a few weeks. If teachers knew their pupils longer, their expectations could not be changed so easily by external "information." In primary studies, such a conclusion is difficult to reach without hundreds of participants.

Because meta-analyses are based on numerous decisions about collecting, coding, and analyzing the pertinent studies, meta-analytical results, in turn, need to be replicated as well (Lytton, 1994). Even if replications of meta-analyses yield the same results, they will never constitute the final argument in the spiral of scientific research. On the contrary, only meta-analyses leading to new hypotheses for further primary study can be considered fruitful (Eagly & Wood, 1994).

In Figure 8.1, a process model of progress in research programs through different methods is presented. Meta-analyses have not been positioned in a more crucial role than any other systematic form of inquiry. Meta-analyses are part of a series of connected steps in the description and explanation of human behavior, which never reaches a final point. In this respect, the model is a revised version of an earlier model in which meta-analysis was proposed to provide a more or less definite answer to the original question (Van IJzendoorn, 1994).

The scientific and public debate on the effects of daycare on children's socioemotional development may be illustrative. In 1974, Blehar compared 20 daycare-reared toddlers with 20 home-reared toddlers in the Strange Situation procedure (Ainsworth, Blehar, Waters, & Wall, 1978). She found that toddlers in daycare showed more insecure-avoidant behavior than the home-reared comparisons. It was the first study to suggest potentially negative effects of daycare on attachment in a middle-class sample. The study was criticized because participants were not assigned randomly to the experimental and control groups. Furthermore, the Strange Situation procedure had been validated for infants from age 12 to 24 months, and it was not considered to be valid for toddlers.

Figure 8.1. Process model of different types of replications. (Adapted from van IJzendoorn, 1994)

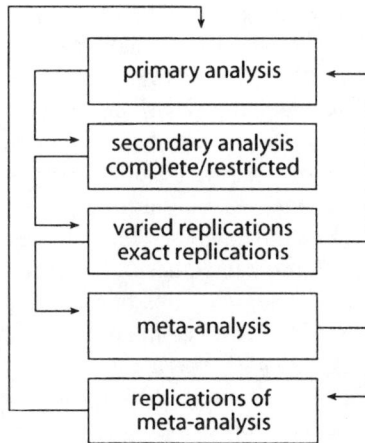

Blehar (1974) did not establish patterns of attachment, but relied instead on unstable separate behaviors.

Several primary studies were performed to replicate and extend Blehar's provocative results in different age groups, different socioeconomic strata, and with different designs and measures. At least two meta-analyses tried to synthesize the pertinent studies, and each of the meta-analyses could be considered as replications with somewhat different sets of studies and coding systems (Clarke-Stewart, 1989; McCartney & Phillips, 1988). Two conclusions were drawn. First, daycare-reared children appeared to show somewhat more insecure-avoidant behavior than home-reared children, in particular if they entered daycare at an early age for more than 2 days a week. Second, the meaning of avoidant behavior in daycare children was suggested to be different from its meaning for home-reared children because the first group would be used to separations from the parents and therefore might be less stressed by the Strange Situation procedure.

This outcome led in turn to a multimillion dollar study on the effects of nonparental care on attachment in children. In this 10-site American enterprise, not only the Strange Situation procedure but also alternative attachment measures have been used to address both the substantive issue of daycare stimulating avoidance and the measurement issue of daycare children being less stressed by the Strange Situation (Appelbaum et al., 1997). Only the successive application of primary and secondary studies, and meta-analyses leads to accumulation of knowledge in complicated domains of inquiry.

STAGES IN META-ANALYSIS

Meta-analysis and primary studies are structured in similar ways. In fact, meta-analysts should proceed through the same stages as primary researchers (Cooper, 1982). Starting with the formulation of a specific hypothesis, meta-analysts systematically collect the relevant literature. The retrieved papers, dissertations, and unpublished documents are considered to be the raw data to which a coding system is applied to produce the variables to be used in the analysis. The application of the coding system should be tested for intercoder reliability. Data analysis often consists of three steps (Mullen, 1989): First, the central tendency of the study results is computed, that is, the combined effect size. Then, the variability of the results around this central tendency is assessed, and outliers as well as homogeneous subsets of studies are identified. Finally, through a moderator analysis, meta-analysts try to explain the variability on the basis of study characteristics. For example, intervention studies with randomized designs may, on average, yield larger effects than studies without randomization. The interpretation of the meta-analytical outcome leads to new hypotheses and suggestions for further primary research. A meta-analysis is always a spiral process, similar to the process model of a Lakatosian research program. The basic components of a meta-analysis may be summarized as follows:

1. Hypothesis formulation
2. Retrieval and coding of studies
3. Analysis of study results and characteristics
4. Interpretation of meta-analytical outcomes (Adapted from Cooper, 1982)

The most important stage in meta-analysis is the formulation of an attractive and specific hypothesis. The hypothesis should be relevant and attractive to researchers in a broad area (Rosenthal, 1991), and it should cover a domain that one would not be able to review systematically and exhaustively without the help of meta-analytical methods. Nevertheless, the meta-analytical hypothesis also should be specific, because the results are meant to contribute to the falsification or confirmation of a specific theory. In that respect, it may be argued that it is less relevant to document the effects of psychotherapy in general, or even more broadly, of interventions in general (Lipsey & Wilson, 1993), than to describe the effects of parent training programs in early childhood (Cedar & Levant, 1990). It is unclear what theory could make use of the finding that interventions in general are effective.

The tension between broadness and specificity can be solved, however, in a systematic and quantitative manner. In a meta-analysis on the relation between sensitivity of parents and attachment security in their children, Goldsmith and Alansky (1987) used a broad set of studies on parenting to address this hypothesis. Their results were criticized because of the combination of "apples" and "oranges," that is, studies operationalizing sensitivity in a strict way, and studies covering a broader area of parenting. Replicating this meta-analysis 10 years later, De Wolff and Van IJzendoorn (1997; De Wolff, 1996) retrieved more than 60 studies on parenting and attachment security, and asked 20 experts to decide whether the parenting variables included in this set of studies were similar to the construct of sensitivity as defined in attachment theory. The experts also were asked to cluster the parenting variables into a limited set of constructs, and to rate the similarity of these constructs to the original sensitivity construct.

Through Homogeneity Analysis (Gifi, 1990) basic dimensions and clusters of parenting were found, and their distance to the sensitivity construct was established. For example, cognitive stimulation was considered to be less similar to sensitivity than was synchrony in parent–infant interaction. In a series of meta-analyses, the clusters of parenting variables were analyzed separately as well as combined into one set. The total set of studies showed a significantly smaller effect size than the subset of studies that included the assessment of the original sensitivity construct. In fact, a subset of studies most similar to the original Baltimore study on sensitivity and attachment showed a considerable effect size of $r = .24$, which confirmed a core element of attachment theory (De Wolff & Van IJzendoorn, 1997). We conclude that it is not problematic to combine apples and oranges in an overall set of fruits as long as we know which subset of fruits consists of apples, and which subset consists of oranges. Expert ratings can assist in providing a quantitative basis for the differentiation of a broad construct into smaller and more homogeneous subsets.

The second stage in meta-analysis is the retrieval of studies. The retrieval of pertinent literature should be a systematic and replicable part of the meta-analysis, and it should make use of a multimethod approach. The most important data collection procedures are the "snowball" method, the "invisible college" approach, and computer searches of subject indexes such as ERIC, PsychLit, Medline, *Dissertation Abstracts*, or citation indexes such as SSCI or SCI. The snowball method uses the references lists of previous reviews or meta-analyses to retrieve relevant publications. In the invisible college method, key figures in the field are asked to provide relevant papers, in particular, papers in preparation, conference papers, and other unpublished documents. Computer searches help to trace published papers and dissertations across a wide range of years, with an emphasis on publications in the English language.

The basic problem faced at this stage of the meta-analysis is the "file-drawer" problem (Rosenthal, 1991). Primary researchers know that it is easier to get papers published in which they report significant results than to guide papers into print with null results—regardless of the quality of the study (Begg, 1994). This may lead to the unfortunate situation that the majority of papers remain in the file-drawers of disappointed researchers, whereas only a minority of papers with significant results are published (Cohen, 1990). In that case, the progress of a research program is at risk because a review of the field would incorrectly be based on published papers and would suggest the rejection of null hypotheses, where, in fact, the combination of unpublished and published results would lead to the opposite conclusion. It is, therefore, crucial to retrieve published as well as unpublished papers for meta-analysis, even when the quality of the two sets of studies is different: Quality of study design and measures can be assessed, and moderator analyses can make clear to what extent it influences the overall outcome. The file-drawer problem, of course, can be radically solved by changing the review process of scientific journals: Editors should decide to accept or reject papers for publication only on the basis of a description of hypotheses, design, and measures of the study, without considering the results (Cooper & Hedges, 1994).

It will take some time to change our reviewing habits, however. In the meantime, meta-analysts are able to estimate the number of unpublished papers with null findings that are needed to make the meta-analytical outcome insignificant (the "fail-safe number") (Rosenthal, 1991). Unfortunately, the fail-safe number is based on combined p-values, and when the set of published studies is quite large, the conventional alpha-level of .05 may yield statistically significant but practically or theoretically insignificant outcomes. More recently, fail-safe numbers were estimated on the basis of a minimally acceptable effect size (e.g., Nye, Foster, & Seaman, 1987).

It should be noted that the influence of unpublished material is usually rather small. Meta-analyzing 17 sets of studies with and without "gray" literature, Rosenthal (1991) found a rather small mean difference in combined effect sizes of .07. Most problematic are dissertations: If dissertations are left out of the meta-analysis, that might inflate the outcome with an effect size of .20. That is, dissertations contain on average 1/5 standard deviation smaller effect sizes than published papers. Through *Dissertation Abstracts* it should be possible to retrieve most Anglo-Saxon dissertations.

TYPES OF META-ANALYSIS

Ten years ago different meta-analytical approaches were vehemently defended, and indeed different schools or currents of meta-analysis seemed to exist (Bangert-Drowns, 1986). In recent years the convergence of meta-analytical methods is notable. For example, there is no longer a meta-analytical approach based exclusively on the combination of probability or p- values across studies. Because p-values depend heavily on the number of observations, and because meta-analyses usually integrate hundreds of observations, most meta-analytical outcomes would be significant on the conventional alpha = .05 level. Recently, all meta-analytical methods have been focusing on combined effect sizes, although they may differ in the way in which effect sizes are computed and combined. The combined effect size—that is, the combined standardized differences between the means of the experimental and control group—can be computed on the basis of the standard deviations of the control group (Glass, 1976), the pooled standard deviations, or the pooled variance (Hedges & Olkin, 1985). Alternatively, the test statistics (F, t, X) can be transformed into an effect size (Rosenthal, 1991). In practice, different strategies do not seem to make a substantial difference (Johnson, Mullen, & Salas, 1995).

In recent years, most meta-analyses have gone beyond combining effect sizes to estimate their variability and to explain this variability in terms of study characteristics or error components. In this respect, the exhaustive search for pertinent literature is preferred above the best evidence approach (Slavin, 1986), in which only qualitatively sound studies would be allowed to enter a meta-analysis. Because of the emphasis in recent meta-analytical approaches on explanation of variability in effect sizes, it is preferable to test whether the quality of research (which always is a matter of degree, and a matter of different strengths and weaknesses) explains variation in study results, in order to make the process of study evaluation transparent and to maximize the power of the analyses.

A common characteristic of all meta-analytical approaches is the use of a specific set of statistical methods compared with the methods used in primary research. The reason is simple: In primary research the unit of analysis is the individual participant, whereas the unit of meta-analysis is the study result. Study results usually are based on different numbers of participants and are, therefore, point estimates with different precision and confidence boundaries (Mullen, 1989). It would be incorrect to give a significant correlation of .30 in a sample of 40 participants the same weight as a correlation of .30 in a sample of 400 participants. Furthermore, in most meta-analytical approaches, it is highly recommended that several results within a study first be combined before its outcome is combined with other study outcomes, to prevent inflation of the number of participants and confounding of results.

For most practical purposes, current meta-analytical approaches share a substantial amount of common ground and differ only in minor respects. There are two exceptions to this rule: Psychometric meta-analysis (Hunter & Schmidt, 1990) and categorical meta-analysis (Van IJzendoorn & Kroonenberg, 1988). Psychometric meta-analysis considers the observed "between study variance" of the results of a set of studies as the sum of the true variance and the variance caused by sampling errors, errors of measurement, restriction of range, and other research artifacts. Regular meta-analysts do not systematically estimate the error components before computing the combined effect size and performing moderator analyses to explain the heterogeneity of the study outcomes. Hunter and Schmidt (1990) argue, however, that the relevant heterogeneity usually disappears—and the search for moderators therefore would be obsolete—if the study results are corrected for artifacts.

Suppose the study outcome is a correlation between two measures, X and Y, and the reliability of X equals .90, whereas the reliability of Y equals .60. It can be shown that the observed correlation is equal to the product of the reliabilities and the true correlation: r (observed) = .90 × .60, that is, r (observed) = $.54r$ (true). That is, the true correlation is almost twice as large as the observed correlation if it is corrected for attenuation because of unreliable measures. In psychometric meta-analysis, the primary study results first should be corrected for various sources of error, before a combined effect size is computed. If 75% of the observed variance in the study outcomes can be regarded as error variance, the remaining 25% of variance should be considered as small and the studies should be seen as homogeneous. Hunter and Schmidt (1990; Hunter, Schmidt, & Jackson, 1982) argue that in most cases the error component turns out to be responsible for the majority of the observed variance, and that the search for moderators, therefore, is superfluous. They argue that, in fact, the coding of study characteristics requires substantial resources, but the profits usually are marginal.

At least two problems of the psychometric approach to meta-analysis should be mentioned. First, primary researchers are rather hesitant to perform corrections for attenuation in their data, because they are aware of the problem of replicability. In an ideal world of completely reliable measures and flawless research designs, corrected correlations may be the best approximation of real associations between variables. No researcher, however, works in this ideal world (Rosenthal, 1991). For meta-analysts, the challenge should be to depict the state of the art in the real world of research, not in the ideal world of "true" variances. A second problem is that in most primary studies the statistical information is lacking to carry out the required corrections; in many cases missing data will prevent the successful application of the psychometric approach. The use of regression or expert procedures to estimate the missing data may create its own errors.

The categorical approach is relevant when study results entail categorical distributions of educational or developmental characteristics of the participants (Van IJzendoorn & Kroonenberg, 1988). For example, in attachment research, three main categories of attachment relationships between children and their caregivers have been discovered (Ainsworth et al., 1978): insecure-avoidant (A), secure (B), and insecure-ambivalent (C) attachments. In fact, it has been argued that similar attachment categories describe attachment representations in adults as well (Main, Kaplan, & Cassidy, 1985). Many attachment studies have been carried out in various continents and countries. From the perspective of attachment theory, whether and how across studies the distributions of insecure and secure attachments differ between countries and continents, are important cross-cultural questions. The traditional meta-analytical combination of effect sizes is not applicable because categorical data are at stake. Instead, the study samples can be cast in a contingency table, with number of participants (N) in a study as one of the marginal distributions, and frequency of categories (A, B, and C) over all studies as the other marginal distribution (Van IJzendoorn & Kroonenberg, 1988).

Three kinds of analyses can be performed on this type of data. First, standardized residuals uncover deviations in frequency of a given category in a particular study from the expected frequency. Second, to evaluate the extent of cross- and intracultural differences, the overall variation can be partitioned into sums of squared residuals over studies within a country and those between countries. Similarly, the variation between countries may be partitioned further into sums of squared residuals over countries within a continent, and those between continents (Greenacre, 1985; Van IJzendoorn & Kroonenberg, 1988). Third, to investigate similarities and differences in study distribution profiles, correspondence analysis can be used (Greenacre, 1985), which yields a graphical representation of categorical distributions against the background of the total distribution of categories.

The categorical meta-analysis on attachment showed that across 32 attachment studies from eight countries, the intracultural variation was nearly 1.5 times the cross-cultural variation; the cross-cultural variation in attachment patterns appeared to be rather modest compared with the intracultural differences. The categorical approach also has been used in clinical attachment research on children and adults (Van IJzendoorn & Bakermans-Kranenburg, 1996; Van IJzendoorn, Goldberg, Kroonenberg, & Frenkel, 1992). Categorical meta-analysis should not be considered as an alternative to traditional meta-analysis; it serves as a supplement to the traditional approach in the case of categorical data that cannot be summarized into combined effect sizes.

META-ANALYSES IN EARLY CHILDHOOD EDUCATION

Meta-analyses have been performed in several domains of early childhood education. Intervention studies have focused on the stimulation of infants' development or their parents' child-rearing skills. Similarly, a large number of intervention studies tried to enhance academic achievement, or to stimulate the language development of preschool and kindergarten-age children. The most famous example, perhaps, is the Head Start program. Lastly, intervention studies were performed to stimulate the development of disabled or disadvantaged infants and preschoolers.

We are talking here literally about hundreds of primary studies. It is impossible to keep track of this myriad of studies without the help of meta-analysis. In Table 8.1, 25 meta-analyses in the various domains of early childhood education have been listed. We did a computer search of PsychLit and ERIC, with the key words "meta-analysis and early childhood," to trace the relevant meta-analyses. The reference list of Lipsey and Wilson's (1993) meta-meta-analysis was searched for pertinent references as well.

In general, interventions in early childhood appear to be effective. For example, parents and their children can be effectively prepared for a stay in the hospital, so that the children show less psychological disturbance after treatment. Parents can be trained to react more sensitively to their infants' signals. Head Start programs appear to be effective across the board, although it is unclear how long the results remain visible. In particular, language intervention programs with normal and special groups also have been demonstrated to be effective. Other successful interventions could be added to this already impressive list.

Of course, it is not always clear whether a program is equally effective in all circumstances and with all relevant populations. In several meta-analyses, the search for significant moderators is more meaningful than the presentation of the combined effect size across studies. Cultural diversity, for example, may moderate the intervention effects in an educational or developmental area substantively, and meta-analysis may be able to trace the influence of such moderators. Nevertheless, it should be of some comfort to see that children's development early in life can be affected by interventions intending to optimalize their opportunities later in life.

The interpretation of the size of the combined effects is a matter of much debate. The average effect size across the 25 meta-analyses is about $d = .44$, which is less than half a standard deviation difference between the experimental and the control group. This may seem a rather modest outcome for so many intervention efforts. It should be noted, however, that participating in an intervention program certainly can make a tremendous difference in the lives of young children. In terms of the Binomial Effect Size Display (BESD) (Rosenthal, 1991), the effect size of .44 is sizable. The BESD is defined as the change in success ratio because of an intervention. If we equate the combined effect size $d = .44$ with an $r = .224$, the success ratio in the experimental group would be: $.50 + .22/2 = .61$; the success ratio in the control group would be $.50 - .22/2 = .39$. The difference between the experimental and control groups would amount to a substantial difference if we translate this outcome to the millions of children who might profit from the intervention.

In a similar vein, it can be demonstrated that it makes perfect sense to recommend an aspirin a day for certain populations at risk of cardiovascular disease, on the basis of a small correlation of .03 that was found between the use of aspirin and the occurrence of cardiovascular problems (Rosenthal, 1991). In the social, educational, and behavioral sciences, researchers seem to be eager to translate effect sizes into percentages of explained variation, and to be overly conservative

Table 8.1. Meta-Analyses of Early Childhood Education and Intervention

	N	Effect Size(d)
1. Interventions in families with infants		
Training of new mothers about sensory/perceptual abilities of newborns; effects on maternal–infant interaction (Turley, 1984)	20	0.44
Clinically applied vestibular stimulation as a sensory enrichment therapy for infants at risk and developmentally delayed infants (Ottenbacher & Petersen, 1984)	14	0.71
Tactile stimulation of developmentally delayed and at-risk infants (Ottenbacher et al., 1987)	19	0.58
Interventions enhancing sensitivity of mothers to their infants' signals (Van IJzendoorn, Juffer, & Duyvesteyn, 1995)	11	0.58
Interventions enhancing infant-mother attachment security (Van IJzendoorn, Juffer, & Duyvesteyn, 1995)	12	0.17
Parent effectiveness training; all outcomes (Cedar, 1986; Cedar & Levant, 1990)	26	0.33
2. Interventions for academic achievement		
Head Start early childhood education programs; cognitive outcomes (Administration for Children, Youth, and Families, 1983; Collins, 1984)	71	0.31
Reduced class size and academic achievement in grades K–3 (McGiverin, Gilman, & Tillitski, 1989)	10	0.34
Effects of formative evaluation procedures on students in grades K–3 (Fuchs & Fuchs, 1986)	31	0.50
Punishment/reward feedback on preschoolers' discrimination learning; punishment versus reward (Getsie, Langer, & Glass, 1985)	—	0.29
Familiar versus unfamiliar examiner testing preschoolers; effects on test performance (Fuchs & Fuchs, 1985)	18	0.25
3. Language interventions		
Remedial and developmental language programs for linguistically deficient or disadvantaged preschool and elementary students; language ability (Kavale, 1980, 1982)	34	0.39
Language interventions for preschoolers; language and non-language outcomes (Piorier, 1990)	61	0.50
Language intervention with language/learning–disabled 6-year-old children (Nye, Foster, & Seaman, 1987)	61	1.04
Language intervention efficacy in mentally retarded preschoolers (Arnold, Myette, & Casto, 1986)	17	0.34

(Con't)

Table 8.1. (Con't)

	N	Effect Size(d)
4. *Interventions with kindergarten children*		
Intervention programs for kindergarten children; all outcomes (Lewis & Vosburgh, 1988)	65	0.43
Full versus half-day kindergarten; all outcomes (Karweit, 1987)	11	0.48
5. *Interventions with special groups*		
Early childhood special education; all outcomes (Snyder & Sheehan, 1983)	8	0.48
Early intervention programs with handicapped preschoolers; all outcomes (Casto & Mastropieri, 1986)	74	0.68
Early intervention programs for environmentally at-risk (disadvantaged) infants; effects on IQ and other variables (Casto & White, 1984)	26	0.43
Preschool intervention programs for culturally disadvantaged children; follow-up effects on achievement and cognitive outcomes (Goldring & Presbrey, 1986)	8	0.24
Familiar versus unfamiliar examiner testing preschoolers; effects on test performance (Fuchs & Fuchs, 1985)	18	0.25
6. *Interventions for social adjustment*		
Training of social competence in preschoolers (Beelmann, Pfingsten, & Lösel, 1994)	14	0.96
Cognitive and behavioral treatment of impulsivity in young children (4-7 years old) (Baer & Nietzel, 1991)	8	0.35
Preparations and interventions to help hospitalized preschoolers adapt after hospitalization; Posthospital Behavior Questionnaire outcomes (Vernon & Thompson, 1993)	9	0.15

in estimating the (practical) relevance of their results. In a narrative review on parents' storybook reading to their preschoolers, Scarborough and Dobrich (1994) concluded that the effects on literacy and language development were minor, and that they had unmasked the myth of stimulating parents to read to their children early in life. In a meta-analysis, Bus, Van IJzendoorn, and Pellegrini (1995) showed that the association between early storybook reading and later literacy was about $d = .59$, which explains about 8% of the variance in children's literacy skills. In an earlier meta-analysis, Van IJzendoorn and Bus (1994) showed that the phonological deficit explains only 6% of the variance in dyslexia, although it correctly is considered the major cause of dyslexia and the major point of departure for remediation.

Parental storybook reading should be recommended because in terms of BESD it makes a difference for many thousands of preschoolers.

CRITICISM OF META-ANALYSES
ON EARLY CHILDHOOD EDUCATION

Several meta-analyses have been subjected to thorough and sometimes harsh criticism (Cooper, 1993, vs. Vernon & Thompson, 1993; Dunst & Snyder, 1986, vs. Casto & Mastropieri, 1986; Eysenck, 1995, vs. Lipsey & Wilson, 1993). Dunst and Snyder (1986), for example, conclude that the Casto and Mastropieri (1986) findings cannot be the basis for policy: It would be both dangerous and unwarranted to develop policy about early intervention based on their meta-analyses because to do so would be both misleading and misguided. The criticism concerns the heterogeneity of independent and dependent variables across various intervention studies, and the heterogeneity of the interventions themselves. Furthermore, several unsound, nonrandomized studies were included in the meta-analysis. Any meta-analysis would be an example of the famous dictum, *garbage-in, garbage-out*, and would yield only GIGO bytes of pseudo-information.

As we have shown earlier, the heterogeneity of the studies can be productively used to explain variation between study outcomes. Meta-analysts should pay systematic attention to the discrimination of relevant subsets of more homogeneous studies, using quantitative approaches based on expert ratings, for example. Quality of study designs is never an easy all-or-nothing decision; careful ratings of several quality dimensions of the studies should enable meta-analysts to find out whether and to what extent study results are affected by quality issues.

A more important criticism concerns the dependence of effect sizes within a study. Dunst and Snyder (1986) argue that Casto's meta-analyses are based on 1,665 effect sizes from 162 studies, that is, an average of more than 10 effect sizes per study. They show that this treatment of multiple outcomes from the same study blatantly violates crucial assumptions of independence of observations. In this respect they are completely correct in their evaluation. Similar criticism is applicable to the meta-analyses by Fuchs and Fuchs (1986) and Baer and Nietzel (1991). The problem, however, can be solved easily by performing meta-analyses within studies, before combining effect sizes across studies (Beelmann, Pfingsten, & Lösel, 1994; Foster & Seaman, 1987; Goldring & Presbrey, 1986; Vernon & Thompson, 1993). This practice is now recommended in standard introductions to meta-analysis (Cooper & Hedges, 1994), and it would be important to replicate contaminated meta-analyses following this guideline. We conclude that the criticisms uncover the pitfalls and problems of meta-analysis without invalidating this quantitative approach to reviewing.

CONCLUSIONS

Meta-analysis not only provides a summary of research, but it also produces new insights and facts. Through meta-analysis we use the combined power of the primary studies to address issues that otherwise would require hundreds of participants and many different interventions within the same study. Only a meta-analysis could show that the teacher expectancy effect works better when teachers do not know their pupils for more than a few weeks (Raudenbush, 1984).

Combining the results of several meta-analyses, researchers are able to construct models of associations between theoretically important variables that have not yet been combined in any separate empirical study, and to show at what point the model still is incomplete. Elsewhere, we combined meta-analyses on the associations between parents' attachment, parental sensitivity, and children's attachment to document the "transmission gap," that is, our lack of knowledge of the mechanisms that are responsible for the transmission of attachment from one generation to the next (Van IJzendoorn, 1995). New meta-analytical approaches for creating and testing causal and multilevel models have been proposed (Cook et al., 1992).

Primary researchers sometimes feel that their work is underestimated compared with the meta-analytical synthesis. Meta-analyses are highly visible publications that frequently are cited in textbooks and research papers. It is important to note that meta-analyses save many primary studies from oblivion, in particular those studies that did not yield significant results. It is because of the powerful combination of studies that the lack of power in primary studies loses its importance (Schmidt & Hunter, 1995): Even when a small-scale primary study does not yield a significant outcome, and at the same time lacks power to reduce the risk of a Type II error to an acceptable rate, the point estimate and confidence boundaries of the study contain important information. Meta-analysis can make these findings productive for further research. In this respect, meta-analysis may be a solution for the obsession of our field with p-values and asterisks, which lead to an intolerable waste of energy and potential knowledge (Cohen, 1990). Meta-analysis is, however, a complicated method with many pitfalls and problems, and it should be applied with the required expertise. In most undergraduate and graduate methods and statistics textbooks, the meta-analytical approach is conspicuous by its absence. In (under-)graduate education, meta-analysis should receive more attention, because it is a crucial step in every research program.

Acknowledgments. Preparation of this chapter was facilitated by a PIONEER award from the Netherlands Organization for Scientific Research (NWO; Grant No. PGS 59–256) and by a fellowship of the Netherlands Institute for Advanced Study in the Humanities and Social Sciences (NIAS).

REFERENCES

Administration for Children, Youth, and Families. (1983). *The effects of the Head Start program on children's cognitive development (Preliminary report): Head Start evaluation, synthesis, and utilization project.* Washington, DC: U.S. Department of Health and Human Services. (ERIC Document Reproduction Service No. ED 248 989)

Ainsworth, M. D. S., Blehar, M. C., Waters, E., & Wall, S. (1978). *Patterns of attachment: A psychological study of the Strange Situation.* Hillsdale, NJ: Erlbaum.

Appelbaum, M., et al. (1997). The effects of infant child care on infant-mother attachment security: Results of the NICHD study of early child care. *Child Development, 68* (5), 860–879.

Arnold, K. S., Myette, B. M., & Casto, G. (1986). Relationships of language intervention efficacy to certain subject characteristics in mentally retarded preschool children: A meta-analysis. *Education and Training of the Mentally Retarded, 21,* 108–116.

Baer, R. A., & Nietzel, M. T. (1991). Cognitive and behavioral treatment of impulsivity in children: A meta-analytic review of the outcome literature. *Journal of Clinical Child Psychology, 20,* 400–412.

Bangert-Drowns, R. L. (1986). Review of developments in meta-analytic method. *Psychological Bulletin, 99,* 388–399.

Beelmann, A., Pfingsten, U., & Lösel, F. (1994). Effects of training social competence in children: A meta-analysis of recent evaluation studies. *Journal of Clinical Child Psychology, 23*(3), 260–271.

Begg, C. B. (1994). Publication bias. In H. Cooper & L. V. Hedges (Eds.), *The handbook of research synthesis* (pp. 399–409). New York: Russell Sage.

Blehar, M. C. (1974). Anxious attachment and defensive reactions associated with day care. *Child Development, 45,* 683–692.

Bornstein, M. H., & Sigman, M. D. (1986). Continuity in mental development from infancy. *Child Development, 57,* 251–274.

Bus, A. G., Van IJzendoorn, M. H., & Pellegrini, A. D. (1995). Joint book reading makes for success in learning to read: A meta-analysis on intergenerational transmission of literacy. *Review of Educational Research, 65,* 1–21.

Casto, G., & Mastropieri, M. A. (1986). The efficacy of early intervention programs: A meta-analysis. *Exceptional Children, 52,* 417–424.

Casto, G., & White, K. (1984). The efficacy of early intervention programs with environmentally at-risk infants. *Journal of Children in Contemporary Society, 17,* 37–50.

Cedar, B. (1986). A meta-analysis of the parent effectiveness training outcome research literature (Doctoral dissertation, Boston University, 1985). *Dissertation Abstracts International, 47,* 420A. (University Microfilm International No. 86-09263)

Cedar, B., & Levant, R. F. (1990). A meta-analysis of the effects of parent effectiveness training. *American Journal of Family Therapy, 18,* 373–384.

Clarke-Stewart, K. A. (1989). Infant day care: Maligned or malignant? *American Psychologist, 44,* 266–273.

Cohen, J. (1990). Things I have learned (so far). *American Psychologist, 45,* 1304–1312.

Collins, R. C. (1984). *Head Start: A review of research with implications for practice in early childhood education.* Washington, DC: American Educational Research Association. (ERIC Document Reproduction Service No. ED 245 833)

Cook, T. D., et al. (1992). *Meta- analysis for explanation: A casebook.* New York: Russell Sage.

Cooper, H. M. (1982). Scientific guidelines for conducting integrative research reviews. *Review of Educational Research, 52,* 291–302.

Cooper, H. (1993). Commentary. Children and hospitalization: Putting the new reviews in methodological context. *Developmental and Behavioral Pediatrics, 14,* 45–49.

Cooper, H., & Hedges, L. V. (Eds.). (1994). *The handbook of research synthesis.* New York: Russell Sage.

Cooper, H. M., & Rosenthal, R. (1980). Statistical versus traditional procedures for summarizing research findings. *Psychological Bulletin, 87,* 442–449.

Craig, J. R., & Reese, G. C. (1973). Retention of raw data. *American Psychologist, 28,* 723–730.

De Wolff, M. (1996). *Maternal interactive behavior and infant attachment: A meta-analysis.* Unpublished doctoral dissertation, Leiden University, Leiden, The Netherlands.

De Wolff, M., & Van IJzendoorn, M. H. (1997). Sensitivity and attachment: A meta-analysis on parental antecedents of infant attachment. *Child Development, 68*(4), 571–591.

Dunst, C. J., & Snyder, S. W. (1986). A critique of the Utah State University early intervention meta-analysis research. *Exceptional Children, 53,* 269–276.

Eagly, A. H., & Wood, W. (1994). Tying research synthesis to substantive issues. In H. Cooper & L. V. Hedges (Eds.), *The handbook of research synthesis* (pp. 485–502). New York: Russell Sage.

Eysenck, H. J. (1995). Meta-analysis squared—Does it make sense? *American Psychologist, 50,* 110–111.

Fuchs, L. S., & Fuchs, D. (1985). *The importance of context in testing: A meta-analysis.* Washington, DC: American Educational Research Association. (ERIC Document Reproduction Service No. 255 559)

Fuchs, L. S., & Fuchs, D. (1986). Effects of systematic formative evaluation: A meta-analysis. *Exceptional Children, 53,* 199–208.

Garfield, E. (1979). *Citation indexing. Its theory and application in science, technology, and humanities.* New York: Wiley.

Getsie, R. L., Langer, P., & Glass, C. V (1985). Meta-analysis of the effects of type and combination of feedback on children's discrimination learning. *Review of Educational Research, 55,* 9–22.

Gifi, A. (1990). *Non-linear multivariate analysis.* New York: Wiley.

Glass, G. V. (1976). Primary, secondary and meta-analysis of research. *Educational Research, 5,* 3–8.

Goldring, E. B., & Presbrey, L. S. (1986). Evaluating preschool programs: A meta-analytic approach. *Educational Evaluation and Policy Analysis, 8,* 179–188.

Goldsmith, H. H., & Alansky, J. A. (1987). Maternal and infant temperamental predictors of attachment: A meta-analytic review. *Journal of Consulting and Clinical Psychology, 55,* 805–816.

Greenacre, M. J. (1985). *Theory and applications of correspondence analysis.* London: Academic Press.

Habermas, J. (1981). *Theorie des kommunikativen Handelns. Band 2. Zur Kritik der funktionalistischer Vernunft* [Theory of communicative activity]. Frankfurt: Suhrkamp.

Hedges, L. V., & Olkin, I. (1985). *Statistical methods for meta- analysis.* New York: Academic Press.

Hoffman, L. W. (1974). Effects of maternal employment on the child. A review of the research. *Developmental Psychology, 10,* 204–228.

Hunter, J. E., & Schmidt, F. L. (1990). *Methods of meta-analysis: Correcting error and bias in research findings.* Beverly Hills, CA: Sage.

Hunter, J. E., Schmidt, F. L., & Jackson, G. B. (1982). *Meta- analysis: Cumulating research findings across studies.* Beverly Hills, CA: Sage.

Johnson, B.T., Mullen, B., & Salas, E. (1995). Comparison of three meta-analytic approaches. *Journal of Applied Psychology, 80,* 94–106.

Kamin, L. J. (1974). *The science and politics of I.Q.* New York: Wiley.

Karweit, N. L. (1987). *Full or half-day kindergarten—Does it matter?* (Report No. II). Baltimore, MD: Johns Hopkins University, Center for Research on Elementary and Middle Schools. (ERIC Document Reproduction Service No. ED 287 597)

Kavale, K. (1980). Psycholinguistic training. *Evaluation in Education, 4,* 88–90.

Kavale, K. (1982). Psycholinguistic training programs: Are there differential treatment effects? *Exceptional Child, 29,* 21–30.

Lewis, R. J., & Vosburgh, W. T. (1988). Effectiveness of kindergarten intervention programs: A meta-analysis. Eleventh Annual Colloquium of the International School Psychology Association. *School Psychology International, 9,* 265–275.

Lipsey, M. W., & Wilson, D. B. (1993). The efficacy of psychological, educational and behavioral treatment: Confirmation from meta-analysis. *American Psychologist, 48,* 1181–1209.

Lytton, H. (1994). Replication and meta-analysis: The story of a meta-analysis of parents' socialization practices. In R. van der Veer, M. H. van IJzendoorn, & J. Valsiner (Eds.), *Reconstructing the mind: Replicability in research on human development* (pp. 117–150). Norwood, NJ: Ablex.

Maccoby, E. E., & Jacklin, C. N. (1980). *The psychology of sex differences.* Stanford: Stanford University Press.

Main, M., Kaplan, N., & Cassidy, J. (1985). Security in infancy, childhood, and adulthood: A move to the level of representation. In I. Bretherton & E. Waters (Eds.), Growing points of attachment theory and research (pp. 66–106). *Monographs of the Society for Research in Child Development, 50*(1–1, Serial No. 209).

McCartney, K., & Phillips, P. (1988). Motherhood and child care. In B. Birns & D. F. Hay (Eds.), *The different faces of motherhood* (pp. 157–183). New York: Plenum Press.

McGiverin, J., Gilman, D., & Tillitski, C. (1989). A meta-analysis of the relation between class size and achievement. *Elementary School Journal, 90,* 47–56.

Mullen, B. (1989). *Advanced basic meta-analysis.* Hillsdale, NJ: Erlbaum.

Noblit, G. W., & Hare, R. D. (1988). *Meta-ethnography: Synthesizing qualitative studies.* Newbury Park, CA: Sage.

Nye, C., Foster, S. H., & Seaman, D. (1987). Effectiveness of language interventions with the language/learning disabled. *Journal of Speech and Hearing Disorders, 52,* 348–357.

Ottenbacher, K. J., Muller, L., Brandt, D., Heintzelman, A., Hojem, P., & Sharpe, P. (1987). The effectiveness of tactile stimulation as a form of early intervention: A quantitative evaluation. *Journal of Developmental and Behavioral Pediatrics, 8,* 68–76.

Ottenbacher, K. J., & Petersen, P. (1984). The efficacy of vestibular stimulation as a form of specific sensory enrichment. *Clinical Pediatrics, 23,* 428–433.

Pearson, K. (1904). Report on certain enteric fever inoculation statistics. *British Medical Journal, 3,* 1243–1246

Piorier, B. M. (1990). The effectiveness of language intervention with preschool handicapped children: An integrative review (Doctoral dissertation, Utah State University, 1989). *Dissertation Abstracts International, 51,* 137A.

Raudenbush, S. W. (1984). Magnitude of teacher expectancy effects on pupil IQ as a function of the credibility of expectancy induction: A synthesis of findings from 18 experiments. *Journal of Educational Psychology, 76,* 85–97.

Rosenthal, R. (1991). *Meta-analytic procedures for social research* (rev. ed.). Newbury Park, CA: Sage.

Scarborough, H. S., & Dobrich, W. (1994). On the efficacy of reading to preschoolers. *Developmental Review, 14,* 245–302.

Schmidt, F., & Hunter, J. E. (1995). The impact of data-analysis methods on cumulative research knowledge. Statistical significance testing, confidence intervals, and meta-analysis. *Evaluation and the Health Professions, 18,* 408–427.

Slavin, R. E. (1986). Best-evidence synthesis: An alternative to meta-analytic and traditional reviews. *Educational Researcher, 15,* 5–11.

Smith, M. L., & Glass, G. V. (1977). Meta-analysis of psychotherapy outcome studies. *American Psychologist, 32,* 752–760.

Snyder, S., & Sheehan, R. (1983). Integrating research in early childhood special education: The use of meta-analysis. *Diagnostique, 9,* 12–25.

Turley, M. A. (1984). A meta-analysis of informing mothers concerning the sensory and perceptual capabilities of their infants (Doctoral dissertation, University of Texas, Austin, 1983). *Dissertation Abstracts International, 45,* 1B. (University Microfilms International No. 84-14461)

Valkenburg, P. M., & Van der Voort, T. H. A. (1994). The influence of TV on daydreaming and creative imagination: A review of research. *Psychological Bulletin, 116,* 316–339.

Van IJzendoorn, M. H. (1994). Process model of replication studies: On the relations between different types of replication. In R. van der Veer, M. H. van IJzendoorn, & J. Valsiner (Eds.), *Reconstructing the mind: Replicability in research on human development* (pp. 57–70). Norwood, NJ: Ablex.

Van IJzendoorn, M. H. (1995). Adult attachment representations, parental responsiveness, and infant attachment: A meta-analysis on the predictive validity of the adult attachment interview. *Psychological Bulletin, 117,* 387–403.

Van IJzendoorn, M. H., & Bakermans-Kranenburg, M. J. (1996). Attachment representations in mothers, fathers, adolescents, and clinical groups: A meta-analytic search for normative data. *Journal of Consulting and Clinical Psychology, 64,* 8–21.

Van IJzendoorn, M. H., & Bus, A. G. (1994). Meta-analytic confirmation of the nonword reading deficit in developmental dyslexia. *Reading Research Quarterly, 30,* 266–275.

Van IJzendoorn, M. H., Goldberg, S., Kroonenberg, P. M., & Frenkel, O. (1992). The relative effects of maternal and child problems on quality of attachment: A meta-analysis of attachment in clinical samples. *Child Development, 63,* 840–858.

Van IJzendoorn, M. H., Juffer, F., & Duyvesteyn, M. G. C. (1995). Breaking the intergenerational cycle of insecure attachment: A review of the effects of attachment-based interventions on maternal sensitivity and infant security. *Journal of Child Psychology and Psychiatry and Allied Disciplines, 36*(2), 225–248.

Van IJzendoorn, M. H., & Kroonenberg, P. M. (1988). Cross-cultural patterns of attachment. A meta-analysis of the Strange Situation. *Child Development, 59,* 147–156.

Vernon, D. T., & Thompson, R. H. (1993). Research on the effect of experimental interventions on children's behavior after hospitalization: A review and synthesis. *Journal of Developmental and Behavioral Pediatrics, 14,* 36–44.

Wolins, L. (1962). Responsibility for raw data. *American Psychologist, 17,* 657–658.

CHAPTER 9

Research in Early Childhood Education: A Look to the Future

Bernard Spodek and Olivia N. Saracho

As noted in the introduction to this volume, there has been a continuing increase in the amount of research being conducted in early childhood education. We expect that increase to continue and that the research reported will be increasingly diverse. As we look at the field, we can see certain trends that we expect will continue into the foreseeable future.

WHAT RESEARCH METHODS WILL BE USED?

More and more, researchers are studying the actual experiences that children receive in early childhood programs. Descriptions of teaching practices and of teacher–child and child–child interactions in programs are being reported. Larger numbers of observational studies are being done in early childhood education. Some of these studies are quantitative in nature, but a growing number of qualitative studies are being reported in the field. It is expected that the number of such studies will increase in the future.

A variety of qualitative methodologies are being used today. Many of these have built on qualitative research methodologies developed in the fields of sociology and anthropology, for example, ethnography. Ethology is a methodology that was developed in biology and has been used to study animals in their natural settings. One would have difficulty characterizing any early childhood educational setting as "natural" since they are all contrived. However, we use the term *natural setting* to contrast such a setting with a laboratory setting where children are taken out of the situations where they normally function and placed in an environment specifically designed for conducting research. While much qualitative research is based on observation, it also may include interviews and artifact analysis. Hatch, in Chapter 3, also included narrative studies, feminist studies, and poststructuralist studies in his analysis of qualitative methodologies.

Some of these qualitative approaches apply methodologies from a number of fields of inquiry to research questions in early childhood education. Many qualitative methodologies also represent a change in research ideology. To some extent the move to qualitative research was a reaction to the logical positivist point of view that underlies most quantitative research. Questions were raised about whether there really is an objective truth that can be discovered through research and whether only observable phenomena are worthy of study. Qualitative research does not assume the objectivity of the data collected or the data collector. In fact, those using this methodology have questioned whether any research can be objective. Instead, researchers are admonished to identify their biases in their reports. Some of this research seeks to find out how individuals interpreted experiences and to uncover the meanings that the various actors in a setting gave to experiences, rather than to look for "facts."

In addition, many researchers feel that the voices of only a few were being heard within the positivist approach to research. Feminist research, for example, is viewed as valuable because it gives voice to the interests of women. Considering the fact that the vast majority of practitioners in early childhood education are women, this is certainly a valid concern.

Many issues are raised by the increased interest in qualitative research. One major issue relates to the quality of the research done. Issues relating to the validity and reliability of qualitative studies persist. There is also the issue of how to apply findings of such studies to the field in general. Since qualitative studies deal with unique individuals or settings, and since these studies are not generalizable, the field will continue to need to address the meanings that qualitative research has for the rest of the field. Perhaps, just as early childhood educators are concerned with the need to respond to individual differences among children, researchers will need to respond in newer ways to the individuality of research studies and how we can create a useful body of knowledge from these studies.

WHAT WILL BE RESEARCHED?

Program Outcomes

The research of the 1960s and 1970s consisted mostly of outcome studies. The concern was to test whether the experimental programs developed at the time were effective in achieving their goals. Most often the goals were related to cognitive processes and/or to readiness for learning at the elementary level.

Researchers continue to conduct outcome studies in early childhood education. Some of the current studies are not very different in their purposes from the earlier ones. Program effectiveness continues to be an important issue, but researchers are becoming more systematic and more sophisticated in their view of outcomes and in their selection of assessment tools. In addition, outcomes are being defined more broadly, beyond cognitive and academic goals, to include the social-emotional areas of development. Social competence, an important goal of early childhood education, continues to be difficult to assess in programs.

Nancy Karweit (1993) provides an overview of outcome research done on preschool programs over the years—at least for at-risk preschool and kindergarten children—and summarizes the instruments used and the outcomes found. She concludes that there are limitations to our knowledge in this area. She suggests that we lack empirical studies of the relative effectiveness of alternative ways of combining preschool and other services for young children. There is also not enough empirical data to be sure of the effects of major approaches to preschool curricula. In addition, the methodologies used in these studies are limited. Finally, she suggests that current studies fail to consider how preschools are connected to kindergarten and elementary grades. Thus, the field is ripe for future studies to provide a basis for policy decisions that we need to make regarding early childhood educational services. Certainly, more research needs to be done on the transition from preschool to kindergarten and from kindergarten to first grade.

A number of years ago, it became apparent that if we really want to understand early childhood program outcomes, we need to go beyond assessing outcomes only at the completion of a program. It is important to determine whether a program's effects outcomes persist over time; thus the need for longitudinal studies. The Consortium for Longitudinal Studies (1978) published a 10-year, follow-up study of the early intervention programs of the 1960s. The High/Scope Educational Research Foundation has continued to follow up the subjects of the Perry Preschool Program, one of those included in the above study. The most recent of these studies assesses the benefits of the program to these individuals at the age of 27, going much beyond the time span of the Consortium study (Schweinhart, Barnes, & Weikart, 1993).

The findings of these follow-up studies are impressive. However, the small number of individuals who were in the original programs suggests the need for additional longitudinal studies to provide a broader base on which to determine the benefits of early childhood education programs. In spite of the importance of the kinds of longitudinal research noted above, little such research is being conducted today, nor would we expect a great resurgence of this research.

There are practical difficulties to conducting longitudinal research studies, including design problems, as noted in Chapter 6. It is also difficult to establish experimental programs and randomly assign young children to particular treatment groups or control groups, especially with the range of programs available and the variety of preferences that parents might have. In addition, the problems of finding children for follow-up study long after a program is over, along with the expected attrition in such a follow-up, create difficulties in determining comparability of groups in such a design.

Curriculum

With the development of the cirriculum reform movement of the 1950s and 1960s and the experimental preschool programs of the 1960s and 1970s, an increased concern about the nature of the experiences provided to children was voiced. New curriculum proposals for the education of young children were put forth, sometimes in the framework of a program model (e.g., Evans, 1982). Many of the models were framed in terms of a particular developmental theory; some were in terms of organizational principles.

Today, few existing programs function within a particular conceptual framework; exceptions are Montessori programs and those following the High/Scope approach. More often, the discourse is framed in terms of practices rather than program models, especially in connection with the Guidelines for Developmentally Appropriate Practices (DAP) of the National Association for the Education of Young Children (Bredekamp, 1987). While some research has been done on the uses of DAP, the guidelines themselves are neither rooted in a particular theoretical orientation to human development nor based on a review of curriculum research.

An alternative approach to curriculum research in early childhood education has been research related to the content of preschool and kindergarten programs that is related to elementary school subjects. Some of this research can be found within the programs developed as part of the curriculum reform movement, especially in the area of science (American Association for the Advancement of Science, 1967; Education Development Corp., 1967; Karplus, 1967). The stimulus for this earlier research was the recognition of what were then newer conceptions of development—especially in relation to constructivist theories of cognitive development—and the hypothesis put forth by Jerome Bruner in his book, *The Process of Education* (1960), which suggested that any subject can be taught to any child at any level of development in an intellectually honest way.

The developmental theories of Jean Piaget and those of psychologists interested in information processing theory stimulated educators to develop and test new ways of teaching science and mathematics (Price, 1982). More recently, the theories of Vygotsky stimulated reading specialists to move away from a conception of readiness that had framed reading instruction for a long time and that saw a break between language activities at the preschool-kindergarten level and beginning reading instruction at the primary level. The concept of emerging literacy helped early educators see the process of learning oral and written language as a seamless one, starting at the initial period of language development and continuing into mature literacy skill.

If we look at the various curriculum areas today, we see that considerable research is being done related to literacy activities for young children (Mason & Sinha, 1993). There is also continued interest in research related to fostering children's mathematics learning (Baroody, 1993). The research and development activities of an earlier era are no longer being sustained in the area of science and social studies education for young children (e.g., Howe, 1993), although research is being done on the development of children's social competency, which can be considered part of the social studies program. Even less research is being done on the arts in the early childhood curriculum (Davis & Gardner, 1993; Peery, 1993).

This state of research in these curriculum areas of early childhood education is probably related, to a greater or lesser extent, to the priorities of public education, with its concern that children learn the 3Rs. It is probably due as well to the existence of more evaluation instruments to assess mathematics and language and literacy achievement in young children than achievement in other curriculum areas. However, there has been considerable research related to play in early childhood education. To some extent this is being spurred by newer conceptions of play and its role in the education and development of young children (Saracho & Spodek, 1998).

STUDYING THE EARLY CHILDHOOD EDUCATION SETTING

An early childhood curriculum is not offered to children in a vacuum, but rather within the confines of a school or center. There are three elements that are worthy of study in the early childhood school context: the physical setting, the teacher, and the other children in the class.

Physical Settings

The physical setting of an early childhood classroom includes the physical facilities themselves, including both indoor and outdoor space, the equipment provided, and the materials offered to children. Equipment usually is considered to be the larger, more permanent materials in the school.

Many preschools are established in spaces not originally intended for educating young children on a regular basis. These might include renovated homes or church Sunday school rooms. Even in public schools, preschool classes are often converted elementary classes. These may lack desirable elements or may not provide adequate space. Teachers typically have to adapt these settings for the program they offer. Harms and Clifford developed the *Early Childhood Environmental Rating Scale* (1980, 1988), which is probably the most widely used instrument for assessing the physical settings of early childhood programs. In their review of research on the study of educational settings, Harms and Clifford (1993) identify the diversity of early childhood programs and suggest that settings need to be studied in context. The theoretical framework they propose looks at the interaction of elements within the setting and elements outside the setting, including family, community, and funding and regulatory agencies.

Because physical elements in the educational setting are easily observed, they often serve as the basis for regulatory criteria. Often they also are used as determinants of quality. We need to consider the physical setting in studying early childhood education, but we also need to be sensitive to the importance of certain physical characteristics of schools for young children in a particular cultural context. This is especially important as we do cross-national studies of early childhood education programs.

Teachers

Teachers often are considered the most important element in an early childhood program. For that reason, there have been numerous studies over the years of teachers and of teacher education. As a matter of fact, the first volume in this series was devoted to the preparation of teachers (Spodek & Saracho, 1990). Studies of teaching include research on teacher behaviors, teachers' thought processes, classroom organization, and teaching of different subject matters (Wittrock, 1986). Interestingly, in the third edition of the *Handbook of Research on Teaching* (Wittrock, 1986), there is only one chapter that specifically addresses teachers of young children. Unfortunately, early childhood teachers and elementary teachers are treated together, and this chapter is more a review of research on programs than on teachers.

Considerable research has been done since that time on studies of teachers and teaching, and some of this research has included teachers of young children. This research has used a variety of methodologies, including case study methodologies, studies of teachers' implicit beliefs or thought processes, and teachers' biographies. We would expect an increase in research that focuses on teachers of young children and their preparation, and it would seem that teachers will be studied using an increased variety of methodologies.

Children

Children have always been the focus of research in early childhood education, either directly or indirectly. The child populations of our programs has been changing and becoming increasingly diverse in recent years. In response to that, Volume 5 of this series has focused on early childhood special education (Safford, 1994), and Volume 6 has focused on linguistic and cultural diversity in early childhood education (Garcia & McLaughlin, 1995). In addition, increased attention has been given to at-risk preschool and kindergarten children. This diversity means that we need to commit ourselves to the acceptance of individual differences among the children in our program.

With children in early childhood programs so varied in their abilities and disabilities, it is difficult to frame research questions or to generalize the entire population. Rather, we need to focus more on seeing how different elements in programs interact with different characteristics found in children. Many of the qualitative research methods can help us look closely at what is happening to particular children in specific programs and settings. Perhaps in using these methods, we will be able to paint a richer picture of what happens to children in early childhood education programs and what the consequences of particular configurations of influences might be.

WHO WILL DO RESEARCH
IN EARLY CHILDHOOD EDUCATION?

Much of the research in early childhood education that was conducted in the 1960s and 1970s was done by individuals from the fields of child development and educational psychology. Traditionally, early childhood educators have been primarily practitioners. Their training was practical and related to classroom teaching and supervision, not to theory and research. In the past 2 decades, however, graduate programs in early childhood education, including doctoral programs, have grown. This means that there are more persons who identify themselves as early childhood educators and who have systematically developed knowledge and skills in a variety of research methodologies. It is not that early childhood educators are inherently better researchers than those from other fields. Rather, it is a matter of perspective. Barbara Beatty, in Chapter 1, discusses the difference between "inside" research and "outside" research in the historical research of the field. The same distinction might be made in other areas of research. Insiders—early childhood educators doing research—may consider different research problems worthy of study than may outsiders. Even when they consider the same problem, each group of researchers may view the problem from a different perspective.

Another new set of researchers has been studying early childhood education. This group is composed of classroom teachers. The focus on "teacher as researcher" has been effective in giving teachers a voice in research. Too often, researchers will move into classrooms, involve teachers and children in research, and then leave. When a report appears, the teachers seldom are considered co-authors. In fact, there may be no acknowledgment of the contribution of the teachers or the children to the research. Often the perspective of the teacher is disregarded. Having the teacher function as researcher avoids these problems and lets the teacher control the research process.

Teachers' studies are usually a form of action research, and there may be a problem generalizing from such research, much as in the area of qualitative research. On a practical level, having early childhood teachers function as researchers in their own classroom can be problematic. Teachers of young children generally lack the time for doing even the necessary tasks relating to teaching during the school day. Early childhood teachers seem to have less free time available to them than do teachers at other levels. In addition, many early childhood practitioners are less well trained than teachers at other levels. Both of these concerns place limits on what can be expected of early childhood teachers as researchers.

PUTTING EARLY CHILDHOOD
EDUCATION RESEARCH IN CONTEXT

There has been increasing interest in using the results of research to inform social policy relating to young children. However, this does not happen as often as it might. Too often social policy is established without looking at the degree to which research can illuminate issues. Kagan (1993) quotes Lazar's (1980) comment that only three studies have directly changed policies in our field. She identifies four challenges to applying research to social policy, namely, the different values held by policy makers and researchers, the lack of definitional clarity in much research, the problems with the process and context of research and policy, and the difficulty in measuring policy-relevant outcomes.

Similarly, there are difficulties in applying research to classroom practice. Research often focuses on the general in early childhood education, whereas teachers are more concerned with the specific. In addition, teachers may not have access to research or be able to derive implications for their practice from research.

Too often research in early childhood education is conducted, reported at research conferences, and published in research journals, but nothing else happens with it. There is a belief that research should inform practice. Yet practitioners seldom read books or journals devoted to research. Perhaps it is too much to expect practitioners and policy makers to access research reports and abstract particular meanings that are relevant to them.

The gap between researchers and practitioners is wide, yet research can inform practice, just as it can inform social policy. There is a need for a level of reporting that abstracts research and identifies implications for policy and practice. To some extent the ERIC Clearinghouses serve such a purpose. In addition, there are newsletters that serve this function, and columns often appear in journals for practitioners that attempt to summarize research related to particular topics so that it is more accessible to nonresearchers. It seems to us that more of these efforts are needed.

REFERENCES

American Association for the Advancement of Science. (1967). *Science—A process approach*. New York: Xerox Educational Division.

Baroody, A. J. (1993). Fostering the mathematical learning of young children. In B. Spodek (Ed.), *Handbook of research on the education of young children* (pp. 151–175). New York: Macmillan.

Bredekamp, S. (Ed.). (1987). *Developmentally appropriate practice in early childhood programs serving children from birth through age 8*. Washington, DC: National Association for the Education of Young Children.

Bruner, J. S. (1960). *The process of education*. Cambridge, MA: Harvard University Press.

Consortium for Longitudinal Studies. (1978). Lasting effects of early education. *Monographs of the Society for Research in Child Development*. Chicago: University of Chicago Press.

Davis, J., & Gardner, H. (1993). The arts and early childhood education: A cognitive developmental portrait of the young child as artist. In B. Spodek (Ed.), *Handbook of research on the education of young children* (pp. 191–206). New York: Macmillan.

Education Development Corp. (1967). *Elementary science study*. Newton, MA: Author.

Evans, E. D. (1982). Curriculum models and early childhood education. In B. Spodek (Ed.), *Handbook of research in early childhood education* (pp. 107–134). New York: Free Press.

Garcia, E. E., & McLaughlin, B. (Eds.). (1995). *Yearbook in early childhood education: Vol. 6. Meeting the challenge of linguistic and cultural diversity in early childhood education*. New York: Teachers College Press.

Harms, T., & Clifford, R. M. (1980). *Early childhood environmental rating scale*. New York: Teachers College Press.

Harms, T., & Clifford, R. M. (1988). *Early childhood environmental rating scale* (rev. ed.). New York: Teachers College Press.

Harms, T., & Clifford, R. M. (1993). Studying educational settings. In B. Spodek (Ed.), *Handbook of research on the education of young children* (pp. 477–492). New York: Macmillan.

Howe, A. C. (1993). Science in early childhood education. In B. Spodek (Ed.), *Handbook of research on the education of young children* (pp. 225–235). New York: Macmillan.

Kagan, S. L. (1993). The research–policy connection: Moving beyond incrementalism. In B. Spodek (Ed.), *Handbook of research on the education of young children* (pp. 506–518). New York: Macmillan.

Karplus, R. (1967). *Science curriculum improvement study*. Lexington, MA: Raytheon.
Karweit, N. (1993). Effective preschool and kindergarten programs for students at-risk. In B. Spodek (Ed.), *Handbook of research on the education of young children* (pp. 385–411). New York: Macmillan.
Lazar, I. (1980). Social research and social policy: Reflections on relationships. In R. Haskins & J. J. Gallagher (Eds.), *Care and education of young children in America: Policy, politics, and social science* (pp. 59–71). Norwood, NJ: Ablex.
Mason, J. M., & Sinha, S. (1993). Emergent literacy in the early years: Applying a Vygotskian model of learning and development. In B. Spodek (Ed.), *Handbook of research on the education of young children* (pp. 137–150). New York: Macmillan.
Peery, J. C. (1993). Music in early childhood education. In B. Spodek (Ed.), *Handbook of research on the education of young children* (pp. 207–224). New York: Macmillan.
Price, G. G. (1982). Cognitive learning in early childhood education: Mathematics, science and social studies. In B. Spodek (Ed.), *Handbook of research in early childhood education* (pp. 264–294). New York: Free Press.
Safford, P. L. (Ed.). (1994). *Yearbook in early childhood education: Vol. 5. Early childhood special education*. New York: Teachers College Press.
Saracho, O. N., & Spodek, B. (Eds.). (1998). *Multiple perspectives on play in early childhood education*. Albany: State University of New York Press.
Schweinhart, L. J., Barnes, H. V., & Weikart, D. P. (1993). *Significant benefits: The High/Scope Perry Preschool study through age 27*. Ypsilanti, MI: High/Scope Press.
Spodek, B., & Saracho, O. N. (1990). *Yearbook in early childhood education: Vol. 1. Early childhood teacher preparation*. New York: Teachers College Press.
Wittrock, M. C. (Ed.). (1986). *Handbook of research on teaching* (3rd ed.). New York: Macmillan.

About the Editors
and the Contributors

Lillie R. Albert is Assistant Professor in the Department of Curriculum, Instruction, and Teacher Education at Boston College. She received her Ph.D. from the University of Illinois at Urbana–Champaign. Her research interests include pedagogical implications of writing to learn; application of Vygotskian psychology in the area of mathematical problem solving; and the impact of cultural relevant teaching on children's learning of mathematics. Her writings have appeared in journals and a contributed volume.

Barbara Beatty is Associate Professor of Education at Wellesley College. A former kindergarten teacher and campus-laboratory nursery school director, she is the author of *Preschool Education in America: The Culture of Young Children from the Colonial Era to the Present.* Her interests and research focus on history and policy in early childhood education, psychology, and teacher education, and she is the author of various publications on these topics. She currently is working on a book on the history of teacher education and on an edited volume on the history of the applications of psychology in education, child rearing, and child welfare.

Renee T. Clift is the Executive Director of the Council on Teacher Education and Professor of Curriculum and Instruction at the University of Illinois at Urbana–Champaign. She is the lead author of *Collaborative Leadership and Shared Decision Making: Teachers, Principals, and University Professors,* and the author or co-author of numerous articles on teacher education and continuing professional development. She has twice received the Conference on English Education/National Council of Teachers of English, Richard A. Meade Award for Outstanding Research in English Education. She currently is working on a study of the career paths of teachers who were academically successful students.

M. Elizabeth Graue is Associate Professor in the Department of Curriculum & Instruction at the University of Wisconsin–Madison. She received her Ph.D. in research methodologies from the University of Colorado at Boulder in 1990. She is the author of *Ready for What? Constructing Meanings of Readiness for Kin-*

dergarten, and, with Daniel Walsh, of *Researching Children in Context: Theories, Methods, and Ethics.* Her academic interests include readiness, with a particular focus on academic redshirting; assessment; and parent relationships with schools.

J. Amos Hatch is Professor of Inclusive Early Childhood Education at the University of Tennessee, Knoxville. Since completing his Ph.D. at the University of Florida, he has conducted several qualitative research projects, reporting findings and discussing research issues in numerous articles and books. He served as executive editor of the *International Journal of Qualitative Studies in Education* and recently published two edited volumes: *Qualitative Research in Early Childhood Settings*, and *Life History and Narrative* (co-edited with Richard Wisniewski). In collaboration with colleagues from Australia, he currently is involved in a cross-national study of early childhood teachers' work.

Penny Hauser-Cram is Associate Professor of Developmental and Educational Psychology in the School of Education at Boston College. She received her doctoral degree in Human Development from the Harvard Graduate School of Education. Her research includes evaluation studies of early education and family support programs and the development of children with disabilities. Her publications include *Early Education in the Public Schools: Lessons from a Comprehensive Birth-to-Kindergarten Program* (co-authored with D. P. Pierson, D. K. Walker, and T. Tivnan), and *Essays on Educational Research: Methodology, Testing, and Application* (co-edited with F. C. Martin).

Richard M. Lerner is the Anita L. Brennan Professor of Education at Boston College and Director of the Boston College Center for Child, Family, and Community Partnerships. A developmental psychologist, he received a Ph.D. in 1971 from the City University of New York. Lerner is the author or editor of 32 books and more than 250 scholarly articles and chapters. He is known for his theory of, and research about, relations between life-span human development and contextual or ecological change. He is the founding editor of the *Journal of Research on Adolescence* and of the new journal *Applied Developmental Science.*

Erez C. Miller is a doctoral candidate in Developmental and Educational Psychology in the School of Education at Boston College. Born in Israel, he has bachelor's and master's degrees in deaf education and has worked for a number of years as a teacher of children with and without disabilities. Currently, he is a teaching fellow and clinical supervisor of teachers-in-training at Boston College. His research interests are social development of children with special needs, the development of children with chronic illnesses, and the impact of child abuse on children's development.

Anthony D. Pellegrini is Professor of Educational Psychology at the University of Minnesota, Twin Cities Campus. His research and teaching interests center around observing children's social behavior and early literacy development at home and at school. He is co-editor of this volume.

Olivia N. Saracho is Professor of Education in the Department of Curriculum and Instruction at the University of Maryland. Her areas of scholarship include cognitive style, teaching, and teacher education in early childhood education. Dr. Saracho's most recent books are *Teachers' and Students' Cognitive Style in Early Childhood Education*, *Right from the Start: Teaching Children Ages Three Through Eight* (with Bernard Spodek), *Dealing with Individual Differences in the Early Childhood Classroom* (with Bernard Spodek), and *Foundations of Early Childhood Education* (with Bernard Spodek and Michael J. Davis). She is also the co-editor, with Roy Evans, of *Early Childhood Teacher Education: An International Perspective*, and co-editor of this volume.

Peter K. Smith is Professor of Psychology at Goldsmiths College, University of London, England. He received his bachelor's degree from the University of Oxford and his Ph.D. from the University of Sheffield. He has researched extensively on children's play and is co-author (with K. J. Connolly) of *The Ecology of Preschool Behaviour* (Cambridge University Press, 1980) and editor of *Play in Animals and Humans* (Blackwell, 1984). More recently, he has researched the topic of school bullying and is co-editor (with S. Sharp) of *School Bullying: Insights and Perspectives* and *Tackling Bullying in Your School: A Practical Handbook for Teachers* (both Routledge, 1994).

Bernard Spodek is Professor Emeritus in Early Childhood Education at the University of Illinois, where he has taught since 1965, having been invited to start the early childhood education program there. Prior to that time he was Assistant Professor at the University of Wisconsin–Milwaukee. He began his career in 1952 as an early childhood teacher at the Beth Hayeled School. He also taught children in the New York City Public Schools and at the Brooklyn College Early Childhood Center. Spodek received his doctorate from Teachers College, Columbia University. His research and scholarly interests are in the areas of curriculum, teaching, and teacher education in early childhood education.

During his career he has written and edited 31 books, 48 chapters, and 65 scholarly articles. Dr. Spodek's most recent books are *Right from the Start: Teaching Children Ages Three Through Eight* and *Dealing with Individual Differences in the Early Childhood Classroom*, both with Olivia Saracho; *Handbook of Research on the Education of Young Children*; and *Foundations of Early Childhood Education*, with Olivia N. Saracho and Michael J. Davis. He is co-editor of this volume.

Marinus H. van IJzendoorn is currently Professor and Chair at the Center for Child and Family Studies of the Graduate School of Education, at Leiden University, The Netherlands. His research interests are attachment relationships across the life span, moral education and development, and methodology, including issues of meta-analysis. His writings have appeared in a number of scholarly journals.

Author Index

Subject Index